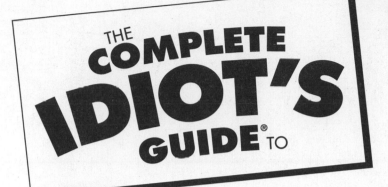

THE COMPLETE IDIOT'S GUIDE® TO

Buying a Home

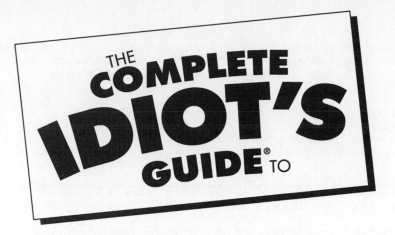

Buying a Home

by Peter Richmond

A member of Penguin Group (USA) Inc.

This book is dedicated to my mother, Edna Dorothy Richmond, and my sister, Paula (Richmond) Adriance. Both were teachers, the most valuable and, unfortunately, most underappreciated position in our society today. Both taught English composition and literature.

ALPHA BOOKS

Published by the Penguin Group

Penguin Group (USA) Inc., 375 Hudson Street, New York, New York 10014, USA

Penguin Group (Canada), 90 Eglinton Avenue East, Suite 700, Toronto, Ontario M4P 2Y3, Canada (a division of Pearson Penguin Canada Inc.)

Penguin Books Ltd., 80 Strand, London WC2R 0RL, England

Penguin Ireland, 25 St. Stephen's Green, Dublin 2, Ireland (a division of Penguin Books Ltd.)

Penguin Group (Australia), 250 Camberwell Road, Camberwell, Victoria 3124, Australia (a division of Pearson Australia Group Pty. Ltd.)

Penguin Books India Pvt. Ltd., 11 Community Centre, Panchsheel Park, New Delhi—110 017, India

Penguin Group (NZ), 67 Apollo Drive, Rosedale, North Shore, Auckland 1311, New Zealand (a division of Pearson New Zealand Ltd.)

Penguin Books (South Africa) (Pty.) Ltd., 24 Sturdee Avenue, Rosebank, Johannesburg 2196, South Africa

Penguin Books Ltd., Registered Offices: 80 Strand, London WC2R 0RL, England

International Standard Book Number: 978-1-59257-868-9
Library of Congress Catalog Card Number: 2008937772

12 11 10   8 7 6 5 4 3 2 1

Interpretation of the printing code: The rightmost number of the first series of numbers is the year of the book's printing; the rightmost number of the second series of numbers is the number of the book's printing. For example, a printing code of 10-1 shows that the first printing occurred in 2010.

Printed in the United States of America

Note: This publication contains the opinions and ideas of its author. It is intended to provide helpful and informative material on the subject matter covered. It is sold with the understanding that the author and publisher are not engaged in rendering professional services in the book. If the reader requires personal assistance or advice, a competent professional should be consulted.

The author and publisher specifically disclaim any responsibility for any liability, loss, or risk, personal or otherwise, which is incurred as a consequence, directly or indirectly, of the use and application of any of the contents of this book.

Most Alpha books are available at special quantity discounts for bulk purchases for sales promotions, premiums, fundraising, or educational use. Special books, or book excerpts, can also be created to fit specific needs.

For details, write: Special Markets, Alpha Books, 375 Hudson Street, New York, NY 10014.

Publisher: *Marie Butler-Knight*
Editorial Director: *Mike Sanders*
Senior Managing Editor: *Billy Fields*
Acquisitions Editor: *Karyn Gerhard*
Production Editor: *Kayla Dugger*
Copy Editor: *Krista Hansing Editorial Services, Inc.*

Cartoonist: *Steve Barr*
Cover Designer: *Becky Batchelor*
Book Designer: *Trina Wurst*
Indexer: *Johnna VanHoose Dinse*
Layout: *Chad Dressler*
Proofreader: *John Etchison*

Contents at a Glance

Contents

5 Steps to Approval — 65

6 Mortgage Loans — 83

Introduction

Congratulations! Either you're about to buy a home or you're giving serious thought to doing so. Buying a home can be one of the most exciting things you will ever do—but it can also be one of the scariest, since it's likely to be the biggest financial investment you'll ever make. However, as you'll find from following the advice and ideas contained in this book, you *can* handle the daunting parts and really take pleasure in your home-buying process. And of course, it all leads up to you being handed the keys to your new home and finally moving in!

You'll find many different home-buying subjects covered here, all of them important parts of the process—deciding what you want and need in your home, meeting with a Realtor, securing a mortgage, finding a home, placing an offer, going through the inspections, obtaining certain documents, and getting through the closing.

We lead you through this process by sharing personal experiences in both banking and real estate. Good luck! See you at the housewarming!

How to Use This Book

We've organized this book into five easy-to-follow parts, each covering a specific part of the process of buying a home, to help you successfully find and purchase your home.

Part 1, "Home Buying 101," examines your goals and concerns about buying a home. Included in this part is a discussion of terminology you'll need to be familiar with, how to find a Realtor, and how to determine exactly what kind of a home you want to buy—including location, style, and size of home. By the end of this part, you'll have a completed dream list of what you want your home to look like!

Part 2, "Money Talk," is all about the financials of buying a home. From the money you'll need—down payment and closing costs—to how you'll pay for it—cash, mortgage—to the money you'll save—tax breaks and more—this part covers it all. First, you'll figure out how you're going to pay for your home. You'll learn about various types of mortgages and mortgage lenders, and you'll discover options from government-supported institutions; you'll also come to understand the interest rates and costs associated with a loan. You'll learn about your credit history and score, and how both affect your purchase and your mortgage. If your credit hasn't always been stellar, you'll find valuable information on how this affects your loan and what you can do to improve it before buying a home.

Part 3, "Finding Your Home," focuses on finding your dream home. You'll learn about traditional open houses and how you can find your home—and take tours—through the Internet. This part also shows you how to understand whether it's a seller's or buyer's market and what that means to you. You'll examine the home and its surrounding area to see if it fits your criteria, and then learn how to place an offer on the home. And since not every home purchase is picture perfect, you'll learn how to handle any obstacles that come along.

Part 4, "Getting Closer," gives you a primer on home inspections. Now that you have the home you're interested in, this part shows you how to find out if it's in good condition and, if there are any problems, how to use them to your financial benefit. You'll also learn about the disclosure documents you'll need and the benefits of seller financing and seller concessions—the latter of which can save you hundreds, if not thousands, of dollars in closing costs.

Part 5, "Taking Possession and Moving In," gets you to the finish line. It focuses on everything you need to know about the closing. You'll learn the differences between escrow and attorney closes. You'll also find out everything you need to know about moving into your new home, including the potential advantages of using professional moving companies versus the advantages of doing the move on your own.

Separately, when we feel something should be highlighted for you, we do it with a sidebar, set in a special box such as this:

Tips and Traps

Pay attention to this information. It can be very useful!

Warning!

Be very careful about what we share in these sidebars. Don't take this information lightly.

def•i•ni•tion

This tells you in plain English exactly what something means.

Quotes and Facts

Here you'll find quotes from experts and buyers about their home-buying experiences, or helpful facts related to the subject being discussed.

Acknowledgments

I'd like to thank a number of people for their help, guidance, and ideas on this book, for without them it would not have happened. As always, my agent Marilyn Allen, absolutely the best agent anyone could ever have, tops the list. Lisa Iannucci, an excellent writer in her own right, kept me on point and was always a great source of ideas and suggestions to keep the project on track. Her edits were very valuable to me as well. For his friendship, ideas, and information on the latest in the mortgage industry, Alan Garber continues to be invaluable. I also want to thank Ellie Besancon of the California Association of Realtors, as well as Lily Ruiz and Tim de Wolfe of the San Francisco Federal Reserve Bank for their assistance with some of the documentary forms you see in this book.

Also not to be forgotten by any means are the following members of the greatest organization of practicing Realtors anywhere, The Allen Hainge CyberStars: Ken Deshaies, Tucker Robbins, Elaine Lawson, Sven Andersen, Cheryl Scott-Daniels, Sandra Nickel, Jackie Safran, Allyson Hoffman, Henri Gutner, Nick Molnar, Stephanie Evelo, Alice Held, and Tim Kinzler. If you, dear reader, ever need a Realtor, you can do no better than any of these folks.

Finally, to my wife Jane and my daughters Jenn and Sara for their continuing love, help, and inspiration. Words are never enough, but will have to suffice for your constant support and understanding.

Special Thanks to the Technical Reviewer

The Complete Idiot's Guide to Buying a Home was reviewed by an expert who double-checked the accuracy of what you'll learn here, to help us ensure that this book gives you everything you need to know about buying a home. Special thanks are extended to Grant Munroe.

Trademarks

All terms mentioned in this book that are known to be or are suspected of being trademarks or service marks have been appropriately capitalized. Alpha Books and Penguin Group (USA) Inc. cannot attest to the accuracy of this information. Use of a term in this book should not be regarded as affecting the validity of any trademark or service mark.

Part 1

Home Buying 101

When you enjoy a fine meal, each course is special in its own right—but each course also helps you look expectantly and eagerly toward the next. By the end of the meal, you're full and satisfied, content to know that you got your money's worth and then some. Think of this book as a literary meal.

Consider this first part your appetizer—it gives you a taste of the many things to come in buying a home. In this part, we examine not only your goals, concerns, and boundaries, but also what you need to address at the beginning of your search. We discuss the terminology used in the home-buying process, and describe how you can find a Realtor. We also help you to create your dream home wish list. So bon appétit!

An Introduction to Buying a Home

In This Chapter

- Why now is the right time to buy
- The benefits of owning a home
- Are you ready to buy?
- Home-buying myths
- Mistakes to avoid

Congratulations on your search to buy a new home! If this will be your first home, you might think that all you need to do is connect with a good real estate professional. If you've purchased a home before, you might think that you already have enough experience with the home-buying process to get the job done. Working with a real estate professional, or going through the process once before, is a great first step to finding your new home, but there's so much more to it. Reading this book will make you a much more educated buyer.

Buying a home involves more than reading ads in the local newspaper or online, and going to open houses. It also involves understanding your budget and your current financial situation. Have you looked at your credit report recently? Do you know what you can afford? You also need to thoroughly understand your needs, your wants, your finances, and the current real estate market before you get started.

Even if you've bought a home before, have your needs changed since then? Is your family bigger or smaller? Has the real estate market or the economy changed since then, which might affect your purchase? You need to know many things so you don't make mistakes or fall into traps and pitfalls.

Tips and Traps

One thing that many buyers, new or experienced, overlook is the amount of stress that home buying can generate. You're making a major purchase and you should be aware of all the important things that this implies. Be careful, diligent, and deliberate and you'll be successful.

This book guides you through all the steps to buying a home. It also provides tips and suggestions to make the task easier and less stressful. As a result, you'll have an easier time finding your dream home. First, let's focus on the basics, including why this is a perfect time to start looking, how to decide whether owning a home really is the right decision for you, and how to spot and avoid the most common home-buying mistakes. While you're at it, don't forget to investigate if a home you're interested in has a workable floor plan for you, or the right number of various types of rooms that you need for your lifestyle. Let's get started!

Now Is a Good Time to Buy

The time is ripe to explore the housing market. We currently are in a "buyer's market," which means prices of homes are lower than they've been in years—you're bound to find homes more affordable. It's like being able to buy a $500 brand-name suit for $375. Perhaps that pricey two-story colonial that you've adored from afar (you know, the one with the extra bedroom, bathroom, and home office) has now become much more affordable.

In addition, the lending industry has lowered mortgage interest rates. What does that mean to you, the buyer? It means that you save money. For example, a reduction in a mortgage interest rate of just a quarter percent can result in hundreds of dollars in savings on your monthly mortgage payment. That savings can make all the difference in the world when it comes to daydreaming about owning a home and actually owning one. A smaller mortgage payment may mean that you can now afford that beautiful brown-shingle period home that you've been eyeing since it went on the market a few months ago!

Tips and Traps

Make sure you establish a positive credit history. If you don't have a credit card, apply for one immediately so you can begin to establish credit—the sooner you do it, the better. Use it responsibly. This cannot be stressed enough. Keep the balance low and make payments on time. If you have other loans, such as a car loan or student loan, or if you rent an apartment, be sure to make those payments on time, too. The more responsible you are with your money, the easier time you'll have getting approved for a mortgage.

Along with providing a sense of stability for you and your family, a home is an investment that grows over time and offers several tax deductions, including mortgage interest, property taxes, and possibly closing costs, points paid, and loan application fees (you learn more about these later in the book). If you want to see how these tax breaks affect you personally, ask your financial advisor to go over the numbers with you. You can also visit the Internal Revenue Service's website (www.irs.gov) for the latest information on tax breaks for buying a home.

First-time home buyers are also entitled to special tax credits. For example, a first-time home buyer tax credit was included in the American Recovery and Reinvestment Act, signed into law in early 2009. The bill offers a tax credit of up to $8,000 for the purchase of a home (which must be your principal residence) between January 1 and December 1, 2009. You can claim the credit on your tax return in order to reduce your tax liability.

Most important, as you repay your mortgage, your *equity* increases. You have no equity in a rental. Real estate is a great investment. Need proof? Consider that some of the largest fortunes in history are based on real estate—Donald Trump, the late Harry Helmsley (Leona's husband), and billionaire Sam Zell.

def•i•ni•tion

When it comes to buying your home, **equity** is the current market value of your home after you deduct the outstanding mortgage balance.

Am I Ready to Own a Home?

Before you go through the process, it's best to first ask yourself, "Is owning a home for me?" There are just as many responsibilities of owning a home as there are benefits. For example, these responsibilities include, but aren't limited to, maintenance, upgrades, and remodeling; homeowners also pay additional expenses such as property taxes and homeowner association fees. Although home ownership is the so-called American dream, some people are truly not cut out for it and are better off renting.

Tips and Traps

To keep from being short on cash when an unexpected repair comes your way, it's best to put aside at least 10 percent of each paycheck into an account that is earmarked for these unexpected expenses.

For example, are you ready to deal with a furnace or electrical system that goes on the blink at 3 in the morning? Can you afford an unexpected, and costly, plumber's or electrician's bill? Or are you more comfortable calling your landlord and letting her deal with the aggravation and expense?

Consider another example: a huge storm carrying torrential rains and gale-force winds reveals leaks in your home and causes a tree to crash into your den. Can you deal with such upset and expense? If not, perhaps you're not ready to own a home right now. It's okay—this could change. You may be ready for home ownership after some time has passed. Only you can know for sure when you're ready.

Also, if you think that your life circumstances might change within the next five years, think carefully about whether you should buy a home. Most homeowners of less than five years lose money or barely break even in typical markets. If you know you are probably going to be transferred, taking care of a parent or relative, or simply thinking that you'll upgrade in a few years, slow down and carefully consider your purchase before moving ahead.

If you're ready to enjoy all the benefits and handle all the responsibilities of owning a home, that's great! Before we move on, let's bust some of the most popular home-buying myths out there.

Home-Buying Myths

When you tell someone you're buying a home, you'll often hear one of their "bits of wisdom." But that advice is often as substantial as the fertilizer you'll be spreading around your lawn next spring. Remember, everybody's experience is different, so don't listen to the advice of other home buyers without checking it out to see if it's true. We analyze a few of these nuggets, but remember that you also need to look into what others tell you so you can decipher truth from fiction. After all, it's your home—make your own decisions.

However, when it comes to recommendations for realtors, mortgage brokers, home inspectors, and other professionals you'll need to depend on to buy your home, advice from others can be worth its weight in gold.

Buying Costs More Than Renting

In most cases, it does cost more to buy a home than to rent, but in the end, the financial advantages outweigh the expense of buying and keeping up the home. You do need much more money for a down payment and closing costs than you do for a security deposit. You also need money to keep the home maintained. When you're renting, the landlord takes care of those items.

Although the real estate market over the last few years has significantly decreased in value, some markets are starting to see a turnaround. Later in the book, you'll learn how to do your basic research so you can avoid buying in areas that are still falling in value. For the most part, if you buy a home in an area that is starting to see an increase in values, your home's value should increase over time, too. This increases your overall net worth, something you can't do by renting. As a result, buying a home may cost more money outright, but it typically saves you much more money in the end.

I Can Just Call the Seller's Agent

If you've never bought a home, you might think that all you do is call the agent who is listing the house you want to see. Like another house? Call that agent, right? Not quite. The traditional method of buying a home is to find one Realtor who is going to work for you—the buyer's agent. Feel free to contact several agents and interview them before you select one to work with. When you've decided on an agent, that agent contacts the sellers' agents for you and sets up your appointments. Agents frown upon buyers who call several agents and ask them to set up appointments; it's a professional no-no. That's why you have one agent to represent you.

I Don't Need a Real Estate Professional

Although over 85 percent of all buyers use the web to do their own research on buying a home (which is a great way to find some basic information and scope out the homes you like), you really need a real estate professional to help you close the deal.

A real estate professional can give you market and neighborhood information, do your research for you while you work and take care of your kids, and set up appointments on homes that fit your specifications. In addition, most sellers won't even show their homes to a buyer unless the buyer is accompanied by a real estate professional.

The beauty of modern real estate practices in this country is that using an agent usually doesn't cost you a dime. In the vast majority of cases, your agent will be paid from a commission of the sale through the seller. You have everything to gain and nothing to lose when you use an agent.

Getting a Mortgage Is Complicated

Looking at mortgage information can be overwhelming—having so many choices and trying to understand all the financial mumbo-jumbo can be a daunting task. Securing a mortgage doesn't have to be difficult, though. Take advantage of the many experts in the lending industry. Talk to several lenders before making a decision. Talk to your friendly banker where you have your checking account, or interview experienced mortgage brokers and choose one who can explain all your options to you and sell you a mortgage loan. These professionals will do the "heavy lifting" and walk you through the approval process for your home loan. Along the way, they will explain the details to you in simple, easily understandable terms.

Tips and Traps _____

Federal and state laws on privacy mandate that any personal information—bank account numbers, Social Security information, and so on—that you provide to your real estate or banking professional stays with them.

I Have to Pay an Agent's Large Commission

In most cases, the seller of the property pays the commissions for both the seller's agent and the buyer's agent. Exceptions to this are usually on an individual property basis.

Foreclosures Are a Much Better Deal

Don't believe that foreclosures—homes from owners who went into default on their mortgage loans—are necessarily a much better deal than a resale or even a new home you're having built. They might sound like they are because the price of a foreclosed home is low, but there can be several problems with foreclosures.

The bank that owns and is selling the foreclosed property really has no knowledge about its history, including any serious defects. Since foreclosures are sold as is, you get what you get—problems and all—and you'll need money to fix those problems. As a result, depending on the situation, you might be paying more money overall once you factor in closing costs, upgrades, and repairs. Make an informed decision before you buy a foreclosed property by getting inspections and finding out the cost of any needed repairs.

You may discover some of the repair issues from normal due diligence during the inspection process, but that's a lot riskier than being able to talk with the individual who currently owns the property.

I'll Be Denied a Mortgage Due to Bad Debt

Approval for a mortgage application depends on a number of factors, bad debts being just one of them. If the bad debts are far enough in your past, many lenders may be willing to overlook them, particularly if your subsequent credit history shows that you pay your obligations now in full and on time.

Do Your Homework

Whether it was deciding where to go to college, what car to buy, or what profession to choose, you probably researched the subject, questioned many people, and consulted a variety of sources before making a final decision. Buying a home is no different. To buy a home that meets your needs, you have to do your homework.

Learn the real estate market, and carefully interview and select a financial professional and a mortgage lender to determine what size home you can afford. You also need to compare different types of loans and interest rates, and find out what the local ordinances and tax structures are. That's a lot of homework, but doing it will help you avoid many of the potentially aggravating pitfalls that can come with buying a home.

Just like when you were in school, consequences arise when you don't do your homework. Let's look at some of the most important things you should do as you move through the home-buying process.

Read the Fine Print

A serious error that too many buyers make is failing to read all the documents they're signing. Let's say that you aren't the type of person who understands mortgages.

You're being transferred to a new city, and when you talk to the mortgage lender that your human resources manager has recommended, he tells you about a great low-rate adjustable mortgage loan that is so cheap it will save you hundreds of dollars on your monthly mortgage payment. Since you don't understand mortgages too well, you trust his judgment, don't research further, and sign on the dotted line.

If you had taken time to read the fine print (or had a more trustworthy mortgage lender), you would have learned that after three years, the loan rate initially increases by 2 percent *per annum* and can further increase every year thereafter up to 1 percent annually, whether you can afford it or not. Let's say you found out in the third year of a 30-year mortgage, so you wanted to refinance into another mortgage loan that was better suited to your needs. But since you didn't read the fine print, you didn't notice that there's a prepayment penalty that you're liable for if you want to pay off the loan within the first 10 years.

def•i•ni•tion

Per annum is another way of saying "by the year" or "every year." It's a term that's usually used when discussing money.

At the fast-paced closing, many people say that they don't have enough time to read the many documents they have to sign. Unfortunately, you can't use that excuse if you find something wrong after the fact. Instead, your mortgage lender should be supplying you with, and explaining, the papers beforehand. Also, your agent can—and should—provide you with a copy of any other documents you will be signing a few days in advance. You can read them carefully, take note of any items you don't understand or don't agree with, and ask your agent to explain or get additional information. A good agent always does this for his clients. It can save a great deal of aggravation later.

Check Out the Location

You've heard the old adage, "location, location, location." It really means that the value of a property, both in absolute terms and in comparison with other properties, comes from where it's located. There are reasons people refer to areas as "good neighborhoods" or "the wrong side of town." Location in real estate is everything—if you don't check out the area thoroughly, it could cause problems down the road.

For example, let's assume you're being transferred from New Hampshire to Oklahoma. You visit Oklahoma on a look-see trip, and while there, you drive past a new subdivision that is being built. If you choose to have your home built there, it will be ready a month before you move to Oklahoma for good. During your trip, you visit with the development's on-site salespeople and, without any further research, you are impressed enough that you sign on the dotted line. You return home happy that you bought a home.

Unfortunately, a few months after you move in, you discover that the area traffic is horrible. You also learn that the city's new multipurpose athletic center will be built a half mile down the road, both worsening the traffic situation and bringing crowd noise when the local team is playing a night game. The price might be a great deal, but just wait until it's time to sell. Whatever negative factor existed when you bought the home will likely still be there when you sell.

Tips and Traps

While scouting locations, read the area's newspaper on its website. Your agent could give you important economic information on the area—job market, real estate market, and so on—but here you can keep on top of all local news and any important facts you may need in making your decision.

You won't be in the greatest situation if you buy a home that's an architectural classic if it's located in a center for gang activity, or if that great new ranch on a half-acre just north of downtown turns out to be on the site of a former manufacturer of toxic chemicals. (In such cases, the seller should inform you about information like this before you buy. If she doesn't, you'll likely have a good reason for legal action against her and her agent.)

Check Out the Local Economy

Perhaps the area you're moving to has just lost one or two of its largest employers. The increased unemployment that results from these closures may adversely affect many things in the community. If you didn't do your homework ahead of time or read about it on the area's town government or newspaper website before you purchased your home in this area, this area's economic problems can affect the value and resale of your home. Again, your real estate agent should tell you about important information, but if she doesn't, make sure *you* ask. In fact, compile a list of such questions about the locale and any buying-related subjects to ask about. You may also want to ask local residents what they know about such things.

Remember, though, real estate agents are very limited with what they are allowed to say about areas for fear of discrimination and fair housing laws. Even if the agents know it has gang problems or is not a safe place to be, as agents they have to be careful as to how they describe the area.

Here's another example. One of the things that attracts you to a particular house is the large open space behind what would be your lot. All that greenery is just beautiful, and you think, "No one would ever be allowed to build there." But you don't verify that with the local authorities. Bad move. If you had done so, you'd have learned that the new regional high school is due to start construction next year exactly on that spot. Yes, it's something your agent should've told you, but it was overlooked.

Never, ever assume that the real estate agent will tell you everything. Although it's her job to explain this information to you, your agent simply may not know the facts because she may not know everything about every area. It's also your responsibility to ask important questions that will help you make the right decision. For example, your agent may not know details about crime statistics for a certain area. However, some police departments maintain websites that provide information of this nature. For example, Oakland's police department has a website that allows you to input an address, then "draw" a radius around it and choose which crime you're concerned about. Then, you hit "Enter," and bingo—it all shows up on the map of the area you've chosen.

Don't Pay Too Much

Your real estate professional will help you decide on a fair purchase price, but if you try to do this without an agent, you could pay way too much for a home. An agent will compare the home you're interested in buying to what other homes are worth in that area. These comparisons, or "comps," will give you a better picture of a fair bid; otherwise, you might bid too high. The result? The seller is happy and you're out a nice chunk of cash.

Don't fall into the trap of going over your budget because you've fallen madly in love with a house. You might think, "It's only a few dollars more per month" or "It'll be a bit tight, but I can make it work somehow." Unfortunately, you'll probably end up struggling financially. *Richmond's Rule:* Never let a house own you!

Get Your Inspections

Some people make the mistake of not obtaining enough home inspections or not following up when further inspections are recommended. For example, your termite inspector might find no active infestation during the routine examination, but he might recommend another in-depth inspection to be sure there's nothing going on in a certain part of the house. You're hesitant to spend the extra money and you're trying to move quickly to closing, so you don't heed the inspector's advice. Two years later, you make the unfortunate discovery that there really was an active infestation exactly where he had recommended further inspection. Never skimp when spending a few dollars now can save you thousands of dollars later!

Think Resale

Yes, this book is about buying a home, but the entire time you're looking at a home, you should be thinking about when the time comes to sell it. Yes, a sale might likely be years away, barring the unexpected, but failing to look at a house now in terms of possible future issues can cost you.

Ask your agent or the local authorities in the new area about any plans for development that could affect your home, both positively and negatively. For example, plans for a new mall, even a few miles from your home, could add extra noise and congestion on your now-quiet street. Being near good shopping is a plus when it comes to selling your home, but having all that new traffic and noise near you may not be. On the other hand, if you find out that the town is building a new manufacturing facility on the opposite side of town, it won't add traffic and noise to your neighborhood, but it can lead to an increased demand for homes in your neighborhood. This is a good thing, because it improves the likelihood of selling your home in the future, possibly for a higher price.

You may also want to take a look at the current trends for new construction in your area. If you are in a city or town that has been doing a lot of building, how will your home compare if the builder wants to build near your neighborhood? Will your home sell if the buyer sees that there are brand-new homes available only one block over? You should know the future plans.

Get It in Writing

Get any verbal agreements with the seller in writing. Most states require that any agreements involving the sale of real estate be in writing. If you've got your heart set on that beautiful antique crystal chandelier and sconces in the dining room and the seller agrees, get it in writing and make sure both parties sign the agreement. If you fail to do so and notice that the items are missing when you're moving in, you'll probably be out of luck. To be sure everything you want is left, compile a list of these items as a reminder, and then cite them in your offer.

Get to Know People

Another thing to do is get to know your neighbors. Take a stroll around the area and knock on a few doors. Introduce yourself as the potential neighbor, and ask if they mind answering a few questions you have about the area in general and the home in particular. Talk to local business owners to find out about the local economy, or take a trip over to the local government offices and find out about the neighborhood. It can add a great deal of information about where you're thinking of buying.

Get to Know the Area

Drive by any potential homes a few times during the day. Is there a lot of traffic to turn left onto your main street in the morning? What are typical commute times to and from the home? After school, are neighborhood kids outside playing and exercising? On Friday night, does the home across the street have 10 cars out front and loud music blaring from the backyard? Does the neighborhood feel scary or safe at night?

Don't Be Afraid

It might sound like you have to avoid many mistakes when buying a home. But don't be afraid. We take you step-by-step through the entire process, and we give you tips and suggestions so you won't let these situations happen to you.

It can be overwhelming and hard to stay focused and relaxed when you're trying to buy a home. After all, you already have other things on your mind—your job, kids, housework, hobbies, and more. You have to go through houses, meet with lenders and real estate agents, do research, the list goes on …. It's okay. Take it one step at a time and breathe. We'll get through this together. Remember, this is an exciting time in your life!

The Least You Need to Know

- Don't listen to the advice of other home buyers without checking it out first.
- Check with your tax expert to see what other new tax breaks you're eligible for.
- Location, location, location is important, but so is read, read, read … read documents thoroughly before you sign them.
- Spend some time in the neighborhood to see what kind of community it is.

Chapter 2

Getting Started

In This Chapter

- ◆ Determining your wants and your needs in a home
- ◆ Identifying the different types of homes
- ◆ Figuring out how many bedrooms and bathrooms you need
- ◆ Looking at the land
- ◆ Checking out the neighborhood

Although it happens, most people don't just wake up one day and say, "I think I'll buy a new house." The decision is usually the result of one or more changes in your life. In some cases, the catalyst may be a change in your employment situation—you accepted a new job, you were promoted and received a sizeable pay increase, you were transferred to a new city, or your apartment lease is due to expire in a few months. In other cases, the number of family members in your home is increasing or decreasing. These changes are either forcing a change in your housing situation or giving you the necessary push to start an earnest search.

Whatever the reason, after you decide to buy, you must figure out exactly what features you desire in a home. Will it be a condominium, a cooperative, or a single-family home? Do you want a newer home with less upkeep, or do you want a home in an established neighborhood with charming bungalows? Do you want a lot of land and a small house, or a big home and a little plot of land to call your own? It's time to start planning!

Whenever you embark on a big project, it's best to make a plan and a list of what you want to accomplish. This chapter helps you figure out your wants and your needs. It's about deciding what kind of a home you want to live in and how many bedrooms and bathrooms it has to have. By the end of this chapter, you'll know exactly what you want your dream home to be.

Your Dream Home

Some buyers have an idea of what their dream home should look like. This idea may be so clear that if the mind were a Nikon camera, you could hook it up to your computer and print a poster-sized, full-color picture in all its glory. Other buyers have no idea what they want in a home. A former colleague once said that the first thing to consider in whatever goal you are trying to achieve is your "ultimate"—in other words, what you want if there were no limitations or barriers to that goal. He called this ultimate his Big Hairy Audacious Goal, or BHAG. So what would you want if there were no limitations? You could have anything you want in the home, any features. The house you ultimately buy may not have everything that your BHAG lists, but it's a good starting point from which you can work backward.

Your Wants

Wants are what you'd *like* to have in your home, without any monetary or other constraints, whether reasonable or taken from your BHAG. Examples of wants include a specific view, jetted bathtubs, a wine cellar, a swimming pool, wood floors or carpeting, and so on. Make a list of what you want and then prioritize that list. It's okay to dream about the perfect home—that's the point of this exercise. It doesn't mean you'll find a home that has all your wants, but it's a great way to get started.

Your Needs

Now let's get real. Your list of wants is ready, but your needs are determined by the actual requirements of your personal life and your budget. Make a prioritized list of your needs and your wants on a piece of paper. Of course, it's perfectly fine to have both, as long as they both fit into your budget.

For example, you may want a home with five bedrooms, a study, and a library. But the reality is you may *need* only three bedrooms; a bathroom; and a decent-sized backyard for your kids, for your dog, and for entertaining. Determining your needs list depends on such factors as these:

- ◆ **The size of your family**—You need enough square footage, bathrooms, and bedrooms to live comfortably.

- ◆ **Family health requirements**—For example, do you need to live in a one-story home for accessibility purposes?

- ◆ **Location**—Do you need to live in a certain area?

- ◆ **Your lifestyle**—For example, do you need space for frequent entertaining?

- ◆ **The number of cars you have**—Do you need a one-, two-, or three-car garage?

- ◆ **Your and your family's hobbies**—For example, do you need garage space for bicycles or a yard for your award-winning tulips?

- ◆ **Your career**—Do you run a business from home?

Determining your needs will help you cut costs and narrow your selections to exactly what fits your requirements.

Types of Homes

When choosing the type of home you want to live in, you have many options, each with its advantages and disadvantages. Types of homes to choose from include a condominium, a townhome, a cooperative, a single-family detached home, tenants-in-common, a duplex, and a fixer-upper.

Condominium

First and foremost, you need to consider what you can afford. Usually, a first-time home buyer starts with something that is a step up from what they're living in now. For example, if you're living in an apartment, you may look for a small single-family home. However, that may not always work out. If the place you've been renting already comes with a number of amenities—for example, access to a common club-house and pool—you might want your new single-family home to have such amenities, too. That may be cost-prohibitive, depending on your budget, so you may want to think about purchasing a condominium.

A condominium, often referred to as a condo, is a single housing unit within a group of housing units in a complex. Owners of a condo have exclusive ownership of the space within the four walls of the unit but share the *common areas* with the other condo owners. Condominiums can be individual units in a larger building, like an apartment building, or they can be smaller clusters of two to four housing units per building in a larger group of such buildings spread over a larger parcel of land.

The exterior and all the common areas are the responsibility of the homeowners' association, or HOA. The HOA membership is made up of the unit owners in the complex. Governing officers are elected from this membership according to rules established and periodically updated by vote of the membership. Each owner pays a monthly dues fee to the HOA, which holds these funds to pay for repairs or upgrade work on the complex. This charge isn't included in your mortgage payment, so make sure your budget allows for this. If the HOA doesn't have enough money for a repair, it collects an *assessment fee*.

def•i•ni•tion

Common areas are sections of the property outside the four walls of your home that you share with other members of the association. These may include hallways, roads, lobbies, the roof, a pool, gyms, and more.

Sometimes collected dues aren't enough to cover an expense. For example, the association's tennis court might be cracking and in need of repair, or the clubhouse roof might be leaking and need to be replaced. In this case, the membership will be asked to approve by vote a special **assessment fee,** in which money is collected to specifically cover the expense of the task at hand.

Assessments can sometimes be an unpleasant surprise for owners, but they are no different than the owner of a single-family residence unexpectedly finding that he needs to replace the roof or some other component of his home at his own expense.

Warning!

Make sure you have some flexibility in your budget to pay an assessment if one arises—assessments are mandatory payments. Failure to pay them can result in a lien being placed on your condo unit to force payment. If you fail to pay, the HOA can foreclose on the property because of the lien and have your unit sold at auction to get its payment.

Townhouse

A townhouse, or townhome, operates exactly the same way a condominium does. The owner owns the individual unit, with rights covering everything inside the home. The outside of the structure and common grounds are owned jointly by the owners and administered by the HOA. The HOA collects monthly dues and any special assessments. As with a condo, the HOA is administered by officers elected by the general membership of the HOA. The day-to-day tasks, as well as any repairs, are managed and paid for by a management firm engaged by the HOA.

The only difference between a typical condo and a townhouse is that condos are often multiple units in a large building, but townhomes are usually individual residential structures, or structures that include no more than two or three units per building, all arranged together on one large parcel of land. The townhome owners also share the common grounds and facilities. Some associations offer both condominiums and townhomes.

Cooperative

A cooperative, usually referred to as a "co-op," is an individually owned residential unit that is a part of a larger whole. However, it's different from condos and townhomes in that owners own shares of the whole building, with specifically assigned rights to live in and use a unit as their own. Unlike a condo or townhome, owners don't own the living space within the walls of the individual unit. Co-ops are usually more common in Eastern states, especially in New York.

For budgeting purposes, remember that if you want to buy a co-op, you also must pay maintenance charges just as if you were living in a townhome or condo. These charges are determined by how many shares you own in the building. The more shares you own, the more your maintenance charges may be.

Single-Family Detached Home

As the name implies, a single-family detached home is one house on a lot that houses only one family. It is not physically connected to any other home, and the rooms are fully contained in a single structure. Unlike a condominium-type structure, a single-family home shares no common features with any other unit, such as a laundry room, a garage, or storage space. It may or may not have a garage or carport, and if it does, that structure can be either attached or detached from the home.

When you buy a single-family detached home, you are solely responsible for all its maintenance and upgrades, both inside and out. If you want to redo your kitchen, that's your prerogative. If the carpet in the hallway is getting threadbare, that's your problem. If the roof or grounds need maintenance, it's your responsibility. Nobody else will repair it for you. This home is truly your castle, for better or worse. This changes only if the home is part of an association in which someone else takes care of the outdoor property and you are responsible for only your home.

Duplex

A duplex is a combination of two separate areas of living space under one owner. In the case of a duplex, an owner purchases and owns an entire building and then leases the second unit to a tenant for a specific period of time. In this case, you would own the building and grounds—inside and out—just as you would with a single-family detached home, and you would have full control and responsibility for the property.

One important note is worth mentioning here: although duplexes have been referred to as one building with two units inside, some duplexes actually are separate structures sold together, with each structure being an individual living unit. The units have separate keyed entrances, utilities, and mail delivery; if parking is included, they also have separate parking facilities. Inside, each has its own kitchen, bedrooms, bathrooms, and other rooms. You could lease the second unit or keep it vacant, use it for storage of your personal possessions, or use it as your place of business, depending on the local zoning codes.

Buying a duplex offers an additional benefit. Because you can rent out the second unit, this allows you additional savings on your income tax because that second unit becomes an investment property, with all the potential tax savings such a property receives. However, some states exact higher property taxes for investment property; ask your agent or financial representative. We cover this more in Chapter 8.

Just keep in mind that a duplex isn't the same as a "mother-daughter," mother-in-law, or in-law home. These homes have additional space for a family member to live with you and share some of the features of the home. It has its own entrance and maybe its own kitchen, bathroom, and living room. Depending on the zoning laws in your area, you may or may not be able to rent it. You may use the area for an elderly relative who is staying with you or for an older teen who needs or wants her own space. Presumably, the arrangement could also have the relative living in a guest cottage or carriage house on the grounds. The physical structure isn't as important as the arrangement.

Tenants-in-Common

Another way of buying a home isn't as common but is gaining popularity, particularly on both coasts and in a few major cities throughout the country. In a tenants-in-common, or TIC, arrangement, you purchase a share in a building and simultaneously own your area and jointly share ownership in the overall building, based on your percentage of the original purchase.

A TIC arrangement involves at least two separate owners, although there is no limit on the number of owners of a TIC property. Each owner has a legal ownership to some part of the whole, but not every owner must have an equal share in the property. Each owner's share is mutually exclusive of the others and may be sold independently of the other shares. An immediate benefit to each of the common owners is that a TIC arrangement allows ownership at a lower entry cost than if any single owner had to pay for the entire home.

For example, let's say three unrelated people agree to buy a three-bedroom home as a TIC purchase. If they're smart, they'll have a legal document drawn up for them, laying out the details of their purchase, including who owns what rights and the size of each person's share. Each person will obtain his own mortgage financing for his share of the purchase and contribute his percentage share of the down payment. The sum of these contributions will add up to 100 percent of the purchase price. When the purchase closes, the three buyers will own the building in common with each other.

If an owner wants to sell after a period of time, the others do not have to agree to sell as well. The owner who wants to sell places his share of the property on the market. Whoever buys that share becomes a common owner of the property along with the other two existing owners. If this sounds confusing, don't worry: many real estate professionals don't understand the concept either. Some won't get involved in a TIC just because of its unique details. Nevertheless, it is a viable option in some areas.

Fixer-Upper

A fixer-upper is a home that is in less-than-perfect condition at the time of purchase. Fixer-uppers generally require less up-front cost and can be almost any type of home—a single-family detached home, a condominium, a townhouse, or a duplex.

Usually the price is lower than for similar properties in the area that don't need as much work. A fixer-upper can be a cosmetic fixer or what's charitably known as a teardown. This should give you a loose idea of how much will be necessary to get the property into what you think is satisfactory condition. Some people buy fixer-uppers to save money and then do the repairs over time. Others buy them because they enjoy the creative outlet and want to give the home their own personal touch.

Whatever the reason, cosmetic fixing of a fixer-upper can be as simple as repainting the interior, changing some of the landscaping, or replacing such items as the wall-to-wall carpeting or the baseboard and ceiling moldings. The work is relatively inexpensive, not structural, and is designed to improve the appearance of the home. If the home needs only cosmetic fixing, you can probably live in it while the repairs are being made. On the other hand, if the repairs are more extensive—for example, the home needs a new electrical system, plumbing system, furnace, or ducting system (especially in the winter), or an entire new foundation—keep in mind that the price of the home may be lower, but the cost of the repairs will be substantial. You will also probably need to live somewhere else until the repairs are made, so add that into your budget, too.

Tips and Traps

Before settling on any price for a fixer-upper, have your contractor come by and look at what needs to be done to the house. Then get a bid for the required work and consider it along with the purchase price to see how much the total amount will be for the home and the repairs. Compare that total to comparable homes in the area that aren't fixer-uppers. When making the cost comparison, don't forget to include your temporary residential costs if it's a major fixer-upper that won't be habitable for some time. Be aware also that some banks offer special combined repair/purchase mortgages for just this situation.

Inside the Home

The inside of your home can loosely be referred to as the floor plan. The floor plan governs the size of the living space inside the home, the "flow" of the house (how easy movement inside the house is), the functionality of the home, and, to some degree, the suitability of a particular home to your lifestyle.

Does the home have adequate bedrooms and bathrooms for the size of your family? Is the kitchen sufficient for your needs in assembling meals for you, any family members, and guests that you may have from time to time? Is there adequate space for your hobby? Remember, a poorly designed floor plan can be one of the most costly things to change in a home. In general, if you do not like the floor plan, you should look further or have a skilled professional take a closer look. Making changes could require moving *load-bearing walls*, and that can be a very serious issue.

def•i•ni•tion

Load-bearing walls are interior walls that structurally support the weight of the upper floors and roof of the structure. You must be very careful when considering moving or altering these walls.

Square Footage

When you're reading listings of homes for sale, you will see the size of the home measured as square footage—for example, "Colonial-style home with three bedrooms, two baths, and 1,500 square feet." The square footage of a home is the living area of the house inside its walls. It is also one of the bases for calculating the value of a home. Generally, a home with a larger living space is worth more than a home of similar design that has fewer square feet in its interior.

There really is no typical size of living area from one home to the next. However, it is safe to say that any floor plan with fewer than 1,000 square feet of living area is considered a small home, no matter how many rooms the home has. It is also safe to say that any home over 4,000 square feet of interior space is a large home.

Tips and Traps

To calculate square footage of a room, multiply the length of the room by the width of the room. For example, if the living room is 15 feet long by 12 feet wide, the square footage of the room is 180 square feet. Square footage of a house is generally a little more than the total of the area of each of the interior rooms. The reason it totals more than the sizes of all the rooms taken together is that it also includes the thicknesses of the walls separating one room from the next.

Bedrooms

Now that we know how much living space the home has, let's take a look at how that living space is divided. Usually, the first feature buyers look at is the number of bedrooms. Obviously, how many you need depends on two basic considerations: the number of people in your family who will be occupying the home and, based on your lifestyle, the frequency and number of overnight guests.

A single adult with few planned overnight guests may require only one or two bedrooms, while a family of five or six—especially a family with older children who may require their own rooms—may need at least four or five bedrooms for family, and more if they want a guest room. The largest bedroom in the home is usually called the master bedroom. If it has a bathroom accessible from the bedroom, it is referred to as a master suite. However, there are some instances where the bath in a master suite also has access from a hallway or other bedroom. Your seller may still consider this to be a master bedroom. In my opinion, as well as that of many other experts in the field, this outside access effectively removes it from "master" status.

> **Warning!**
>
> To qualify as a bedroom, a room must have its own separate entrance from the hallway and a closet. From time to time, sellers call rooms bedrooms even when they are accessed through another bedroom or do not have a built-in closet. You can certainly use this as a bedroom, but it can't officially be called a bedroom in a sale.

You may also want to consider the location of the bedrooms. If you are single, a bedroom at the end of the house away from everything else is probably just fine. However, if you have children, bedroom placement can be more of an issue. For example, if you have a baby or youngster, you may want your child's room close to your master bedroom. If your kids are into or beyond their teens—or if you have an adult child or elderly parent living with you—you might want a master bedroom located on a separate floor from the others.

Consider the bedroom size next, especially if you or a child has a hobby or interest that requires extra space. For example, if your son makes and collects model airplanes, a slightly larger bedroom with space to display his collection may be desirable. Or perhaps your daughter is a gymnast and has won a number of awards that she'd like the space to display in her room.

Also, family size and particular use requirements should be considered. Will siblings share a bedroom, or does your high school–aged daughter need a desk and bookshelf area for her studies?

Something else to consider, but often forgotten, is emergency exit safety. Does each bedroom have easy access to the outside in case of an emergency? Some municipalities have ordinances that require second-story bedrooms to have some form of installed exit method, such as a collapsible fire escape outside a window. Ground-floor bedroom windows should be large enough for someone inside to escape. This may save your life.

Bathrooms

Along with bedrooms, it's important to consider how many bathrooms the home has. Again, the number you need depends on how many people are living in the home. If you are a single homeowner, one *full bath* or one full and one *half-bath* might be sufficient. If you have a guest room, you may want a home with two bathrooms.

def•i•ni•tion

A bathroom is a **full bath** if it has a toilet, a sink, and either a tub or shower (or both). A **half-bath** has a sink and a toilet, but no bathtub or shower. There is also a three-quarter bath, but the general definition of it fits a basic full bath. The distinction is that sellers who claim a three-quarter bath are saying it has either a bath without a shower or just a shower, but not both. A quarter-bath has a toilet only, with no sink to wash afterward. Although this lack of sink usually goes against our concepts of personal hygiene, the quarter-bath format occasionally shows up in a house. Usually, however, this format occurs in an older home where a subsequent owner has added another bathroom.

If you are a family of four, at least two baths may be necessary to keep everyone happy. Yes, a family of four can survive and thrive with only a single bath, but it can make for regular moments of tension when everyone is trying to get moving to work and school in the morning, or preparing for evening plans out on the town. The larger the family, the more bathrooms you may want.

Kitchen

When considering the kitchen, you need to take many things into account beyond what you'll have on the menu for dinner tonight. When looking for a new home, try to find a home that has a kitchen that meets your needs. Altering a kitchen can be one of the most expensive remodeling projects out there. Also, a kitchen probably has more effect on resale value than any other part of a home.

The size and capability of your kitchen depends on your lifestyle and the number of people living in the home. A larger family, and even a single homeowner or couple that frequently entertains, may need a bigger kitchen. If the kitchen comes with a small dining area, it is called an eat-in kitchen. Kitchens can also include a small room, called a pantry, off the kitchen where the foodstuffs are stored.

Home Office/Den

A den is an extra room that can be used for relaxation or socializing. A den can also be converted into a home office where you can handle personal or work-related activities or into a home gym. It can also be a playroom for the kids to hang out and play. Usually a home office or den is located away from the kitchen, to minimize distractions by the cooking or mealtime activity. Sometimes, in larger homes, a den or office may also have its own separate entrance, as well as interior access.

Living and Family Rooms

A living room is usually a formal room for family events or entertaining. Frequently, it is one of the largest, if not the largest, room in the home.

A family room can be located in any part of the home, and it's usually in addition to having a living room. Think of it as an extra space for entertaining. Here's where it gets a little interesting. When you're looking around, the home might have what's called a "great room." This is a living area that connects to the kitchen or dining room, making it one big space. A great room can be a family room, but a family room is not necessarily a great room.

Dining Room

A dining room is used for exactly what the name suggests. Typically bigger than an eat-in kitchen area, the dining room serves as a formal sit-down area for full meals and is often near or connected to the kitchen, with access by a doorway or a pass-through area. Usually, the room is large enough for intimate family dining or for larger gatherings of friends and guests, such as holidays or celebrations.

Other Rooms

In addition to the basic rooms we've already discussed, you can buy a home with other rooms, depending on how much you want to spend and your wants and needs.

For example, if you are a painter or sculptor, you may buy a home with space for an art studio. Are you into photography? Consider a room for a photo lab. Do you like dance or martial arts? You might want a room large enough to practice. In today's market, it's common in middle- to upper-priced homes to have a wine cellar. You may also need an attic or extra room for storage.

In many parts of the country, homes commonly have basements, which can vary from a large empty area used mostly for storage, to an area that is further divided into a number of rooms. Included among these basement rooms may be a media room, set up with a TV and other electronic entertainment equipment, and an exercise room, equipped with various exercise equipment such as a treadmill or stationary bike and weights. A basement can also be used for a home office, a playroom, a game room, a bedroom, or any combination of all of these. Basically, the only limitation is your imagination!

The laundry room, which can be located on any floor in the house, usually has a washer and dryer, and possibly a closet or other storage area for washing supplies. It may also have counters for folding clothes and an area for ironing. In some homes, the laundry room may be connected to the upper floor of the home by a laundry chute, to aid in getting the dirty laundry to the laundry area. In some higher-end or larger homes, there may even be two laundry rooms for convenience.

Garage

Once made to keep a car out of the elements, today's garages are far more than just a simple covered parking space. The mere existence of a garage now adds value to a home. A garage can be an extra storage space with beautifully planned shelves and cabinet systems for storage. Some garages also have a workshop area, a half-bath, and even laundry appliances.

Consider whether the garage is attached or detached from the home. If it's attached, you won't have to haul the groceries from the car through the rain or snow to get to the house. If the garage is detached, how far is it from the entrance of the home? Also, make sure the garage has a fire-retardant door leading into the home. Due to the potential for automobile- or workshop-related fires, the connecting door should be a certified fire-retardant to slow down and protect the home from a garage fire. This is often missing in older homes because the door was installed before building codes were updated to require this type of safety door.

When looking at a garage, see if there is outside access other than through the main garage door, and ask if the garage comes with a remote electronic door opener.

In some of the warmer climes in the nation, a carport is a common alternative to a garage. It provides coverage from rain for the family car and, like a garage, allows parking off the street. However, because it does not have the wall structure of a garage, it does not usually offer the storage capabilities of a fully enclosed garage.

Quotes and Facts

Climate could be a concern when deciding on whether to buy a single-family home with an attached or detached garage. I grew up in New England, with its severe winter weather, and had to cross a large backyard from the rear of my house to get to the garage. The guy next door had a heated garage that was connected to the interior of the home through the kitchen. He never had to put on his overcoat to get from his home to his car.

—Peter

Land

No matter what type of home you buy, it sits on a piece of land, and the price you pay for most homes usually includes the cost of that land. However, if you're buying a condo, it includes the fractional share of the overall condominium site that is deed-apportioned to your unit. The only exception to this is in a few local areas where homes may be built on leased land.

You should look at the land the same way you look at the home. Generally, the most important thing to consider is the size of the parcel. Usually measured in either square feet or *acres*, the general rule is that the larger the land, the more expensive the home. For example, in the same neighborhood or area with comparable home values, a three-bedroom, two-bath home of 1,500 square feet will be more valuable on a one-acre lot that backs up to woods than the same house on a small quarter-acre lot that is surrounded on all sides by other homes.

When envisioning your home, you need to envision the land it will sit on, too. Maybe you've always dreamt about a home on a hill overlooking a nearby ocean. You might have always wanted a home that sits on a large tract of open land or is in the middle of a forest. Maybe you want land so you can create the perfect garden. Choosing the land is almost as important as choosing the home. Why? A home sitting on a half-acre lot overlooking a nearby ocean is generally worth more than the same home situated on a half-acre lot that looks onto a vacant lot.

def•i•ni•tion

An **acre** of land is 43,560 square feet. If you want to convert square feet to acres, divide the number of square feet by 43,560. The answer is the number of acres. For example, 21,450 square feet is 0.4924 acres. A lot of 11,500 square feet is 0.264 acres, and so on.

Keep in mind, however, that there isn't much you can change about your land. If it doesn't overlook the ocean, it never will, and if the yard is too small, sits at the foot of a cliff, or is surrounded by other homes, it will always be that way.

Your Yard

The yard is like an outside room. It's where a majority of your outside activities will take place. Just as you would decorate a room within the walls of your home, you have free rein to do the same to the area in your yard. You can fence it in, thereby limiting access to anyone else outside the home. You can—subject to local zoning regulations—build outbuildings or recreational facilities on it. You can also landscape it with trees, shrubs, and flowers to your own personal taste.

The yard also may be one of the reasons you choose one home over others. Perhaps you like to garden in your spare time. You may see an unused yard and envision rows of tomato plants, peppers, cucumbers, squash, and maybe a few sets of blueberry or strawberry bushes. Or the yard may be the perfect place for your young children or dogs to safely run around. Maybe you're the type of person who isn't interested in maintaining a large yard, so a small yard requiring minimal maintenance will do just fine.

Pools, Patios, and Decks

You may want to have other features and amenities in your home, including a swimming pool, a patio or deck (with or without a gas barbeque), a gazebo, garden potting sheds, storage sheds, or detached artist studios. These extras may increase the price of the home. If they don't exist but are something you want after you move in, make sure the yard has enough space to build on.

Tips and Traps _____

If you're thinking of adding on to the home or building something in the yard, contact the local permitting authorities before you sign the purchase contract. This way, you'll know ahead of time whether you'll be allowed to add these amenities.

Location, Location, Location

Where do you want to live? Your new home's real estate value will be affected by its location. A home in a neighborhood with low crime statistics or with owners who are upper-class wage earners is worth more than a home in a lower-income neighborhood with higher crime statistics.

Although it's not always the case, some neighborhoods are less expensive because of their past history. Perhaps the area once had a reputation as a crime-riddled area, was once an industrial site, or is located near a busy railroad or highway. On the flip side, the home might be in an area that's experiencing a renaissance after some hard times. If there has been some renewal and growth to the area, it may be an opportunity for you to get an excellent home for a more affordable price. This will lead to an increase in value over time.

If you're looking for a less expensive home, you can also check out past military housing that has been converted into housing units. The former site of Hamilton Air Force Base, located in northern California, is a good example of this. It's also possible to find an affordable home, such as a fixer-upper, in a pricey neighborhood. You'll buy it at a lower cost, upgrade and repair it, and earn equity almost immediately simply because of the neighborhood it's in. Again, however, keep in mind you will need the money to repair and upgrade the home.

The Commute

Unless you work from home or are retired, your commute is a very important factor to consider when buying a home. How far do you have to travel to get to work, and how much time will it take? You should also investigate the public transit system to see if buses and trains have stops in your area. Your real estate professional will be able to advise you or direct you to sources for this information, or you can visit the public transit websites to check routes and schedules. If you do need to use the public transit system, add in the cost of your commute to your home-buying budget.

If you're transferring to a new office, talk with your new colleagues and the human resources department for the real scoop on commuting issues in your new hometown.

Neighborhoods

Unless you're buying a home in a rural or mountain area with plenty of land around you, you're likely to buy in a neighborhood.

Some neighborhoods are close enough to the town center that you can walk. Others may lie farther from downtown, but feature less traffic and larger plots of land. Others offer easy access to local recreational venues or to a freeway for your commute. Choosing a neighborhood depends on your wants and needs.

Talk to your real estate professional about what type of neighborhood has more added value where you want to live. For example, you may want to buy a home close enough to walk to town, but consider that this location might also be very traffic congested. The home might also be harder to sell later because of this. In other towns, homes that are located close to town actually command higher prices. It all depends on what's on your list of must-haves and where you're looking.

Buying a home in some neighborhoods might cost you more simply because of their historical significance or the fact that there are restrictions on remodeling the homes there. A good example of this is in the Brooklyn Heights section of New York, where homeowners are restricted from altering the outside of their historical brownstone homes. If they want to repair or upgrade the inside of their home, they must follow specific guidelines. As a result, the value and costs of these homes are higher, so think about this if that's the type of neighborhood you want to live in. Keep in mind, however, that you can check in advance with local authorities if you plan to make any modifications after you close—find out your limitations before you buy.

Schools

Even if you don't have children, the quality of the local schools is a major factor in determining what you'll pay for your home. Communities with good school systems always command higher home prices. This can be further extended within an individual community if one school has historically better test scores than all the others. When you narrow the areas where you want to live, ask your real estate agent for school information. When it comes to budgeting, also factor in that, if you have kids and you have chosen a home where the local school system isn't particularly good, you may have to consider a private school.

Tips and Traps _____

Another way to assess the local school district, and any particular school, is to talk with local school officials and ask to see the schools' test scores. If you're checking out a high school, ask for the most recent number of graduates and college acceptances. You can also find out what colleges the students were accepted to.

Shopping

Are you looking to buy a home that's accessible to a grocery store and mall, or are you looking for a home that's as far away as possible from the nearest mall? If shopping proximity is important to you, you can do three things. First, ask your Realtor for information. She'll be able to tell you where all the major stores are located and how to get there. Second, once you find a home you're interested in, take a drive from its location to the stores where you'd likely be shopping. See how long it takes, how easy it is to park there, and how traffic is along the route. Third, call the local Chamber of Commerce and get information and recommendations on local businesses. This will help you determine what's available in your neighborhood or town, and when you will have to travel. To find your local Chamber of Commerce, visit www.uschamber.com.

The Least You Need to Know

- Once you separate needs and wants and then compare them to your budget, you'll know exactly what kind of home you should be looking for.

- The better the school, the more valuable the neighborhood becomes, so ask for test scores and other information.

- Consider how close the home you want should be to shopping and public transportation.

- Doing all this brainstorming now makes the home-buying process easier later. You'll have spent the time necessary to focus on what items really count instead of features you can't afford or those that have nothing to do with your lifestyle.

- You can't buy a home without looking at the whole picture—the house, land, neighborhood, and community.

Chapter 3

Finding a Realtor

In This Chapter

- How a real estate professional can help you
- What agents do and don't do
- How to find the right agent for you
- Real estate commissions—who pays?

When you're looking for your perfect home, you need to have an experienced real estate professional—also known as a real estate agent, broker, or Realtor—leading the way. This professional knows the current real estate market and the values of homes in particular neighborhoods. This professional will also give you all the information you need to make your decision, show you homes in your price range, and guide you through the process of making a bid and signing the final paperwork.

A word of caution: quickly discard the notion of doing a home search and purchase by yourself, no matter what other people may have told you. Although it is perfectly acceptable to look at home listings on the Internet to get an idea of what you'd like—and no laws require you to use a Realtor or agent to purchase a house—we caution you against attempting the entire transaction by yourself. Although many buyers have successfully purchased homes without a real estate professional by their side, the process can be complicated—and real estate laws and contracts are tricky. By using an experienced real estate professional to help you find a home, you get the added bonus of their experience and knowledge of the local market, area homes, laws, and contracts. That is truly invaluable and can save you thousands of dollars in the long run. Best of all, as we said in Chapter 1, it's almost always free, as the Realtor is typically paid by the seller.

In this chapter, you'll discover how to interview and decide on a real estate professional to work with. We discuss the differences between a real estate agent, broker, and Realtor, including the type of education and certification each has. This chapter also explains what an agent does and doesn't do for you. Finally, you'll learn about an agent's commission—who pays and how much.

What's a Realtor?

A real estate professional can also be called a real estate agent, broker, or Realtor—you can use any of these to help find your new home. These terms can be used interchangeably (and are in this book), but each title is based either on the person's amount of real estate education and experience, or in some cases on their individual desire to carry or not carry the additional legal burdens of being a broker. Anyone who has successfully completed a real estate licensing course—licensed by the state in which he lives—to sell real estate is referred to as a real estate agent or salesperson. An agent can list and sell property and is the legal agent for his client, whether it's the buyer or the seller, under the laws of his state. An agent cannot open his own business, but instead must work under a more experienced real estate broker.

A broker is an agent who has passed a broker's exam. She has furthered her education after becoming an agent and may have a few years of real estate experience as well. In some states, earning a college degree can substitute for real-life experience. After earning her degree, the agent can then take a broker's license examination. Be careful, though, because while this is possible, it means that someone can earn a broker's license but have no practical hands-on experience. You want a professional with field experience. Ask the potential agent: "How many years have you been working as a Realtor? How long have you had your broker's license?"

You'll notice that the term *Realtor* is capitalized in this book. That's because the National Association of Realtors (NAR), a trade association of real estate professionals, has copyrighted the title and capitalized the first letter as part of its copyright. If someone is a licensed broker but is not a member of the NAR or your local Association of Realtors, he cannot use the Realtor title.

To become a member of the NAR, a real estate professional must first join his local real estate board. Membership in a local association automatically extends his membership to the state and national associations.

Tips and Traps

Eighty-five percent of sellers were assisted by a real estate agent when selling their home, according to NAR's 2007 Profile of Home Buyers and Sellers. Seventy-nine percent of buyers purchased their home through a real estate agent or broker.

Education and Certification

In the past, an agent with a college or graduate degree in real estate was an exception to the rule. If an agent did possess a degree, it might have been earned in the business field or another subject. Today, thanks to the development of more real estate degree programs at many colleges, it's quite common for someone who is interested in real estate to not only earn a college degree in some area of real estate, but to go on and earn a graduate degree, too. In my own office, a number of Realtors have Master's degrees, at least one has a Ph.D., and a couple agents (myself included) have law degrees. This additional education helps the agent understand legal and financial contracts.

In addition to secondary education and the real estate licensing course they must take, agents must take state-mandated continuing education courses. Each state has its own course requirements for professionals to keep up their knowledge of a changing industry and to better improve their skills. These topics can include marketing, finance, investment analysis, Internet marketing, and international real estate, to name just a few.

Tips and Traps

If you're just starting to browse for a home now but you don't plan to buy until a little later, let your agent know so he can plan accordingly.

If a Realtor continues to take additional courses through either the NAR or other real estate organizations, she can earn various certifications. These designations show that a Realtor is specially qualified in certain areas. Some of these certifications include, but are not limited to, residential, commercial and industrial, and international real estate. The education varies with the designation.

Why is a real estate professional with a designation important to you as a buyer? First, the designation lets you know that your Realtor has gone beyond merely getting his license. He's gone through additional courses to improve his education. Are there excellent agents with no designations? Yes, but the fact that an agent has a special designation says that this agent has broadened his professional knowledge and been in the business for a period of time.

Many designations are used in the real estate industry. Here's a list of many that a real estate professional can earn:

◆ **Certified Residential Specialist (CRS)**—This is the most common designation for agents. CRS training requires that the agent pass several graduate-level courses and maintain a constant level of productivity over a period of years. It is a very distinguished certification: only 100,000 agents out of 1.4 million licensed real estate agents nationwide have a CRS designation. That's barely 7 percent of all agents.

Tips and Traps

Visit the website www.crs.com to search for agents who have earned the CRS designation.

◆ **e-PRO Certification**—This is NAR's online training program to certify real estate professionals as Internet Professionals. An Internet Professional is an agent who not only is a successful Realtor, but also has learned to use the Internet to help his clients successfully buy and sell real property.

◆ **Graduate Realtor Institute (GRI)**—This designation from the NAR's Institute shows that the Realtor has done much studying to improve his ability to service and market real estate.

◆ **Certified Commercial and Investment Member (CCIM)**—This is typically a designation for commercial agents, but some residential Realtors also earn this designation because investment property can include investment in residential property. The two are linked by the concerns any investor in real estate has, regardless of the type of real property involved.

◆ **CyberStar**—The CyberStar designation is given by invitation only to agents known for their expertise in using cutting-edge technology in their practices. Virtually all CyberStar agents are tops in their geographic area, and many also hold the CRS designation. Their expertise is sought after by home buyers, sellers, other Realtors, and Realtor associations. Visit www.cyberstars.net for more information. Only about 200 U.S. agents and a half-dozen overseas possess the designation of CyberStar.

Two international designations indicate that the holder focuses at least a portion of his professional activity in the international arena, servicing property in many different nations or assisting buyers and sellers in more than one country.

♦ **Certified International Property Specialist (CIPS)**—This course is offered by the CCIM Institute. It's a curriculum that distinguishes CIPS designees as individuals who have had hands-on experience in international real estate transactions.

♦ **Transnational Referral Certification course (TRC)**—This is another international certification course that is developed by the International Consortium of Real Estate Associations (ICREΛ).

These certifications will give you an idea of how much additional education your agent has had. However, this doesn't mean that agents who lack a CRS—or any of the other designations, for that matter—are not good agents. Quite the contrary! Many agents faithfully pursue many avenues of continuing education but never attempt to attain any of these designations. They may be focused on practical experience and take some continuing education courses along the way. Others do extensive continuing education study, but not enough in one program to qualify for the designations.

Agents Who Specialize

A real estate agent can also specialize. Some specializations are noted in an agent's designations, as we just discussed. An agent can also specialize in the sale of a particular type of real estate. For example, some agents list and sell only condos or townhomes. A former colleague specialized in this type of property to the extent that she was sometimes referred to as the "condo queen."

Some agents specialize in estate properties—these are entire estates of someone who has passed away and the home is just part of the package. Some agents specialize in ranch or "equestrian" properties, which are properties that commonly have a lot of acreage and a varied assortment of structures conducive to owning and, in many cases, breeding horses. Finally, some agents specialize in the sale of foreclosed properties, which has recently become much more common. In this case, the agent's seller is a bank instead of a person. The buyer is typically someone just like you who's merely seeking a place to call home. No matter what type of property you seek, there likely is an agent who specializes in that specific type of property.

A relocation agent is one who specializes, at least as a part of his practice, in helping clients who are relocating from one part of the country, or world, to another. He is usually specially trained in the unique demands that a relocation calls for—buying a home long distance, moving your goods to your new home in time for your arrival, helping with your familiarization to the new area, and just assisting your move overall.

Tips and Traps

If you're relocating to a new locale, agent interviews needn't necessarily wait until you are in the area where you'll be purchasing. Once you've asked around for referrals, searched online listings and association websites for potential agent names, and narrowed your list, you can begin the process of interviewing agents by telephone or e-mail. You may not have quite as formal of an interview this way, but you can get a basic idea of whether you want to have this person work for you.

With all these specializations, you might think it's difficult to choose an agent, but it's really easy. You just need to ask the agent during the interview, "Is there a particular type of real estate you specialize in?" If the answer is yes, you may find that he's the type of agent you need. If his real estate specialization isn't exactly what you're looking for, don't be so quick to cross him off your list. He may still be extremely capable of finding other types of properties and probably can do a good job of helping you find your home.

What Does an Agent Do?

Basically, all an agent has to do is take you to see homes, hoping that one of them will suit you and you'll want to purchase it. Then he helps you write up an offer to present to the seller. If you're lucky, the seller will accept the offer. If everything goes well, the agent will accompany you to the closing, where you'll sign many documents and receive the key to your new home. Your agent has earned his commission when you become the owner of the house.

A good agent does much more than that, though, such as meet you at the airport and take you to your hotel, if you're relocating and have come to visit. She will arrange for school visits to meet administrators and get the latest test scores for each school.

If you're interested in a particular recreational activity—for example, tennis or cycling—she'll obtain information for you about local facilities or clubs that accommodate your sport. If you are a commuter, count on your agent to have all the commuter information about the local public transit options ready for you—costs, availability, and scheduling. In short, a good agent will help you in any reasonable way possible to learn as much about your new home locale as she can, to make your purchase a successful one in every way, not just in the physical structure of your home.

Beyond these items, there are additional benefits gained from using an agent. An experienced Realtor is likely to notice possible defects that could escape an untrained buyer's eye. Perhaps he'd recognize the signs of a roof nearing the end of its functional life or an outdated electrical system for a home. You might walk into a home with a lovely fountain in the backyard, not recognizing that the *real* reason isn't appearances—it's to mask the traffic noise from the interchange two blocks away. You might think that the wooded hill behind a home affords privacy, but your agent may point out that it also could be the source of potentially damaging water running toward your home every time it rains. There are many possible examples, but these few should serve to point out additional reasons to find and use an experienced agent in your search.

Warning!

Once you have established a relationship with an agent, do not call the seller or the seller's agent to set up appointments on your own. That's what you have contracted with your agent to do. Doing so will jeopardize your relationship with your agent and often hurt your bargaining powers. Inadvertently, you can "say too much" and thereby harm your chances in any negotiations in the course of your purchase. I often say, "He who speaks first loses."

Takes You on Home Tours

The agent will build a profile of your likes and dislikes so she can find the right home for you. She'll ask you how many bedrooms and bathrooms you want; what other rooms you want, such as an office or artist's studio; your preferences about garage size, land, and architectural style of the house; and about the size of your present and future family. She'll ask about your kids—their ages and interests, and whether they have any special needs. She'll ask many questions about your lifestyle, your work, and your commute. She isn't being nosey; she simply wants to find the perfect home for your needs without wasting your time. Once your talk is finished, she'll search her inventory and find you some homes that meet your needs.

Before your agent takes you out to look at a home, or several homes, she will either call the seller's agent for more information or visit the home on her own to see if it meets your requirements. She'll also get copies of the disclosure papers for you. All of this is to see if the homes match what you said you're looking for. Sellers don't write everything in a listing, and your agent usually will check it out first just to make sure it's really what you might like.

When your agent accompanies you to visit a home, she will watch your reactions. This is so she can see if this is the type of home you really want. For example, say you tell Jane, your Realtor, that you are looking for a turn-of-the-century brown-shingle home with lots of exterior design molding on a large flat, grassy lot. However, when she takes you to a home that meets those specifications, she can see that you're not quite thrilled with the style. When she takes you to see a new glass-and-steel-trimmed "high-tech" design home located on the edge of a cliff looking over a valley, you're very excited about the design. The agent might discuss your reactions with you and see if you want to focus on high-tech homes instead of older turn-of-the-century homes. Perhaps you just didn't like that particular home and you're still interested in seeing older homes, but a good agent will follow through with you and make sure you're on the right path.

Accesses the Multiple Listing System

The Multiple Listing System (MLS) is the computer-based system most Realtors use to list their own property listings and also to search for information on other listings for their clients. If you are searching for a home in an area where there is public access to an MLS, you can look through the listings on your own, too. This allows you to see what's coming on the market just as soon as the agent does, so if you spot something you're interested in, you can alert her. Otherwise, the agent will check the listings daily. The MLS updates constantly as new listings are added or sold, or as changes to a listing are made. Changes might include price reductions, changes in a property's status, or new property information that has been added.

Be aware that just because the MLS in your area has a public feature doesn't mean that you'll have all of the options that are available to a Realtor. There are some informational and/or search capabilities that are open only to Realtors. This is one more reason to have a Realtor help you in your search.

Writes and Presents an Offer

Once you find a house, your agent will work with you to craft the best possible offer (although there's much more you need to know before you get to this point—we cover all this in later chapters and include a sample purchase contract in Appendix E).

To do this, your agent will first provide a comparative market analysis, which is an analysis of other property values in the neighborhood based on relevant comps from the recent and current market. Based on this, she will recommend an appropriate price range for the house and then let you make the final decision on how much to offer.

The agent can print the comparisons, then sit with you in front of the computer and show you the various properties. It's your agent's job to then present the offer to the seller or the seller's agent, whichever the seller has specified. In most cases, it will be to the agent. If the offer is accepted, you'll begin inspections to make sure that the home has no hidden problems. A good agent will not only arrange for the inspections, but she'll also notify you of when they are so you can attend if you choose to do so. In some cases, an agent may be prohibited by his firm or liability insurance carrier from arranging the inspections, for fear of any conflict of interest, but this is the exception. However, regardless of who arranges the inspection, the contract with the inspector for the job is between you and the inspector, and you will pay for it. We strongly advise that you attend, but if you are unable to do so, your agent will also be at the inspection to ask further questions as the inspectors move through the process.

If the inspections uncover major issues with the home, your agent will explain them to you and help you understand the reports. If you're still interested in this property, she'll help you get bids on any necessary repair work. She'll also advise you on how to negotiate the cost of the repairs as a condition of remaining in contract to purchase the home. However, understand that while a thorough inspection will uncover all types of defects, major and minor, its purpose is to simultaneously show you what the major issues with the home are and to better help you negotiate the price for major issues that may have turned up. [A collection of little things that collectively can be cured with a few hundred dollars is not expected to be the basis for a renegotiation of the contract.]

If your offer is not immediately accepted, you may receive a counteroffer from the seller. Your agent will help you decide whether you want to respond to the seller's counteroffer by increasing your offer a bit. The process will go back and forth until an agreement has been made or you move on to another property.

Closing

If you continue into contract to purchase the home, you'll probably need a mortgage. If you're using your own mortgage broker or bank, the agent's duties will be limited to getting complete copies of the contract to the lender so they can tie the loan to the property. During the process, she'll arrange to meet the *appraiser* at the property.

def•i•ni•tion

An **appraiser** is a licensed professional who estimates the worth or value of your property based on various factors. These include values of other comparable properties, as well as size, location, and condition of the properties analyzed. Usually, your bank or mortgage broker chooses the appraiser to value your intended home.

As you get closer to closing, your agent will obtain a copy of a title report (more on the title in Chapter 16) that tells you everything that exists on record about the property that will affect your title as owner. If you have any questions or issues, your agent will call the title insurance firm and ask that these items be clarified. If they cannot be rectified, you may decide to cancel the purchase.

If everything is agreed upon, you'll have closing documents to sign. Your agent will accompany you to the signing, in case you have any questions that arise as you go through the documents.

After you get the keys, a good agent doesn't stop working. She may give you a closing present to help you celebrate your new home. Then she'll check in a few weeks after you've moved in, just to see if anything has come up that you'd like explained or taken care of. She'll also maintain a complete file on the transaction for whatever number of years the law in her state requires. This protects you in case any disputes arise some time after the closing of the sale. All of this is what a good agent does.

What an Agent Does *Not* Do

No matter how much you trust your agent, an agent legally cannot do some things. Your agent won't sign any documents for you, including your offer for the property. Similarly, an agent will not release any contractual contingencies for you, which means that the agent can't sign an approval to let the contract proceed forward. Such releases, including approving your inspection results or obtaining a loan to purchase the property, are things that only you can do.

Your agent also will not make an offer or negotiate the price or any contract terms without your approval of the specific terms he's offering for you. Your agent will not hold your money for the purchase, with the possible exception of temporarily holding, in his firm's trust account, your initial *earnest money* deposit. Even that is held, if at all, only until the seller accepts your offer. Then it goes to the escrow, the place holding your funds until closing, that is handling the sale.

Your agent will also learn a great deal of confidential information about you, including financial information, account balances at a bank or securities firm, Social Security numbers, and more. He will not divulge that information to anyone without your written consent. Another thing an agent will not do is reveal to anyone other than the seller's agent the terms of your offer for a property. This is to protect you from others knowing the details of your offer, and then submitting a better competing offer and getting the house.

def•i•ni•tion

Earnest money is money given by a buyer to a seller to bind a contract. This legally can be any amount of money, but usually is at least $1,000. It may be higher in some areas as a matter of custom or in relation to the size of the purchase price.

An agent cannot require you to use a specific bank or inspector. They'll usually offer recommendations based on their past experiences, but any agent who wants to tell you that you have to use someone might be breaking the law.

Choosing the Right Agent

There are almost as many ways to find the right agent to represent you as there are agents. Well, that may be a bit of an exaggeration, but not by too much, especially in the more populous areas of the country. So how do you find one? Let's find out.

Past Experience

The easiest way to find a Realtor to work for you is if you already had a successful relationship with one in a prior transaction. If you've purchased or sold property previously in the same area where you're now looking for a new home, and you were happy with that agent, it is in your best interest to use the same agent again. You and she already know each other, and she is familiar with your housing likes and dislikes. She can use that knowledge as a base from which to start your current search, perhaps tweaking it as she updates herself with any particular changes in your likes and dislikes over the years.

If your relationship wasn't comfortable but she was able to still find you what you wanted in a house, you may still want to use her again, but you should consider interviewing other agents.

Recommendations

You wouldn't pick your doctor's name out of a phone book, so don't pick your agent's name that way, either. You're looking for someone you can trust with the biggest financial purchase of your life, so ask for recommendations from several people you trust—friends, co-workers, family, and neighbors—who have bought or sold houses in the area. If you're moving to a new area, you can ask a local agent for a recommendation in your new area.

Ask the person giving you the recommendation why she likes the agent she is recommending. Did the agent always go beyond the call of duty to make sure she was satisfied? Did the agent return calls promptly? Does the referred Realtor have an unusual area of expertise that will prove valuable to you in your search? Is the agent knowledgeable about the community—its schools, shopping, museums, and local economy?

If you're being relocated and your company has a relocation service, it may be able to recommend a Realtor. Once you get all your recommendations, compare the names you received from each of your sources. You may find one or two names continuing to crop up. That's an indicator of a good agent.

Surf the Web

Just as you can find a house on the Internet, you can find an agent there, too. Most professional agents in the country have a website. You can visit Realtor.com for recommendations, which is owned and operated by the NAR. This is the largest real estate website in the world and allows searches for agents as well as for property.

When you're searching for a home on Realtor.com, you can also find the names of agents right on the listing page. This can give you a sense of who the real estate leaders are in the local area, but this will give you only an idea of who may be doing the largest amount of business. While that's important, an agent doing a large amount of business may not have the time to give you enough attention and address your specific needs. That all depends on the agent, but it's at least worth a call.

Finally, you can do a basic search for Realtors by searching Google. Type in the location you're interested in moving to followed by the word "Realtors" (for example, "Oshkosh, Wisconsin AND Realtors"), and you'll likely come up with plenty of names, complete with contact information. You can then visit their individual websites, but a word of caution: the best website in the world says nothing about a person's real-life skills or experience. It simply shows that he knows how to market himself online.

Interview

You're now ready to do a face-to-face interview (or one over the phone, if necessary) in the agent's office so you can see how he works. Before the interview, compile a list of questions to ask the agent. See Appendix D for a jumping-off point for your interview questions.

If the agent hasn't come to you from a friend, co-worker, or family member, ask for references from buyers or sellers who have used the agent. Call and find out what the clients liked and didn't like about the agent.

Warning!

Your agent may represent the seller on some of the homes you want to see. As a result, the real estate company, or broker, is called the dual agent. It's like being stuck in the middle; the agent can't act exclusively in the interests of either you or the seller. This may lead to a conflict of interest. If you proceed on this basis, you and the seller must sign a document approving of the dual agency situation before actually proceeding. One possible solution is to have another agent in the same firm represent you or the seller for this transaction.

Experience

In the end, just as important as an agent's area of specialization and education is his experience. While it's all well and good to find an agent who, based on references, designations, and specializations, appears to be perfect, an agent's experience also counts for a great deal.

Real estate is like anything else. The longer someone deals with it, the more likely she is to be more knowledgeable and capable. This is not to say that a Realtor who's been in the business for only two or three years won't be a good agent or won't be able to help you find a home. It's just that an experienced agent likely will have learned a few more tricks of the trade than a newer agent.

In many cases, it is far better to benefit from an agent's years of experience than to have him develop his experience at your expense. Experience can make the difference in a particular buyer getting a home if there are multiple offers competing for the same property.

However, the fact that an agent is relatively new is not always a disqualifying factor. If she is part of a large firm with an ongoing thorough training program and has close broker oversight, sometimes a newer agent will work fine for your needs. She very well may be more willing to investigate many more potential homes for you than a more experienced agent, and may be more willing to look at a lower price point than another agent who specializes more in high-end homes. This can be a subject to broach during your initial interview process.

Errors and Omissions Insurance

Ask the potential agent whether she has ever been sued or forced into mediation or arbitration. If so, how many times? If she has, inquire why and what the outcome was. Ask if the agent has Errors and Omissions (E&O) insurance. This insurance covers her for any nonfraud liability she may make due to negligence while representing her clientele.

Commission and Agent Contract

If you like the agent, usually you simply tell the agent you want him to represent you. Most often you don't need a contract with an agent unless it is the buyer-broker agreement, which is discussed later in this section.

The commission is how your agent gets paid for all the hard work she does for you. The most common question about this, particularly from first-time buyers, is "Who pays her?" In most cases, the answer is that the seller pays both agents.

Usually, your agent's commission comes from the overall commission paid by the seller to her agent.

Let's say the overall commission is 6 percent. This figure is not a set figure for all transactions; in some areas it's higher, and in others it's lower. Commissions are always subject to negotiation between the agent and seller. This is the amount the seller has agreed to pay the agent for the sale of his property. Some portion of that amount is then passed on at closing to the buyer's agent. Most often it is an even split of the total of 6 percent, although, in some circumstances, it may be a little more or less than equal.

If your agent is not being compensated by the seller's payment for the sale, your agent will then expect to be paid by you. A good agent will notify you immediately upon learning that a particular property you have an interest in is not a seller-paid commission. He will then explain that if he represents you in purchasing this particular property, you will be expected to pay his commission.

To avoid all misunderstandings, the agent usually has buyers sign a contract stipulating that they'll be paying the commission. This agreement is called a buyer-broker agreement. These agreements are relatively rare, varying with local market and economic conditions.

Warning!

There may come a time when you have a problem with your agent. Maybe he isn't working up to your satisfaction—he isn't listening to what you said you wanted in a home or land; he isn't returning your calls in a timely manner; or, worse, he is doing things that are either unethical or illegal. You have the right to let him know you are dissatisfied and end the relationship. Should this be necessary, protect yourself with a written release from the agency.

The Least You Need to Know

◆ Finding the right agent to work for you is pivotal in making your home-buying experience a success.

◆ Just because a friend or co-worker liked an agent doesn't mean the agent is right for you; interview the agent and find out for yourself.

◆ Your agent works for you. If you're not happy with the work he's doing, sit down and talk with him.

◆ When you're searching for an agent, look for education, training, and on-the-job experience.

◆ Typically, the seller pays your agent's commission, but occasionally you are responsible for the payment in a buyer-broker arrangement.

Part 2

Money Talk

You've probably heard the old expression "Money is the root of all evil." Well, it is also the root of the home-buying process. As you work your way through this part of the book, you'll learn all the financials you need to know about buying a home, including mortgages and mortgage lenders and interest rates and how to find the lowest one.

This part of the book discusses cash purchases, gifts, and other forms of liquid assets. You'll also read a primer on what to do if you have bad credit, previous mortgage defaults or foreclosure, or bankruptcy, and what your chances are for buying a home now.

Chapter 4

Financial Talk

In This Chapter

- Considerations when shopping for a loan
- Choosing a loan from a mortgage broker, a bank, or a credit union
- Prequalification versus preapproval
- Figuring out how much you need to borrow
- Understanding how debt-to-income ratios affect your approval

You may be asking why this chapter focuses on financing your new home when you haven't even found the house you want to buy yet. The earlier you begin to think about how you'll finance (that is, pay for) it, the better. Finding out how much money you'll qualify for and whether you'll even be approved for a loan will make your search easier and quicker. No sense looking for more than you'll be able to spend.

Over the next few chapters, you'll read about the types of mortgage loans that are available, learn about how much money you'll need for a down payment, and walk through the approval process. Right now, though, you need to take your first steps in financing your new home—finding the right lender and getting preapproved or prequalified.

This chapter focuses on helping you find a lender by asking the right questions; explains the differences between a credit union, a bank, and a mortgage broker; and tells you how to get preapproved for a mortgage. You're getting closer to your dream home!

Lenders

Unless you're paying cash for your home—and some people do—you'll have to finance your home by taking out a mortgage loan. This loan will come from either a bank or credit union, or a mortgage broker, sometimes referred to as a loan broker. Each has its own advantages and disadvantages.

Mortgage Broker

A mortgage broker is an individual who, in most states, is licensed by the state in which he practices. Licensing requirements vary from state to state. For example, California requires that the mortgage broker be licensed as a real estate salesman, and his activities are regulated by the same agency that regulates Realtors: the California Department of Real Estate.

Tips and Traps

Check out Bankrate.com, where you can do your own research on different mortgages and interest rates.

def•i•ni•tion

A **credit score** is a number based on your credit experience. The higher the number, the more responsible you are with your credit and debt. You'll find more on this in Chapter 5.

A mortgage broker presents your loan application to any number of lending institutions that he feels can give you the best loan based on your financial situation. He may feel that he has to approach only a single institution to achieve the best results, or he may decide that you would be better served if he presents your application to a number of lenders. His decision is usually based on a combination of factors, such as your *credit score*, loan amount, type of loan, desired interest rate and other loan costs, and, in some cases, a particular bank's ability to meet time frames as they relate to your purchase agreement. In addition to qualifying you for a mortgage, a good broker will discuss with you the advantages and disadvantages of one loan over another.

A broker maintains contact with the lender(s) throughout the process and, if they need further information, obtains it from you. Once the loan is approved, he maintains contact throughout the appraisal process and closely follows the drawing of loan documents.

If you have used a mortgage broker in the past and you're happy with her, contact her again for this purchase—unless, of course, you're moving out of state and she's not licensed to practice in the state where you're buying. However, if you need a broker, finding one isn't any different than locating and choosing a Realtor. Start by asking friends, family, or co-workers for references; ask them what they liked or didn't like about that particular broker. Ask your real estate agent for a referral, too. Most agents know or have worked with a number of mortgage brokers.

Quotes and Facts

Internet lenders, called "counselors," arrange mortgages the same way a mortgage broker does—and they must be licensed in the states where they are arranging mortgages. You contact them through e-mail or by phone. The first, and best known, is LendingTree.com. Others include Priceline.com, E-Trade Group, and Quicken Loans. Some are independent; others are affiliated with a particular lender and arrange loans with more than just their own firm. All are reliable, but do your due diligence.

Once you have some names, whittle them down by comparing pluses and minuses. For example, if one broker received many good reviews but only one bad review, that's a plus, but if another broker has a few more bad reviews, it might be best to remove that broker from the list. Once you have your short list, set up an interview with each broker and discuss the following:

◆ **Experience**—Find out how long the broker has been in the business. If you've had past financial problems or have a unique financial situation, ask if he's had experience obtaining loans for others with similar experiences. For example, if you've declared bankruptcy or had *liens* held against you, is the broker used to working with situations like this? We go over liens in more detail in Chapter 5.

If you are applying for specialized financing such as from the Veteran's Administration (VA) or the Federal Housing Administration (FHA), ask if he is experienced in those types of loans (we discuss these loans in Chapter 6). You can also see if he is a member of the National Association of Mortgage Brokers (www.namb.org), an association of individual brokers, not mortgage companies.

def•i•ni•tion

A **lien** is an encumbrance or burden upon a piece of property, such as real estate. It is for the protection of the party placing it upon the property. One example of a lien is a mortgage given by the buyer in exchange for the mortgage loan used to buy the property.

◆ **Community**—Ask if he is a member of the local Chamber of Commerce. Most chambers are quite familiar with their members and can even give you a few names of mortgage broker members. Being a member of a Chamber of Commerce typically shows that a business cares about the community and wants to work hard to provide good service to its members. However, chambers don't police their members, so this doesn't guarantee legitimacy of your broker; it's still best to complete other reference checks.

◆ **Fees**—Ask what the broker's fees will be. Broker's fees are included in overall loan fees and related expenses the borrower agrees to as a condition of his loan. The borrower pays them as part of closing costs when the closing occurs (more on the closing in Chapter 16).

These fees include processing and loan fees, credit report fee, and more. The size and location of the mortgage loan also have some effect on the amount of the fees.

◆ **References**—Ask for contact information of several past clients who have used the broker. Do not be surprised if some brokers will not give out references, as this is a violation of their client's privacy. It varies from agent to agent.

Ask what the previous customers liked and didn't like about the mortgage broker, and how he handled their transaction. Also ask if they'd use him again. Another approach is to ask for some real estate agents that they've worked with in the past. This doesn't violate anyone's privacy, and most agents will tell you which brokers got them to closing and which ones dropped the ball.

Beyond these standard issues, you can learn about the broker by asking some questions that pertain to his methods. You might want to ask what his most difficult client situation has been in terms of getting a loan. Why was it so difficult and how did he deal with it? What were the results? What was the most unusual property or property location he had to deal with? These answers can help give you a fuller picture to determine whether this broker is the right one for you.

Warning! _____

If you're concerned about a bank's financial health, ask for information on it from your mortgage broker. She has an incentive to deal with only quality institutions. However, even if the bank ultimately fails or is taken over by another bank, it won't affect your loan. Under the Federal Deposit Insurance Company (FDIC), the loan will be taken over by the succeeding bank.

Bank

When deciding on a lender, you can try a bank. Although you're not obligated to use your current bank for your mortgage, the benefit of this is that you will be dealing with a familiar entity. Assuming that the relationship to date has been a good one, using a familiar bank for your mortgage is a plus.

If you're not crazy about your bank—maybe you were turned down for a credit service because you were delinquent on past loans with them or you simply aren't pleased with their customer service—you can try another bank. Trying another bank will not successfully hide any previous delinquencies that your credit report shows, but a new bank might be more lenient and willing to approve you for a mortgage.

Keep in mind that mortgages are lengthy—often 15 or 30 years long—so you need to be happy with the lender you choose if you plan to keep that loan for that long. Of course, many homeowners refinance their loans throughout the time they own the home, so you could use that time to switch lenders if you aren't happy.

Credit Union

Whereas a bank is a for-profit company, a credit union is owned by its members. Typically, credit unions charge lower interest rates and fees, but that's not always the case: read the fine print and weigh your options carefully. Most credit unions are open to anyone, but some have membership restrictions. For example, a credit union may require that you work at a particular company where there is a credit union just for those employees. Some credit unions require that you live in a particular area where that credit union is located. Others are limited to those who attend church in that particular city or county. In those cases, you won't be able to apply for a home loan with that credit union unless you meet the qualifications.

The Credit Union National Association can help you find a credit union by calling 1-800-358-5710. You'll hear an electronic message that includes the name and telephone number of a person at the credit union league in your state who can help you find a credit union to join. You can also check its online database of credit unions.

Tips and Traps

Note that some credit unions require you to maintain a specific amount of money in your savings account in order to use their services. Check the credit union's requirements before applying.

Prequalification and Preapproval

When you first spoke to your Realtor about looking for a home, she may have asked you if you're already prequalified or preapproved for a loan. To get prequalified or preapproved for a loan, you must submit some basic information to your lender, including your Social Security number, employment details, asset and liability information, and more. Your lender then reviews this information to give you an idea of whether you will get his blessing as a potential borrower. If you get this blessing, you're in good shape to receive a final mortgage loan approval, but—this is *very* important—this is *not* an official approval.

If you receive a preapproval or prequalification, share this information with your real estate agent, who can then share it with the sellers so they know you're a serious buyer. You can then make a bid on a home you're interested in based on the preapproval or prequalification. As a matter of fact, some sellers won't even allow a buyer to see their home if the buyer has not gone through the prequalification or preapproval process or has been denied. If your offer on the home is accepted, the lender will move forward with a more detailed approval process at that time, to give you the final okay on your mortgage loan.

It's important to understand that these two terms have vastly different meanings. Each is good to get from a lender or mortgage broker, but one carries far more weight than the other.

Prequalification

A prequalification is the most basic form of lender approval. It doesn't carry nearly as much weight as a preapproval, but it's a good start. Written on the lender's letterhead, it says that you have given that lender or broker some basic financial information about yourself (and your spouse, if this is a joint application) and, based on that information, it appears likely that you'll be able to obtain a mortgage loan at some time in the near future. It also specifies either the maximum amount of a loan or the maximum purchase price that you might qualify for when you actually complete a formal application. The letter also clearly states that it is not meant in any way to constitute a commitment to lend or a guarantee of a loan being approved. You'll still have to go through that final approval process, and you can still be denied.

Consider a prequalification as "mind candy" for potential sellers of property and you, the buyer. It will make both of you more comfortable with your chances of having a loan granted to you.

Preapproval

A preapproval, however, states that you have undergone a full loan underwriting and analysis and have been approved for a loan of a specific amount. A preapproval also means that the lender will fund the loan based on your credit, but it also depends on the results of an appraisal of the property, *title report*, and purchase contract of the home you decide to buy once you find it.

def•i•ni•tion

The **title report** describes the location, dimensions, and size of the piece of property that is the subject of the report. It also lists any liens or other claims against the title that are on record in the county where the property is situated.

Cost vs. Comfort

When you apply for a mortgage, you may find out that you qualify for a much larger loan than you'd ever thought possible. For example, let's say you are interested in a $225,000 home. When you apply for the loan, the lender tells you that, thanks to your excellent credit and your ability to pay bills on time, you are eligible for a $350,000 loan. On one hand, it's good to know that you qualify for that large of a loan. It means that you're doing well with your credit and will likely sail through to approval on a home in your preferred price range.

However, this information opens up the possibility that you can now buy a bigger home. For example, instead of the house with three bedrooms, two baths, and a living room on a 10,000-square-foot plot of land, you can now afford the four-bedroom house that also features a spacious family room, fully equipped home office, and in-ground pool on an acre of land. Sounds great, doesn't it? Maybe, but it really depends on your current financial situation. Remember, a bigger mortgage means that unless you offer up a much larger down payment on the loan, you'll be making bigger mortgage payments every month. Is that something you can afford? If so, will you have any money left over to pay your everyday bills and to put away funds in case of unexpected expenses or circumstances, such as a job loss?

In my book *Save Your House From Foreclosure!*, I note the four largest causes of default and foreclosure: "Life, Wife, Health, and Wealth." If your spouse dies, if you or an immediate family member has a major health crisis with inadequate or no insurance, if you get divorced, or if either one of you loses a job, it can seriously impact your ability to pay your mortgage.

All of these are common occurrences, and any one can place your home in jeopardy. When you're deciding whether to buy a bigger home because you were approved for it, think about this—it is better to have a smaller obligation to your mortgage lender in case something like this occurs. As has been said before, it is far better to own your house than to have your house own you. Only borrow what you're financially and emotionally comfortable with.

Tips and Traps

You should be able to afford your monthly mortgage payment and still put money into an emergency fund. This fund should have three months' worth of living expenses, including your mortgage, debt, food, and car payments. It's important to be prepared so you don't lose your dream home now that you've found it.

Debt Considerations

Banks use two debt ratios to see if you will be able to carry a mortgage loan: debt-to-income and debt-to-equity. The first, debt-to-income ratio, is the relationship between the total amount of debt you have at a particular time to the amount of income you are earning. The higher the percentage of debt, the more difficult it can be to get approved for your loan. This is because the banks are concerned that something could impact your income and reduce your ability to pay your debts. The second, debt-to-equity ratio, is the relationship between the amount of debt you have at any one time and your net worth. Net worth is the amount of money left over when you subtract all your debt from the value of all your assets. This debt-to-equity ratio is sometimes also referred to as the debt-to-worth ratio.

Debt-to-Income

Debt-to-income is used to figure out the percentage of debt you have compared to your total amount of income. In the past, a debt-to-income ratio of as much as 50 percent of income was an acceptable maximum ratio. Today, as lenders have tightened up on lending standards, it has shrunk to the low 40 percent range.

In some cases, a borrower has only housing debt, so a housing debt-to-income is used. This tells the lender how much of your overall debt specifically belongs to your current rent or mortgage payment. This is a lower percentage than total debt-to-income, since most people have other debt beyond housing. In other words, for these folks, the debt-to-income ratio tells the lender what the relationship is of overall debt to an individual's income. If the housing debt-to-income is too high, this gives the lender an indication that you may not be able to handle your mortgage payments. Theoretically, if you have no debt other than housing, your ratio could be as high as 45 percent of your income.

The actual ratio on a particular loan also takes into account your overall financial picture. And, of course, having more liquid assets is much more attractive to a lender.

When lenders are making a decision, however, they look at both ratios, usually beginning with housing debt-to-income, to get a sense of how much you're allocating for your housing costs. Then they apply the tougher standard of total debt-to-income because it provides a more accurate picture of your overall situation and allows lenders to determine whether you can still comfortably pay the mortgage if all your debt is taken into consideration.

These standards apply regardless of what type of loan you're applying for. Either you have the ability to pay it or you don't. If you're within a lower ratio, you've got more of a cushion in case something goes wrong financially for you. It's just more prudent lending.

Quotes and Facts

Are you a member of the military? If so, you may be able to take advantage of the GI Bill's advantageous mortgage program to buy a home. The Department of Veterans Affairs administers programs such as the GI Bill and various other benefit programs. Visit www.gibill.va.gov or call toll-free 1-888-GI-BILL-1 (1-888-442-4551) to speak with a Veterans Benefits Counselor.

Debt-to-Equity

Debt-to-equity, sometimes referred to as debt-to-worth or loan-to-value (of the home), is the relationship of the mortgage debt to the amount of money you're investing in it with a down payment. Yes, you're spending the money, but, as with buying stock or any other investment, the money you're spending is to purchase the investment involved. In the case of a home, your purchase is definitely an investment— possibly the biggest one you'll ever make. It's a simple mathematical ratio. In the early 1970s, the standard debt-to-equity ratio was 70/30, which meant that the buyer had to come up with 30 percent of the purchase price of the home. That 30 percent was considered the equity portion of the purchase. As an example, if your home cost

$100,000, you'd borrow $70,000 and have $30,000 in equity from your own funds to complete the purchase.

By the 1980s, mortgage lenders commonly financed at least 80 percent of the purchase price, with some loans going as high as 90 percent. There was so much growth in the number of potential borrowers that the competition to lend to them led lenders en masse to loosen their limits on the loans.

In the early 2000s, in some cases, loans of as much as 130 percent of value were available. For example, imagine that you bought a home for $200,000, but your loan was for 130 percent of that, or $260,000. No equity was required, and more than the purchase price was loaned because it was thought that continuing increases of the prices would cover the excess loan amounts. None of these loans include "special" loan programs, such as loans from the VA or the FHA. These loans meant that you were able to obtain a larger loan and thus have a higher debt level; you would also be able to obtain more than 100 percent financing of the property. Both *FHA loans*, at 97 percent debt, and *VA loans*, at 100 percent debt, were made because the organizations making the loan had the guarantee of repayment by the federal government, no matter what happened.

def•i•ni•tion

> **VA** and **FHA loans** are special loan programs guaranteed by the U.S. government. If the borrower fails to repay, the government makes good on the debt to the lender and then ends up with the home. Because of this guarantee, lenders can still safely make the loans with little or no down payment. We cover this in more detail in Chapter 6.

Over the last few years, relaxed lending standards caused a major upheaval in the mortgage markets. As a result, a number of lenders got federal financial assistance, while some lenders were forced to close their doors. However, this chaos accomplished one good thing: it virtually eliminated from the marketplace nonfederal guaranteed loans of 100 percent of value.

In other words, as regulators have forced lenders to tighten lending limits, lenders who previously made loans of 100 percent or more of value are no longer able to do so. Larger banks have cut these loans from their product lists, while smaller lending institutions that made these loans have been forced out of the market. It's not completely impossible to find such a loan, but it's rare. In the few relatively rare cases, some mortgage brokers are placing the loans with what are called "hard money" lenders to get them funded. Although these are perfectly legal, the sources of funding for these "hard" lenders are not the traditional bank deposit type. Instead, they are investors willing to carry extra risk found in such loans in exchange for a higher rate of return through the interest they'll earn. This is a classic example of how higher risk generates a higher interest rate.

Standards have now generally returned to buyers' equity participation of between 10 and 20 percent of the purchase price. So when you buy a home, unless you obtain an FHA or VA loan, you will be required to put up more of your own money as part of the purchase price than before. If you're buying a house for $200,000, you now will probably have to put down at least $20,000, and possibly $40,000, of your own money at closing.

Being Denied

The worst news … you've been denied for a preapproval or a prequalification. If this happens, you need to find out why. Are there mistakes on your credit report? If so, you'll need to get these mistakes remedied (we talk about this in Chapter 5). You can still attempt to buy a home, but it may take a bit longer, as you'll have to start the loan process all over again. Usually, if your credit score and history are at least minimally satisfactory (again, see Chapter 5 for a full discussion of credit scores), you'll be able to qualify somewhere. However, it likely will be for a much higher rate of interest than someone with a higher credit score and better history would receive.

Tips and Traps

You can improve your credit score by bringing any over-due bills current and keeping them current. Don't start opening new credit cards, as doing so lowers your score. Don't keep moving card balances from one card to another, either—this also adversely affects your score. Lower or pay off your credit card balances, and keep them there.

Good Faith Estimates

Some time ago, buyers would go through the home-buying and lending process and then get to the closing, only to be blown away when they learned how much additional money they had to come up with on the spot to cover several closing costs. Today a good faith estimate prevents this sudden shock and helps buyers to be certain in advance that they have the up-front cash they need to buy their home. The method of payment can vary from place to place and state to state, and sometimes even within a state. Many locales require cashier's checks for these costs, but some allow a personal check. Ask your Realtor what the practice is where you're buying.

A good faith estimate is a federally mandated document that lists all the fees related to the loan that you will have to pay at closing. Included in such fees are, typically, *title fees*, *settlement fees*, and prepaid real estate taxes. This document must be given to you within three days of initially signing your loan application. However, it's best to request it before you even apply for a loan. There may be a big difference between Bank A and Bank B's closing costs and it might be a reason to choose one bank over another if all other things are equal.

def•i•ni•tion

Title fees are costs associated with the title search and title insurance you'll be getting for your new property. **Settlement fees** are fees paid to cover the costs of any settlement issues handled on behalf of the lender. These may be by escrow firm, title company, or attorney, for example, and can vary widely depending on state and services required.

Keep in mind, however, that this may all depend on where you live. California, for example, uses a Mortgage Loan Disclosure Statement/Good Faith Estimate. The document includes all the information mandated by the feds and also shows who will receive each of the itemized fees. For example, your first year's hazard insurance will be itemized here as being paid to the insurance company or broker providing it. It requires that you, the buyer, are told how much money you'll have to pay, lump sum, for such things as property taxes.

Impound Accounts

Impound accounts, also called "escrow" accounts in certain parts of the country—the terms are interchangeable—are established by the lending institution as a condition of making the loan. They are used to collect funds from you to make annual payments of insurance premiums, property taxes, and so on. The idea is that those items are large annual or semiannual payments—possibly too large to count on the homeowner to have the funds available to pay them when they're due. Usually, impound accounts are a requirement of the loan when your FICO is on the lower end of acceptability or you are at the extreme high end of the range of debt ratios that we discussed earlier in this chapter.

Having an impound account means the funds will be there when the bills must be paid, and the lender will make the payments on behalf of the homeowner. Until the early 1980s, impound accounts were standard, no matter how large or small your loan was or what the debt/equity relationship was. The account carried no interest; monies were just collected from the buyer along with the mortgage payment and held until the bill was due.

After a great deal of consumer complaints, followed by state legislation in many states, lenders began paying interest on impound accounts. The interest, where it's paid, won't make you rich—not by a long shot—but it's a little something in return for having the lender hold your hard-earned cash. The lenders also stopped making impound accounts a requirement of all loans, but started tying that requirement to the borrower's overall financial situation and the debt/equity relationship of the mortgage. While not all borrowers are required to have impounds, anyone not required to do so is permitted to have the bank establish impounds for them if they feel it's more convenient.

The Least You Need to Know

- ◆ Depending on your state, your mortgage broker should be licensed. You can check with your Department of Real Estate to confirm.

- ◆ Before you get started finding a mortgage, make sure you are familiar with your entire financial picture, especially your credit report.

- ◆ You can look for a home, but you can't make an offer without getting a pre-approval or prequalification on your loan first.

- ◆ Don't buy more house than you can afford, even if you are told you can get a bigger mortgage.

Chapter 5

Steps to Approval

In This Chapter

- Looking into your credit history
- Learning what credit scores really mean
- Bouncing back from financial mistakes
- Affording the down payment

Have you ever loaned anyone money? You might have asked them if they could afford to make payments, and then set up a payment schedule until the loan was paid in full. When you apply for a mortgage loan, the lender does the same thing. The lender is loaning you a very large sum of money and wants to make sure you're going to pay it back. Lenders can't just give a loan to anyone; they have to do a little investigating into a borrower's background to make sure they're taking a safe risk.

All the previous years of paying your bills (whether on time or late) and running up your credit cards or paying them off every month in full determine whether you get approved for a mortgage now. Past mistakes may come back to haunt you—those bills you paid late when you were fresh out of college could cause the lender to say no to you. Maybe those late bills are so long ago, though, that the lender will overlook it—but you could still be considered a credit risk and offered a higher interest rate.

It's best to find out your credit score early in your house-hunting process so you know where you stand. This chapter helps you decipher all the details in your credit report and how to correct any mistakes *before* you apply for a loan.

Most lenders won't loan you the entire cost for your home, either. They expect you to come up with a portion of the cost. Depending on what mortgage loan you are applying for, you may have to come up with a down payment of as little as 3 percent or as much as 20 percent of the cost of the loan. This chapter helps you figure out how to get that down payment together. This will become even more common going forward as banks are returning to the prudent lending standards of several years ago. As this "return to basics" becomes the standard, it will be the rule rather than the exception for lenders to frequently require 10 to 20 percent of the purchase as buyer's equity. Only government-guaranteed loans, such as FHA and VA loans, will remain with equity levels permitted as low as 3 percent and nothing down, respectively.

Credit History

Your credit history helps the lender decide whether you will be a good or bad risk with their money. It lets the lender see how you've honored your debts and your obligations to repay them. Have you paid in full and on time? Or have you missed payments—one month here, three months there? Years ago, if you filled out a mortgage application, you would also fill out a credit application and list your debts, including your car payment, house payment, credit card accounts, and other bills. Today the credit application process takes place mostly via Internet and database maintained by the credit reporting companies. It includes the following information:

- Your credit score

- Your credit report

- Other documents that provide proof of your assets, including tax returns (especially if you are self-employed) and investment account statements

Your credit history is so important in the mortgage application process that even former landlords are likely to be contacted to see if you paid your rent as agreed. Your lender assembles all this information and makes a final decision about your loan.

Credit Scores

An important part of your credit history is your credit score, which ranges from 300 (poor) to 850 (excellent), although it is highly unlikely for an individual to actually score at either end of that axis. Developed by the California-based Fair Isaac Company, these scores are called FICO scores.

Your credit score not only tells your lender whether you're capable of paying back the loan, but also helps determine the interest rate of the loan. In general, the better your credit score, the lower your interest rate.

Tips and Traps

If you want to find out your FICO score, you can ask your mortgage broker and he'll share it with you when he receives it as part of your credit history. You can also obtain your own history once a year for free from the three reporting agencies—Equifax, TransUnion, and Experian—or by visiting http://myfico.com.

Scores of 720 and up are superior credit scores and generate what industry sources refer to as *A Paper*, to denote the highest quality of the loan. A score between 680 and 720 is considered "excellent" and is well regarded. You will likely get a loan on excellent terms as far as interest and fees are concerned.

Middle-Ground Scores

A score between 620 and 679 is still acceptable to most lenders, but the interest rate and terms offered won't be as good as if your score were higher. Lending industry members refer to the quality of loans in this score group as B Paper. This category is also referred to as *subprime*.

def•i•ni•tion

A Paper consists of loans made to borrowers who have FICO scores of 720 or above. You must have no more debt-to-total-income than 45 percent of income. A loan of 680 to 720 is called A to B Paper.

Subprime describes mortgage loans made to borrowers whose credit is less than the best, or "prime." If you are one of these borrowers, you might have had a difficult time obtaining a mortgage in the past. Under new industry standards, you may be approved for one now, but with much higher interest rates and points up front. These constitute B and C Paper loans.

Mortgage loans are frequently resold to other lenders in what is called the secondary market. This frees up new lendable funds for the lenders who made those loans, so they can make new loans. Historically, what have come to be called subprime loans were very difficult to resell in the secondary market. However, as the demand from borrowers for such loans exploded in the early part of this decade, more of them were made and, due to their higher rates of return, more secondary market institutions were willing to purchase them from the originating institution. Ultimately, Wall Street investment banks expanded this reselling by securitizing them—packaging many loans together and selling individual shares in the package to investors as if they were stocks or bonds. This was fine until prices suddenly dropped and the homes backing these mortgages were worth less than the loans themselves.

If your credit score comes in between 580 and 619, your options become more limited. Perhaps you missed a few payments on a loan or overextended yourself on your credit card. In that case, you are considered a higher credit risk; although some banks will approve you for a loan, others may not. Your loan fees, broker fees, and interest rates will be higher than they would be if your score were at least in the mid-600s. This is known as a C Paper loan, although this term is used less frequently because these loans become harder to obtain at all. C Paper loans are also referred to as subprime. You can get a mortgage, but it might be a little difficult. If you've gotten your finances in order and can afford the payments, take advantage when you get the opportunity.

Poor Credit Scores

If your score is 500 to 579, this is considered a poor risk for credit. Unfortunately, almost no lender will extend you a mortgage loan. If you do happen to find one, it will likely be the only one offered to you, and its high fees and interest rate will curl your hair. If you're able to handle your monthly mortgage payments, home ownership provides you with an opportunity to not only buy your home, but also improve your FICO score. As a result, the next time you decide to finance, or refinance, you may have an easier time of it—depending, of course, on the rest of your payment abilities.

Most loans made to FICOs under 620 are from the part of the lending market referred to as "hard money" lenders. Don't misunderstand the term. We're not talking about loan sharks who would break your legs for missing a payment. Hard money lenders are those mentioned in the last paragraph whose rates reflect the lower-quality credit and, accordingly, charge much higher interest rates and fees. Also, their loan limits are usually much more restrictive. You likely won't be able to borrow more than 50 percent of the cost of the home in this situation.

If your FICO score is under 500, your credit is very poor. Will no lenders take a chance on you? Never say never, but if you can find a lender willing to approve you for a loan when your score is this low, the terms will probably be positively crushing to you and your monthly budget. The best advice for this situation is to forego the home purchase for now, work at fixing your credit in the meantime, and try again in a year or two.

Credit Score Myths

If you're trying hard to get a handle on your finances, kudos to you. Some people do this by seeking debt counseling and cutting up credit cards. This is a step in the somewhat-right direction. However, both of these steps, while admirable, come with serious consequences that could affect your ability to buy a home. Interestingly, consulting a credit counseling service to help resolve your debt problems might seem like a responsible way of improving your situation, but it can backfire on you. Here's why: when you sign up for a program like this, your credit score actually drops a few points.

Simply closing a credit card to reduce the number of cards you have can also have serious consequences on your FICO score. It might seem logical that your FICO score would increase because you have fewer accounts and less open credit available. However, when you cancel a card, your debt ratio goes up because the total amount you owe is now a higher percentage of your potential total available credit. This causes your FICO score to go down.

Warning!

There are some credit counseling services that try to take advantage of unsuspecting, uneducated consumers. Do your research before getting involved with any credit counseling service.

As an example, let's say you have five credit cards with a total available credit of $50,000 ($10,000 per card). You have outstanding debt among these cards of $35,000. That is a ratio of 70 percent of your total available debt. You decide to cancel one of the cards, to reduce temptation and potential debt load. Now your outstanding $35,000 is 87.5 percent of the total available credit you have access to. You haven't increased your debt and you've reduced your possible debt load, but the ratio of debt has risen because your total debt is measured against a smaller amount of available credit.

Applying for new credit also causes your score to drop. The theory behind this is that you're seeking new sources of credit and could be digging yourself into a bigger hole. When you're trying to increase your credit score so you can get approved for a mortgage, avoid applying for new credit.

Credit Report

The lender obtains credit reports from any or all of the three firms that are in the business of providing them. These firms are Equifax, TransUnion, and Experian. Instead of having to get separate reports, you can purchase a comprehensive report of all three agencies. This is known as a tri-merge credit report. These are available from any number of firms across the country. If you go online, you have a multitude of options to choose from.

Thanks to the Fair Credit Reporting Act (FCRA), you are entitled to a free copy of your own credit report if you have received notice within the past 60 days that you have been declined credit, employment, or housing, or if adverse action has been taken against you based on information from a reporting agency. By "adverse action," I mean any denial of credit based on your credit report from any of the credit agencies. You can also visit www.annualcreditreport.com to receive one free copy of your credit report every year from each of the three nationwide consumer credit-reporting companies. This will give you a heads-up on any potential problems you may encounter. If you already received your free copy but wonder whether anything has changed since then, you can either pay for another copy of the report or, if you've been denied credit, write to each credit agency separately asking for another copy. Include a copy of that denial letter. You can reach the agencies here:

- Experian: www.experian.com; 1-888-397-3742

- TransUnion: www.transunion.com; 1-800-888-4213

- Equifax: www.equifax.com; 1-800-685-1111

Credit reports include any name you used in your past when filling out credit reports (maiden and married names included) and list the names of each creditor, past or present, that has had a relationship with you. The report provides details about every creditor, when the account was established, your maximum credit limit, your current balance, and your current monthly payment. Information on this report—both positive and negative—stays on your credit report for varying lengths of time. For example, *bankruptcies* last 10 years. A past *foreclosure* also stays around for 10 years, which, in most cases, is longer than it will take before a lender is willing to consider you for a mortgage to buy another home. "Regular" information, positive or negative, usually lasts for seven years. The report lists your high credit on each account, which is the highest amount you have owed at any time to that creditor. The report also gives the status of each account on a month-by-month basis over the last year and whether you missed any payments.

If an account is closed, it's still on the report, which indicates when it was closed and whether you closed it voluntarily or whether the creditor closed it because of inability to pay, late payments, or something else. If you had an outstanding balance that you never paid when you closed the account, it's referred to as a charge-off. This means that instead of putting in the extra time and expense trying to collect the amount you owed, the grantor decided it would be a waste of time and money and wrote it off. The report also includes any bankruptcies (more on that later in the chapter), *tax liens*, unpaid judgments, and so on.

def•i•ni•tion

Bankruptcy is a court-managed debt-resolution process. **Foreclosure** occurs when you lose your home to a mortgage lender, usually for nonpayment of the debt.

Tax liens are placed against your assets by a governmental body—federal, state, county, etc.—to force payments of taxes you owe to that specific government entity.

Good vs. Bad Credit

Good credit is pretty basic. For example, you have a credit card for your local clothing retailer. It has a maximum limit of $1,000 and you have paid your balance in full and on time every month. If you handle all your bills in this manner, you have good credit.

Bad credit, on the other hand, is a history of missing payments on debt relationships or a past default on a debt along with such items as defaults, foreclosures, *judgment liens*, tax liens, *charge-offs* of debt, and bankruptcy. The more of these situations are in your background, the lower your FICO score goes and the worse your credit will be. Let's examine a few of them and how they affect your chances of being approved for a mortgage.

def•i•ni•tion

Judgment liens are liens placed against you and your assets to force payment of a lawsuit you have lost. Lenders sometimes opt for a **charge-off** if a debt is way past due, knowing that you're never likely to pay it and that the cost of litigation is far more than it's worth.

Defaults

Default refers to your failure to pay a debt in full as agreed. For example, let's say you borrowed $10,000 on a personal loan and had repaid $7,500 when you started having problems making the rest of the payments. As a result, you just stopped making payments, and therefore defaulted on the loan. This will seriously affect your credit rating, and therefore affect your ability to be approved for a home. The bank wants to see that you can pay your debts.

This is particularly important if you've ever owned land and have defaulted on the payments. The lender may have filed a formal document saying that you defaulted on the mortgage loan. If you have a previous foreclosure on your credit report, it's a huge red flag when a lender is looking to grant a new mortgage loan to you.

Mortgage After Foreclosure

If you've had a previous foreclosure, your best chance at getting a new mortgage now is to just wait until some time passes. However, if you've kept your credit in good standing and paid your bills on time since the foreclosure, you have a decent chance of getting financing now. There's no rule on this, but the general industry standard is that it must be at least five to seven years since the foreclosure before you have a chance of being approved for another mortgage loan.

Then, assuming that everything else in your credit history is satisfactory, lenders may take a chance on you. Because that foreclosure makes you an increased credit risk, you probably won't get the best interest rate possible, and you may be forced to pay a *point* or two up front. You'll remain a less-than-healthy credit risk until you can prove things have changed. You produce this proof by maintaining a good record of debt repayment going forward and not carrying excessive amounts of debt.

def•i•ni•tion

Points are fees that lenders may charge at the initiation of a new mortgage loan as a way of earning extra income on the deal. They are usually charged for larger credit risks or as a trade-off for a slightly lower rate of interest on the loan.

Your best chance to get a loan may be through the FHA or Veterans Administration (see Chapter 6 for a full explanation of these loans). These loans may be more accessible and require lower down payments because they carry federal government guarantees of repayment to the lenders. You may also be required to accept impounds on your loan to cover taxes and insurance premiums until the lender gets comfortable with you. If you've faced foreclosure in the past, don't just throw up your hands and assume that you're "damaged goods" forever. Fill out that application. If enough time has passed and you've kept your credit history clean since then, you may be able to get into your own home again.

Liens

If your credit report shows that there is a lien on your property, this means that some-one has obtained a legal right to do so because of some sort of debt or obligation from you to them. They have the legal right to do this if you are not paying an agreed-upon debt. Many types of liens can be placed on your credit report, in these situations:

♦ When you get a mortgage to purchase or refinance a home, take out a home equity loan, or take out a second or subsequent mortgage.

♦ When you borrow money to buy a car.

♦ When you fail to pay your taxes on income or property.

♦ When you have a carpenter, plumber, or electrician do work on your property and then fail to pay the bill. This is a mechanic's lien and, again, will be removed when the debt is paid.

♦ When someone sues you for whatever reason and wins a judgment, but you don't pay. This is a judgment lien and will be removed when the debt is paid.

If you currently own a home, a lien can have a legal effect, called a cloud, prevent-ing you from selling it. Clouds prevent the title from being clear and marketable. If your credit report shows liens or clouds, this could become a huge obstacle in being approved for a loan. Why? Because if you can't sell property because of this lien, it may limit your ability to generate cash for your down payment on your new home. If lenders feel that you cannot produce a down payment, they will be less likely to give you their money.

Bankruptcy

If you've declared bankruptcy before, it will be listed on your credit report. You might have declared bankruptcy to straighten out your financial affairs when you accumu-lated debts so large that you couldn't handle them anymore. Under the federal bank-ruptcy code, various "chapters" specify different forms of bankruptcy filings. The vast majority of all personal bankruptcy filings are done under one of two chapters: Chapter 7 or Chapter 13. Chapter 7 refers to a bankruptcy in which all your property, real and personal, is liquidated and the proceeds are divided among your creditors to pay almost all your debts. Chapter 7 is a more serious bankruptcy because your credi-tors have decided, with the court's acquiescence, that there is no other way to resolve your debt situation. As a result, they are willing to accept what is likely to be only a portion of what you owe, to put the debt behind them.

Chapter 13 refers to a bankruptcy in which you avoid liquidation of your assets. It allows you to adjust your legal debts so that you can repay them over a period of time, as approved by the bankruptcy court. This bankruptcy is used when the court decides, and the creditors agree, that the solution is not limited to total liquidation of most or all of your assets. It is also used to avoid a foreclosure.

As for whether you'll be able to obtain a mortgage with a bankruptcy on your record, it depends on time and history. Each lender has its own standards, but the general rule is that at least two years must have passed since you filed for bankruptcy. In other words, if you're in a five-year Chapter 13 plan under which you will finish paying off your repayments five years later, your two-year waiting period for a mortgage lender to approve you for a loan begins after the five years are completed. For a Chapter 7 bankruptcy, the two-year rule still exists, but lenders are more hesitant about granting a loan as quickly. That is because, with Chapter 7 bankruptcy, the borrower failed to repay his prior debts in full (in Chapter 13, you eventually pay the whole debt). The key will be how well you have re-established your credit.

Quotes and Facts

In 2005, the Bankruptcy Abuse Prevention and Consumer Protection Act was passed to try to reduce the amount of real or perceived debtor abuse of the bankruptcy code. The act specifies limits to filings under Chapter 7 for individuals. If you are considering a filing, discuss its effects with an attorney.

If this is your situation, it's okay if you're still in your waiting period. Take this time to establish new credit references. Apply for a new credit card, finance a car purchase, buy a cell phone, or open a charge account at a local store—but don't go overboard and do all those things at once. Also make sure you pay your accounts *on time*. You are demonstrating to potential mortgage lenders that you are a responsible borrower again and that they can trust you with their funds. Establishing new credit isn't always easy; it takes time, but if you start slowly with a cell phone or a cash-guaranteed low-limit credit card, pay the bills on time, and go from there, you should be able to rehabilitate your credit over time.

Correcting Mistakes with an Explanation Letter

If your credit report has a mistake on it or needs further explanation, you have the right, under federal law, to include an explanation in your record. Use the credit-reporting agency addresses listed earlier in the chapter to contact them. Simply state why you feel that the item reported is erroneous. If you have proof, such as cancelled checks or a promissory note stamped "paid," send along a copy of these items with your letter.

If the debt in question is correct but there are extenuating circumstances for why it was incurred and was delinquent, you can have this explanation included in your credit report, too. For example, let's say that seven years ago, you were laid off from your job and were out of work for six months. As a result, you were delinquent on a credit card debt. Once you got another job, you resumed payments and paid it off without further problems. Or maybe your spouse died unexpectedly and you missed a mortgage payment while you were taking care of funeral arrangements. You caught up as soon as things settled down, but your credit report marked you as "30 days late." In your letter, you would state exactly what happened.

Credit agencies will investigate the situation and, in many instances, will note when an exceptional circumstance prevented you from honoring your obligations in a timely manner or will correct a mistake. The process takes time. Having these explanations on the report will be helpful when your lender is reviewing your application. A reasonable explanation can remove hurdles to getting approved for your loan.

Down Payment

Think of the down payment as a deposit on your home; it's the part of the purchase price that you're going to pay out of your own resources. The amount that you put down on a home is called personal equity. The down payment includes the *earnest money* deposit that accompanies your offer, along with the money you bring along to closing to complete the purchase price agreement. The money for your down payment can come from several sources, including personal savings, investments, loans, your IRA, collectibles, and gifts, to name a few—anywhere you have liquid funds to put to use.

Let's assume you're buying a nice two-bedroom, two-bathroom home for $210,000 in Kansas City. Your plan is to mortgage the home for 80 percent of the purchase price, or $168,000. You are responsible for coming up with the difference, or $42,000. Now where is that money going to come from?

def•i•ni•tion

> **Earnest money** is the good faith deposit you provide along with your offer to the seller. It shows you're serious about your offer, that you offer it "in earnest." While there is no specific required amount, usually it's at least $1,000. I often have my clients put up $5,000.

Personal Savings and CDs

Let's say that in your savings account—at your local bank, credit union, or online bank—you have saved $50,000 from hard work, earnings from stock investments, and interest you've earned on the account. That money is considered liquid, which means you can access it at any time. You can use this money to pay for your down payment on your home.

Your down payment can also come from money you have saved in a certificate of deposit, or CD, that you have at the bank. The downside to withdrawing the money from a CD to fund your down payment is that, unlike a savings account, you'll lose the interest earned and pay a penalty if you withdraw before the term is up.

In such a case, you can avoid the penalty for early withdrawal of the CD by planning, if it's possible. Look at when your CD matures and, assuming it's not too far off, try to schedule the closing on your purchase to come a day or two after the CD's maturity date. That way, you'll not only earn the full amount of interest on the CD, but also avoid any penalty for cashing it in too soon.

Personal Loans

Let's face it—not everyone has thousands of dollars available for a down payment. If you don't have a rich uncle who can give you a down payment as a gift (which we'll discuss in more detail later in the chapter), you may have to borrow it from a friend or family member, or from a bank or credit union. Keep in mind, however, that if you borrow from a bank, the loan will be added to your list of debts. This may push your debt percentage over what the bank requires to write the mortgage. As a result, the bank may refuse to write the mortgage, so figure this all out before you actually apply for the loan. If you need some help with the calculation, talk with your mortgage broker *before* you formally complete the application.

If you are borrowing the down payment from a friend or family member, talk to the person and tell him you're buying a home and need a loan. Tell him how much you need, how long you will take to pay it back, and what interest you are willing to pay, if any, for the favor.

401(k)

You could even loan yourself the down payment money through your company-sponsored 401(k) retirement account. Although most financial planners urge consumers not to touch their 401(k), it is an option in this case. If you withdraw the money from your 401(k), you can withdraw up to half the amount of your balance, up to $50,000, and you have up to five years to repay the loan. Check with your tax advisor for any financial advice that's specific to your situation.

If you do borrow from your 401(k), make sure you can repay the money. Failure to do so could result in having to pay an unplanned tax bill and penalties for early withdrawal. There is one catch, however. If you are self-employed and have your own 401(k), you cannot take out the money for a down payment. The 401(k) must be with a firm in which you are not the only employee. This is to avoid the appearance, or actual fact, of you controlling the 401(k)'s operations as well as investing in it.

IRA

If you want to use your *individual retirement account* (*IRA*) to fund your down payment, there are penalties for early withdrawals. The typical rule is that you are required to forfeit all the interest your money has earned if you prematurely withdraw funds. You must pay a 10 percent penalty as well. Of course, if you're 65 or older, you can withdraw from your IRA penalty-free. So if your purchase is for a retirement place and you want to tap the IRA, go for it!

def•i•ni•tion

An **individual retirement account (IRA)** is designed to be a personal savings vehicle that encourages savings by sheltering your deposits from income tax until you withdraw the money, ideally after your retirement. At that time, you're likely to be in a lower tax bracket and paying less in tax on the funds. The funds are held by a custodian, usually a bank or brokerage firm, until withdrawal, and can be kept in cash or securities. In some cases, you can even own real estate in your IRA.

In addition, when you withdraw the funds, they are treated as normal income and taxed at your present normal income tax rate. For example, if your present tax bracket is 28 percent and you withdraw $50,000, you'll pay the 10 percent penalty, or $5,000, as well as federal income tax of 28 percent, or $14,000. Thus, your total tax liability for the withdrawal would be $19,000.

If you're a first-time home buyer, though, there is good news: you are exempt from these penalties if you use the money to purchase your home. You will pay income tax on the money you have withdrawn, but you will not be charged the 10 percent penalty. If you have a basic IRA, not a Roth IRA, you may make a withdrawal of up to $10,000 for the purchase of your first home. If you are married and your spouse has an IRA, both of you may make the same type of penalty-free withdrawal, for $20,000 total. The taxes due will be at the higher of your two tax brackets.

This is a once-in-a-lifetime benefit, but there is wiggle room in the law. Even though it is said to be used on a first-time purchase, this doesn't have to be your first actual home. As long as you have not owned a home as your primary residence at any time during the two years before this purchase, the penalty-free withdrawal is allowed. One more important condition: you cannot withdraw the money more than 120 days before the closing date on your home.

Warning!

If you do withdraw from your IRA for the home purchase and your closing gets delayed past the 120-day time frame, you lose this free ride and will be liable for the 10 percent penalty. However, if the reason for the delay is not your fault and is clearly out of the ordinary, you may be able to appeal the penalty. Relief from the penalty is not automatic, though; each case must stand on its own.

Roth IRA

If you have a Roth IRA, you must have had the Roth IRA for at least five years before you withdraw the funds to buy the home. If you've had it less than five years, you will probably avoid the 10 percent penalty for early withdrawal, but you may have to pay taxes on the withdrawn amount at your current tax rate, depending on what offsetting deductions on the rest of your tax return you have to help you avoid the tax liability. A Roth IRA is a savings account in which you deposit money that has already been taxed, so you don't get taxed on the funds when they are withdrawn at the proper time. As a result, you may end up paying taxes on funds that otherwise would be tax-exempt. With a regular IRA, your savings are not yet taxed, so this Roth exemption doesn't exist. Unsure what to do? Check with your tax advisor.

Collectibles

Another source of your down payment can come from the collectibles you may own. Just as some people invest in CDs or stocks and bonds, others put at least some of their investment capital in collectibles. They may be stamp or coin collections, or something more exotic, such as works of art or antiques. Some buyers have even sold a classic car they owned to obtain funds for their down payment. If you have a valuable object that you'd like to sell to earn the money for a down payment, keep in mind that there's no guarantee it will sell. It all depends on that item's market. For example, you may have a valuable early *Spiderman* comic book that you think will fetch thousands of dollars, but if the economy is lagging and comic book collectors aren't buying, you may have to wait. This doesn't help if you need your down payment money right away.

Gift Money

Part or all of the down payment can be given to you as a gift from someone else. Perhaps your parents can provide some financial help to you because they don't want to see you struggle for years to save. This gift money is different from the personal loan we mentioned earlier—in this case, the person who gives you the money doesn't want it back. That's okay. You can use gift money for your down payment.

There is no limit on gift money. In most cases, the entire down payment can be a gift. However, if the amount of the down payment is less than 20 percent of the purchase price, you must have at least 5 percent of the down payment from your own funds and the gift must equal the difference. For example, if you're putting down 10 percent, or $20,000, on a $200,000 house, you must pay at least 5 percent of the price from your own funds—or, in this case, $10,000—and the rest can be a gift. However, although people sometimes try to slip it in as a "gift," the donation of the so-called gift cannot be from the seller.

In some cases, buyers will try to borrow money from a friend or family member and call it a gift, even though the donor expects to be repaid. Be careful. Banks are aware of how people try to use "gift" money that really isn't. As a result, lenders have come up with a gift letter for you to submit with your loan application. The gift letter is signed by the donor and states that the funds were nothing more than a gift and that you are in no way obliged to reimburse the donor for any portion of the gift money. Aside from this, there may be some circumstances in which a cash gift could be taxable income. Check with your accountant to avoid possibly receiving "greetings" from the IRS over your gift.

Gift Letter _____

Donor(s): _____

Donor's Address: _____

_____

Recipient(s): _____

Subject Property: _____

_____

Relationship of Donor(s) to Recipient(s): _____

I/We hereby certify that I/We [   ] have given or [   ] will give the above named recipient(s) the amount of $_____ to use for the purchase of the above referenced property. This is a bona fide gift and there is no obligation, expressed or implied, to repay this sum at any time.

_____   _____
Signature of Donor   Date   Signature of Donor   Date

****

- IMPORTANT -

Evidence of transfer of funds must be provided. A photocopy of the check from the Donor with a copy of the deposit slip showing the funds were deposited into the borrower's account is sufficient. The copy of the check or money order, etc. should clearly indicate the name of the remitter and the payee.

Sample gift letter.

Other Assets

You may also have money invested in stocks and bonds, Treasury bonds, U.S. government securities such as Treasury bonds and Treasury bills, state or local municipal bonds, commercial paper, or banker's acceptances. Withdrawing your money from time-restricted accounts too early can result in paying interest and penalties, so carefully weigh your options and know the financial consequences before you make any final decisions.

Should you borrow cash from your credit cards to fund your down payment? It's possible, but it's a mistake. Even if your credit card charges you only 9 percent on your balances, it can be quite a bit more costly than your mortgage interest rate. Let's assume that you borrow $25,000 at 9 percent per annum. That means that, in interest alone, you'll pay $2,250 for those funds—in the first year! Unless you have absolutely no other source of funds for your down payment, don't do it.

Quotes and Facts

The down payment on my first home was from monies invested in a banker's acceptance (BA). This is financing provided by a large bank's financing of domestic and international trade. BAs are extremely liquid, depending on the agreement with the bank at the time. I invested the money in whatever acceptance the bank had on its books at that time. If it matured before I needed the money, I took the cash and the interest and bought a new acceptance. When I found the home I wanted to buy, I liquidated my BAs and used the funds for my down payment.

—Peter

Bottom line when it comes to paying for your down payment—remember to consider where it may come from and the tax implications from withdrawing or borrowing the money.

The Least You Need to Know

◆ Just because you think you have bad credit doesn't mean you won't be able to buy a home.

◆ Get a copy of your credit report ASAP and work on fixing any problems immediately.

◆ If you have a very low credit score and/or have a foreclosure or bankruptcy in your history, simply retreat, repair your credit, and try again.

◆ It's better to use cash and personal assets for your down payment than to withdraw money from your retirement savings accounts early and be charged penalties.

Chapter 6

Mortgage Loans

In This Chapter

- ◆ Learning the vocabulary of loans
- ◆ Comparing terms and interest rates
- ◆ Understanding the different types of mortgages
- ◆ Shopping around for mortgages

Entire books have been written on mortgages because the industry is complicated and there's so much to know about the biggest bill you will probably ever pay. It might seem like mortgage lenders speak another language and you're left trying to understand what everyone is talking about. The whole process can get overwhelming—one wrong move, and you could be trapped in a loan that costs you more than you can afford to pay and only gets worse as years go on.

If you go into the process informed and knowledgeable, however, shopping for and getting a mortgage doesn't have to be scary. This chapter arms you with the knowledge you need. You'll learn basic loan terminology and come to understand the different types of loans and what you might qualify for. You'll also find out about your rights to understand before you sign on the dotted line.

If you wouldn't rush into buying a car or a new piece of jewelry, why rush into choosing a loan before you know all the facts? This chapter gives you the information you need to make an educated, informed decision.

Mortgage Loan Terminology

What you need is this brief tutorial that breaks down the mortgage lingo into an easy-to-understand language. For example, a mortgage is a lien that the lender puts on your home in exchange for the loan. You are putting up your home as collateral in return for the loan you need to purchase it. If you don't make the payments on the loan, the bank can take the house back. You are called the mortgagor and the lender is called the mortgagee. Let's review some more common terms you need to know.

Principal Amount and Balance

The principal amount of the home loan is the actual amount of money that you are borrowing. As you make payments on the loan, the amount that you still owe is called the principal balance or the balance of the principal—the terms are interchangeable. For example, if you buy a home for $200,000 and you put down a $40,000 down payment, you will need to borrow the other $160,000 in order to buy the home. That $160,000 is called the principal amount of your mortgage loan. If your loan is an amortizing loan, a term discussed later in this chapter, a portion of every payment you make to the bank will go toward repaying the principal amount that you originally borrowed.

Term

The length of the loan is called the term (or sometimes called the tenor) of the loan. The term is the maximum amount of time that you will have to pay the loan back. Mortgages come in a variety of terms. Most common are the 30-year and 15-year terms, but they can be in almost any term you need, down to 5 years.

Interest Rate

Like your credit cards, mortgage loans come with interest rates. An interest rate is a percentage of your loan that is charged to you simply because you have the loan. This is the price you pay to have a loan. Expressed in percentages, the rate is calculated on a per-annum basis on the principal amount of money that you owe.

The interest rate can be either fixed or adjustable. Fixed interest rates remain unchanged for the entire life of the loan, no matter how long the term. Adjustable, or floating, interest rates are named because they may change—up or down—over the term of the loan.

An ARM may also come with a minimum rate, referred to as the floor, which means the interest rate cannot drop below this number, no matter how cheap lendable funds may become to the lender. There may also be a maximum rate, called the ceiling, which is the highest that the lender can raise the interest rate. These interest rate adjustments are made in response to the cost of lendable funds to the lender in the open market. If the cost of borrowing funds is climbing, then your interest rate will likely follow suit. However, if rates in the funding market follow a downward trend, then the rate you will be charged for your loan will probably go down, too. Read up on the real estate market and the mortgage loans to get a sense of whether interest rates are going up or down.

Warning!

There's a danger with committing to an adjustable-rate loan—the rate may have a lower starting rate than the fixed rate, but if it adjusts upward too high for your budget, you might have difficulty making the payments. However, with a fixed rate, you always know exactly what your rate and payment will be.

✳ Points

Think of a mortgage point, sometimes referred to as a discount point, as a discount on the interest rate charged to you. When you pay a point up front on your mortgage—equal to 1 percent of the face amount of the loan—you are eligible to get the loan at a slightly lower rate of interest, sometimes referred to as "buying down" the loan.

Many people question the value of paying points on a mortgage. It does have both advantages and disadvantages. Granted, the advantage of paying points is that you have a lower interest rate on your loan. Typically, paying points results in a cut of approximately one quarter of a percent for each point you paid. However, this depends on current market conditions as well as the status of the lender's own loan portfolio.

However, the disadvantage is that there is a higher up-front cost to you to obtain the loan. For example, paying 1 point on a $150,000 loan costs you $1,500 up front.

You may ask if the expense of paying points actually saves you any money. The answer is, "It depends." If you plan to be in your loan for only three or four years, then you probably do not gain any net advantage by paying points. If you're going to stay in a particular loan for a longer period of time, then the reduced rate of interest you'll receive in exchange for paying points will probably save you several thousands of dollars over the life of the loan.

Let's say, for example, that you are borrowing $200,000. Each point you pay will cost $2,000 and you decide to pay 1 point. The loan is a 30-year fixed-rate loan and your point has just earned you that quarter-point reduction in the interest rate. As a result, your interest rate drops from 5 percent to 4.75 percent. Your mortgage payments now drop from $1,073.64 per month to $1,043.29 per month. That means that every month of your fixed-rate loan, you will save $30.35. While that might not seem like much, if you hold the loan on the home for the full 30 years, your net savings will be a whopping $10,926 in interest minus your original $2,000 that you paid for that point—for a net savings of $8,926!

Another thing to consider before you pay points is your cash flow. Of course paying points will reduce your interest rate, but you may not choose to spend the money simply because you don't have it right now or because you don't want to spend more money at the start of your loan. That $2,000 from our example may be better off somewhere else in your budget—reducing credit card debt or buying new furniture that you need—rather than reducing your loan a little bit each month. Deciding whether or not to pay points depends on your own situation.

Keep in mind that paying points is also deductible on your income taxes, so consult your tax advisor. You can read more about how to deduct points on your taxes in Chapter 8.

Annual Percentage Rate

The annual percentage rate (APR) is the interest rate you'll actually pay for your loan. It is the total annual cost of your loan, including all your fees and interest, expressed as a percentage. The APR must be disclosed to you, thanks to the federal Truth in Lending Act, which was passed in 1968 as a part of the broader Consumer Credit Protection Act. The Truth in Lending Act covers many areas of consumer lending, not just mortgages, and covers your rights when receiving credit from lending and other credit-granting institutions. With very few exceptions, the act does not limit interest rates; it simply requires that the lender inform you exactly what you'll pay for the loan. That information is not limited just to the interest rate. Lenders must disclose all of the loan fees, points, and other ancillary expenses connected with the loan. So while APR is the actual effective interest rate you will be charged, the law also requires that you be advised of *all* costs associated with the loan, not just interest rates.

Mortgage Insurance

Mortgage insurance compensates lenders or investors on a loss in case you default on your loan. In essence, this insurance guarantees the lender they'll get repaid by the insurance if you fail to repay the loan. The insurance can be public or private. There is private mortgage insurance and insurance on FHA loans as well.

Private Mortgage Insurance

Private mortgage insurance (PMI) is insurance that lenders require from home buyers when you put down less than 20 percent down payment on your home. If you obtain a loan that is more than 80 percent of your new home's value, you are required to pay PMI. While protecting the lender, it also enables you to buy a home if you can't afford a hefty 20 percent down payment.

The actual cost of your PMI premium depends upon the loan-to-value ratio of your mortgage. In other words, the more you put down as a down payment, the lower your premiums will be. Premiums are payable on a monthly basis, usually along with the mortgage payment. The premium is typically a fraction of 1 percent divided into equal monthly amounts for the first 20 years of a 30-year mortgage. In the final 10 years of the mortgage, regardless of the size of your original down payment, the premium becomes 0.2 percent of the original mortgage amount, divided into 12 monthly payments.

In 1998, a federal law called The Homeowner's Protection Act (HPA) required lenders to tell borrowers when PMI should be cancelled. This is because, years ago, lenders wouldn't automatically stop the insurance payments after a loan balance dropped down to 80 percent of the property value. Instead, the lenders would keep charging PMI until the borrower requested that it stop—and, most of the time, it wasn't something that homeowners would keep track of.

HPA requires that lenders notify you, at closing and on the anniversary of the closing every year, of your right to cancel your PMI. The law also requires automatic cancellation once the loan principal drops to 78 percent of the home's value. You do have the right to request cancellation before that once your principal balance has dropped to 80 percent of the home's original value. The loan must be current at the time of cancellation. HPA doesn't cover Veterans Administration (VA) loans or FHA loans.

Tips and Traps

If you are required to pay PMI on your new home, remember that you have the right to cancel it when you pay down your mortgage to the point that it equals 80 percent of the original purchase price or appraised value of your home. You need to have been a good customer, though—make sure you pay your loan on time and you haven't been late with a payment more than 30 days over the last year. The bank may ask for evidence that the property value hasn't declined below its original value and that the property doesn't have a home equity loan or another mortgage on it.

FHA Insurance

The Federal Housing Administration (FHA) provides mortgage insurance, called a mortgage insurance premium (MIP), for FHA loans. Because FHA-insured loans require little cash down, this insurance provides lenders with protection in case you default on your loan. The cost of the insurance is included in your monthly payment. Typically, this insurance payment stops after five years or when the loan is 78 percent of the value of the property. Put simply in dollars and cents, MIP is calculated as follows: An insurance premium of 0.55% per annum is charged to the combined principal of loan amount and MIP. This annual amount is payable in monthly increments and becomes part of your monthly mortgage payment. For example, if you borrowed $100,000, then added on the MIP of $1,750, you would pay an annual insurance premium of $559.63. Divided into 12 easy payments, this would add $46.64 every month to your payment.

Types of Loans

There are many types of mortgage loans to choose from, and which type you choose depends on your personal financial situation. A loan with a smaller down payment might be perfect if you don't have as much cash available, or you may choose a larger down payment and then have smaller monthly mortgage payments. You might qualify for a specialized program, such as the GI loan, or if you've struggled financially, you may still achieve the American dream of home ownership through an FHA loan. Here we discuss the most common types of home loans, although it's important to have a detailed conversation with your mortgage lender and find out what loan programs you may qualify for.

Conventional or Jumbo

Decades ago, there was one type of mortgage loan: conventional. Today home mortgage loans are broken down into two categories—conventional and jumbo—and cover all types of loans provided by lenders: fixed or adjustable rate, and amortizing or non-amortizing. A conventional loan is a loan with a maximum principal amount of $417,000. However, as part of the restructuring of financial terminology and regulations that has developed since the current financial crisis has arisen, there is a new loan size: the agency jumbo loan. This is a loan made for a principal amount that's larger than a conventional loan and less than a jumbo loan.

An agency jumbo loan is a loan whose principal amount ranges from $417,000 to nearly $730,000. Anything above $730,000 is considered a true jumbo loan.

There are other differences in loans, too. First, a conventional loan must be one that conforms to the parameters for such loans established by either Fannie Mae or Freddie Mac, both semiprivate federal mortgage institutions.

Second, a jumbo loan generally carries a higher rate of interest than the conforming loan. That's because the larger the amount of the loan, the more risk there is to the lender. Any time the risk on a loan increases, the interest on that loan increases, too.

Third, such loans are more difficult to obtain than the smaller conforming ones. Again, it's a factor of risk. Because more money is at risk, fewer people will qualify for the larger loans. Also, these loans are not eligible for guarantees from the FHA or the Veterans Administration. So, as you can see, you can borrow more money, but there are negatives to consider.

Amortized vs. Interest-Only Loans

These two terms—amortized and interest only—refer to whether the principal amount of your loan is decreasing as you make your payments. With an amortizing loan, every payment you make pays the interest on the outstanding loan balance as well as part of the principal balance.

Interest-only loans are just what the name suggests. As you make your payments, you are paying only the interest that is accruing on your loan. Your payments are not being applied to the principal balance of the loan just yet. When the term of the loan reaches the end, you will still owe the same principal amount as you did on the very first day of the loan. You will then have to pay off the entire outstanding balance of the loan.

How do you do that? You'll have two options: either sell the home or refinance the loan with a new loan. Selling is usually done if you just planned to own and live in the home for the term of the loan, while refinancing is used when you plan to be there beyond the term of the loan.

The most common way is to refinance your loan, replacing it with a new loan that repays the old one. The disadvantage is that you are doing nothing to grow equity, unless the market is experiencing an appreciation in values.

You may prefer an interest-only loan if you are banking on the value of your home to increase during the term of the loan. You will still repay the entire amount of principal at the end of the loan, but you'll have earned money in the increased value of the home. An interest-only loan also keeps your current payments at a minimum, which may help your budget.

You may have heard of something called a balloon payment. With a balloon payment, you take out a loan for a period of time that is less than its amortized period is calculated to be. Let's say you borrow for a 10-year term, with equal monthly payments over that period. To keep the monthly payments manageable, your loan is amortized as if it were a 30-year loan. Sounds fine, but when you get to the 10 year mark, the entire outstanding balance is still due in one lump sum—the balloon payment.

So you're probably wondering if you should get an interest-only mortgage or an amortizing fixed-rate mortgage? There's no right or wrong answer. If you cannot afford the higher payments of an amortizing fixed-rate loan and need to start with smaller payments, an interest-only loan may be the loan for you. You can refinance to a fixed rate later when you're able to pay more each month, or you may want an interest rate loan because you don't plan to own the house for more than a couple of years.

Alternatively, a fixed-rate loan may be better for you if you plan to own the home for a longer period of time and can afford the higher monthly payments. If interest rates drop, you can always refinance to a lower fixed rate.

Fannie Mae and Freddie Mac

Known as the Federal National Mortgage Association, Fannie Mae was originally founded in the latter years of the Depression to purchase mortgages from banks and then *securitize* them for sale to investors so that adequate funds would be available to make mortgage loans without too much difficulty. It is publicly owned and its shares trade on the stock market. Freddie Mac is a similar quasi-government entity with the same purpose. Its full name is the Federal Home Loan Mortgage Corporation.

Created by Congress in 1970, its purpose is to put more money into the secondary mortgage market by buying up more loans and then securitizing them for sale to investors.

Fannie Mae and Freddie Mac are major participants in the mortgage-funding market in the United States. Collectively, Freddie and Fannie may effectively guarantee up to half of the current $12 trillion mortgage market. They purchase the loans from the banks that originated the loans, and their parameters can change from time to time. Whether they are fixed- or adjustable-rate mortgages is of no concern for these purposes; only the dollar amount of the principal matters.

def•i•ni•tion

Securitization is a process by which many individual financial obligations of a particular type are bundled together and then certificates representing them are sold to individual investors, much in the way that shares of stock are sold.

Quotes and Facts

Want to make sure your bank is healthy? Carefully read its investor relations materials and filings. Also check with your state's banking department and with the Federal Deposit Insurance Corporation (FDIC), which insures deposits in banks and thrift institutions for $250,000 per individual. While this doesn't directly affect whether your bank makes you a loan, it is still important because it protects depositors' deposits. Those deposits are one of the basic important components of the funds banks use to fund the loans they make—no deposits, no loans.

FHA Loans

If you've been having problems getting a loan, you might turn to The Federal Housing Administration (FHA), which is part of the Department of Housing and Urban Development's (HUD) Office of Housing. HUD provides insurance to the lender, making sure that the loan will be repaid.

FHA loans benefit home buyers who are having problems getting a conventional mortgage. If you've had issues with your credit history, this loan is made-to-order for you. You can use it to purchase up to a four-unit dwelling in order to earn additional income, as long as you plan on living in the building. You can also refinance using an FHA loan for a new loan. You don't even have to have an FHA loan for the existing loan that you're planning to replace.

Tips and Traps _____

If you ultimately refinance your loan, you may want to consider doing so with an FHA loan. There is a possibility that the interest rate may be a bit cheaper. Also, if you're fixing up a property, the FHA 203k is a special loan used to rehabilitate property, and it may be more convenient to get one loan to refinance and rehab at the same time than to get two separate loans.

Three loans make up almost all of HUD's FHA lending support: the 203b, 203k, and 234c programs. Each is specifically offered for a particular home-financing situation, and they are not interchangeable.

203b

The 203b loan program is a fixed-rate loan and the most common FHA loan for first-time buyers. There are several advantages to this loan.

First, the FHA requires only 3 percent of the purchase price as a down payment, which is almost unheard of for conventional-type fixed-rate 30-year loans. Second, FHA loans generally have less stringent income requirements than conventional loans. Third, the monthly FHA-required mortgage insurance premium is generally lower than that charged on conventional loans, made with as little as 3 percent down. The amount you can borrow with a 203b loan also varies within the county where you buy the home, but the general limit is $417,000 for a 30-year fixed-rate loan. In cases where the home prices are generally higher or lower, HUD has different loan maximum amounts available. These vary with the location of the home, but all are fixed rate.

Tips and Traps _____

If you want more information about any special circumstances that apply to your area, check with your mortgage broker, call the FHA at 202-708-1112 or 202-708-1422, or visit the FHA website at www.hud.gov.

In any case, the highest 203b loan amount available anywhere, in what are referred to as high-value areas, is $729,750. High-value areas are those where the typical price of homes is well above the norm in most of the rest of the country. San Francisco; New York; and Washington, D.C., are examples.

An additional benefit comes when it's time to sell your home. A 203b loan is assumable, which means that if your buyer wishes, she may take over your loan, thus saving substantial expense on fees that she'd likely have to pay for a new loan.

203k

The 203k is an FHA loan available when you want to buy any home, from one to four units, that needs rehabilitation or improvement, as long as you live in one of the units. It can be used to purchase or refinance a home, and the loan can include the costs of rehabbing the home after the purchase. A 203k loan can also help to purchase a home on one site, move it to a new foundation, and rehab it once it's on the new site. Caution: the loan portion to be used for relocating the home is not available to you until the home has been moved and attached to the new foundation. The rehab can then proceed with costs coming from the proceeds of the loan.

Maximum loan limits and rate structure are usually limited to regular FHA guidelines. However, for the 203k ARMs, adjustable loans may be used due to the nature of the purpose of the loan. The decision is that of the borrower when deciding which loan to apply for. If the buyer will have rehab work to do, he has this extra option to use. The rehab work must begin within 30 days of closing the loan and must be completed within six months.

234c

If you're planning to purchase a condominium or townhome, the 234c loan allows purchase of any single-family unit in a condo or townhome complex. Your home can be part of a multi-unit structure, detached individual units, semidetached units (two units attached), or row house–style, garden-unit design, or low- or high-rise buildings. However, they must be on HUD's approved condominium list, which is available from HUD by mail or online. For this, or any other HUD information, go online to www. hud.gov.

Eighty percent of the mortgages in the complex must be the owner's principal residences, and the maximum loan amount is the same as with 203b loans, with the additional requirement that loan amounts be in multiples of $50. Minimum investment by the homeowner, maximum term of the mortgage, and the refinancing provisions are the same as with the 203b loan.

What if you're interested in purchasing a condo that's not on the approved list? Are you out of luck? Not necessarily. You may qualify for a spot loan under the 234c program. The spot loan program has an additional nine guidelines that must be met as a condition of the loan. These conditions are not things that you work at to get compliance with. Either they are already compliant or they are not.

- The construction of the complex should be complete by the time you apply for your loan. No additional construction of units or common facilities may be ongoing.

- The common areas must already have been under the homeowners' association (HOA) for at least a year.

- The HOA must be able to show proof that it has adequate liability, hazard, and flood insurance.

- The individual units must be owned in a *fee simple* or *eligible leasehold legal format*. The owners must also be able to have full unlimited use of all common areas and facilities. This must be provided for in the HOA's legal documents.

- There cannot be any restrictions on *conveyance* of the separate units in the association's legal documents.

def•i•ni•tion

Fee simple is a form of legal title. It means the owner has full power of maintaining or disposing of his real property. He can sell it, mortgage it, or give it away. **Eligible leasehold legal format** is the FHA's parameters requiring that the units be lease eligible under local law.

Conveyance means the disposition, presumably by sale, of property from one owner to another.

- At least 90 percent of the units in the project must already be sold.

- At least 51 percent of the units in the complex must be owner occupied.

- No single legal entity may own more than 10 percent of the total number of units in a complex. The term *entity* refers to any legal form of the word: person, partnership, corporation, LLC, and so on.

- The number of units in a complex that may contemporaneously have FHA financing is limited to 10 percent if over 30 units in the complex, and 20 percent if 30 or fewer units comprise the complex.

You can obtain additional information through your mortgage broker, lending institution, or national or local HUD office (www.hud.gov; 202-708-1112).

State and Local Loan Programs

In addition to the federally supported programs, similar types of housing programs often are available at the state or local level. The most common is the state Housing Finance Agency (HFA) that most states have, operated under charters provided by the state in which they are located. However, at the national level, in conjunction with the National Council of State Housing Agencies (NCSHA), a nonprofit organization, there are some federally authorized programs to help individuals purchase homes, including Mortgage Revenue Bonds (MRB) and the HOME Investment Partnerships Program (HOME).

MRBs, also commonly referred to as Housing Bonds, are tax-exempt bonds issued and sold by local and state governments to help finance mortgages for low-income first-time home buyers. Approximately 100,000 low-income families benefit from them annually. These bonds are sold by the government involved with the funds available to the borrowers as a result of their sale.

The program with the largest single impact is HOME. HOME provides federal block grants to be used in the development, maintenance, or rehabilitation of local housing programs. It also may be used for down payment and rental assistance, but all of its uses are directed at low-income families. More information is available from your individual state housing department or from the NCSHA (www.ncsha.org; 202-624-7710).

GI Loans

This loan is properly known as a Veterans Administration (VA) loan, but is more commonly referred to as a GI loan. Signed into law by President Franklin D. Roosevelt on June 22, 1944, the program was officially known as the Serviceman's Readjustment Act and provided a number of benefits to service veterans. These included educational grants for higher education, job training, veterans' hospitals, and home mortgages. Over the years, it has been extended and updated to meet the needs of the country's veterans. Twenty years after the law's original passage, 20 percent of all houses constructed in the United States were financed by mortgages made with GI Bill guarantees.

The GI Bill does not provide mortgage loans. Instead, it encourages the various lending institutions to make the loans and provides a federal government guarantee of the loan. If the borrower fails to repay the loan, the federal Veterans Administration repays the bank making the loan.

Eligibility

GI loans were originally intended only for the benefit of combat veterans but have been expanded to include all veterans. When the draft ended in 1973, the law was changed again to offer benefits relative to the length of time the recipient was in military service.

The eligibility requirements are simple: if it's wartime, you must have had at least 90 days of active military service in some part of the U.S. Armed Forces. If your service was during peacetime, and the law defines the dates of both, you must have had at least 181 continuous days of active duty service. If you have less time than this due to a service-related disability, you may still be eligible. Your discharge must be other than dishonorable.

In some cases, spouses of veterans are also eligible. This applies when the service person was killed in combat or died of service-related disabilities. Spouses of service members missing in action or being held as prisoners of war may also be provided eligibility.

Limitations

GI loans are limited to purchases of a home with a loan guarantee of $417,000. However, since home prices are different throughout the country, the VA has established what are considered county limits, setting specific maximum loan guarantee limits on different counties on a county-by-county basis. The difference in guarantee sizes can be quite large. For example, while much of the nation is covered by guarantees of up to $417,000, other counties have loan guarantees above that figure. In fact, in some counties, the maximum amount is $1,094,625. For your own local limits, check out www.valoans.com or www.homeloans.va.gov. The latter gives a county-by-county breakdown of the maximum loan guarantee amount in all "high-cost" county areas.

Tips and Traps

With a GI loan, you also have to pay a 1.25 percent funding fee of the principal loan amount. This is due at closing.

Another important part of a GI loan is that it eliminates the requirement for a down payment, allowing you to buy a home much faster. However, before you decide to get a bigger loan and home because you don't need a down payment, remember that for every extra dollar on your mortgage loan, your monthly payment will be higher. Make sure you can afford it. Don't GI yourself into a future foreclosure.

Finally, a GI loan is meant for the purchase of a primary residence, but you can use it to purchase investment properties. You can buy a duplex or triplex, for example, as long as you occupy one of the units as your principle residence. Also, because you purchased a multi-unit building, the loan guarantee limits carry a higher dollar value. For more information, including contact information for your local VA office, visit www.gibill. va.gov.

Warning!

GI loans require a termite report before purchase, and the house has to be certified as termite free in the report. If termites are found, they have to be removed and so certified before the GI guarantee can be provided.

State Veterans Loan Programs

In some cases, individual states have also enacted their own versions of loans for veterans of military service. For example, there is a CalVet program in California (www. cdva.ca.gov/CalVetloans) and a Texas Vet Loan program in Texas (www.tdhca.state. tx.us). Each state that offers special programs has its own restrictions, so be sure to check them out before applying. For example, Texas requires the same eligibility rules as the VA, but a Tex Vet loan requires that you be a Texas resident at the time you are applying and meet Texas Vet residency requirements. These restrictions were established to prevent fraudulent temporary residence by the borrower created solely to take advantage of the system. In California, the CalVet program restrictions include a maximum loan amount of $521,250, including the required funding fee, between 1.25 percent and 3.30 percent, if that fee is financed.

Unlike the GI loan, not all state veterans' loans are permissible up to 100 percent of purchase price. Check with your state to find out its local programs and their eligibility requirements. It's best to research and weigh your options when it comes to financing.

Selling Loans

Once you get loan approval and settle in with a mortgage company, don't be surprised if you suddenly find out that your mortgage is with a different company. Sometimes, without you even being aware of it, your loan is sold to a new institution. It may even be a bank you've never heard of. This is called the secondary market, and it provides a place for lenders to sell off their mortgage loans to other lenders.

Lenders have regulatory limits on how much they can have on their books in loans at any one time. When they make loans, they earn income not only from interest, but also from points and loan fees. If they are unable to make any new loans, their other income is cut accordingly. So by selling off existing loans, they have made their up-front income on those loans, get new money to make new loans and earn additional fees, and get the chance to add interest income on the new loans to their overall income. Lenders also have an opportunity to make additional income in the process. If the two institutions agree, they can retain servicing rights for the sold loans. In other words, the original lender continues to receive and distribute your payments to the new owner of the loan.

Fair Lending

There's such a thing as fair lending when it comes to mortgage loans. The Equal Credit Opportunity Act prohibits lenders from discriminating against credit applicants in any aspect of a credit transaction on the basis of race, color, religion, national origin, sex, marital status, age, whether all or part of the applicant's income comes from a public assistance program, or whether the applicant has in good faith exercised a right under the Consumer Credit Protection Act. The Fair Housing Act prohibits discrimination in residential real estate transactions on the basis of race, color, religion, sex, handicap, familial status, or national origin. Under these laws, a consumer cannot be refused a loan based on these characteristics, nor be charged more for a loan or offered less favorable terms based on such characteristics.

Finding the Best Loan

If you're using a mortgage broker, he chooses the lender and your mortgage shopping has ended. However, if you're planning to apply directly to a bank, then shop around and compare lenders to get the best deal. Talk to as many different lenders as you please to find out the differences in interest rates, loan fees, and types of loan products.

In some cases, a bank will charge a slightly lower interest rate if you maintain your checking account with that bank and agree to have your mortgage payments deducted automatically from the account. Another bank might throw in a credit card with your loan. Some lenders will not make loans on certain types of property, whereas others will. Some lenders take longer than others to process a loan application. It can't hurt to shop around and you will probably be better off as a result.

The Least You Need to Know

♦ Avoid a mortgage that has an interest rate that increases over time if you don't think you'll be able to afford the increased payments.

♦ Your mortgage details depend on your credit history.

♦ You do not need to choose the first mortgage that you find; shop around and decide what's best for you.

♦ There are specialized mortgages that you may qualify for, including GI mortgages, so ask your lender to discuss these options with you.

Chapter 7

Nontraditional Financing

In This Chapter

- ◆ Seller financing options
- ◆ Advantages and disadvantages of seller incentives
- ◆ Using a reverse mortgage to buy a home
- ◆ When you should walk away from a bad loan

As an incentive to move the sale of his home forward, a seller will sometimes indicate he is willing to carry back a mortgage, which means the seller will hold the mortgage and you'll pay him. He can do this for all or part of your mortgage. Why does a seller do this when he is actually trying to sell you the home? It's simple. A seller offers seller financing because he wants to obtain the price he wants for the home, by giving you a lower-than-market interest rate in exchange for a higher price, or he may want to earn some extra income. Seller financing is not automatically available with all home purchases. It enters the picture only if either you or the seller offers or requests it, and both you and the seller agree to it.

Yes, there's the traditional route you can go about getting a loan, but what's good about buying a home is that there are options available to you, and it's important to examine them all before making a decision. This chapter shows you how to collaborate with the seller to obtain a financing package that works for you.

In addition to reviewing what seller financing is, we'll help you decide if this is the right type of financing for you. Just like you can walk away from a home if the features don't meet your needs, you'll learn how to turn away from any financing opportunity, including seller financing, if it also doesn't meet your needs.

We'll also look at reverse mortgages as a vehicle to finance your purchase. This is a new concept because, until very recently, these loans were usually available only to retired folks living on a fixed income with substantial equity in their homes who didn't want the hassle of worrying about making monthly payments to the bank.

Seller Financing

Traditionally, when you bought a home, you would simply get a loan from a bank and buy the home from the seller, case closed. But what if you don't get approved for a loan, or you don't have as much money for the down payment as the bank wants? Or what if the terms of the bank loan don't quite meet what you are looking for? For example, perhaps the interest rate is too high. Have you lost all hope of ever becoming a homeowner? No, fortunately there is another financing option that just might meet your needs.

With seller financing, you are still buying the home from the seller. However, instead of paying the bank, you agree to sign a contract with the seller to pay the mortgage payments directly to him. The title to the home still transfers to you at the closing. In other words, the seller acts exactly like a bank would act when you buy a home.

This unique type of financing offers several advantages for you, the buyer. First, a seller might offer you a more favorable rate of interest than what traditional lenders are offering. The seller can do this because institutional lenders have to make a certain amount of money from the rates and fees that they charge their customers in order to cover their operating expenses and make a decent profit (they report this profit number to their regulators and shareholders). Sellers, on the other hand, don't have to make a specific amount of money and they don't have business operating expenses that they have to cover. They simply are making a deal where they can earn some money and sell their home at the same time.

Keep in mind, however, that just because a seller agrees to seller financing doesn't mean that the seller will just give away the home at rock bottom loan prices just so he can sell it.

The Benefits of Seller Financing

What are the benefits of seller financing? Let's say that you have fallen in love with a Victorian home in a quiet suburban community. It has everything you want—three bedrooms, two-and-a-half baths, a huge backyard, and a price that fits your budget. However, you've gone through some difficulties in your financial life and you have several dings on your credit history, so the bank is offering a substantially high interest rate for your mortgage. Or perhaps you determined that the monthly mortgage payments the bank would require are a bit more than you're comfortable paying. You don't have to give up the home, though.

Instead, this is a perfect opportunity to ask the seller to carry the mortgage. He considers a deal where he will offer you financing for 5 years, amortized (revisit Chapter 6 to review this term again) over 30 years at a rate that is a full percentage point below the rate that the bank was offering you. The seller could also offer you the same rate that the bank has, but with less of a down payment. It all depends on what your terms are.

Another benefit for choosing seller financing is that you won't have to pay points or other fees that you might have to pay with a traditional bank loan. Considering that each point you would have paid would equal 1 percent of your principal loan amount—and loan fees can cost thousands of dollars—you can also save a substantial amount of money.

The bottom line is that you may get to buy that Victorian home that you have been wanting, with a financing package that meets your needs.

But why would the seller agree to seller financing when he can probably find another buyer for his home and be done with the deal? It's simple! In addition to selling his home at or near his asking price, he also gets an opportunity to earn extra income. That extra income is the interest you'll be paying him on a monthly basis. So it works for both of you, and the deal is done.

If your credit score is too low to get a traditional loan or there are other obstacles that prevent you from getting a traditional bank loan, seller financing may be the only way to accomplish your goal of being a homeowner. With this financing option, you can negotiate all repayment terms of the loan.

Warning!

Even with seller financing, the seller can run a full credit check on the borrower and require such items as hazard insurance on the property. A seller can turn you down because of your past credit history as well.

Installment Sales

A seller may also be able to sell you his home by using what's called an installment sale, also called an installment purchase. Installment sales are similar to straight seller carryback financing, but the structure of ownership and financing is different. Unlike a straight purchase with all, or a portion, of your financing carried by the seller, installment purchases allow you to pay an agreed-upon portion of the price to the seller, with him financing the balance for a specified period of time at an agreed-upon rate of interest. This initial payment is usually done at closing, although if both parties agree to some other time frame, that can be done as well. The title does not transfer to you until you have made the final payment on the home to the seller.

Tips and Traps _____

If you're willing to delay full ownership rights for a longer period in exchange for a cheaper financing cost, you may suggest an installment purchase to the seller. Explain to him the potential tax benefits he may receive as a result by agreeing to sell in this way.

Once again, a seller may agree to sell you his property on an installment sale because it affords him a way to sell the property, his main goal, and earn extra income from the sale. He can then spread out his tax liabilities over the years that you are paying him. You benefit from a possible lower interest rate.

Watch Out

If you decide to buy your home by using seller financing or a seller installment plan, you should watch out for a few things, particularly as you get closer to making the final payment and assuming actual legal ownership.

◆ Just as you would in a traditional sale with a bank mortgage, pay to obtain a title report on the property. This is especially important before it's time for the title to exchange hands. This report will provide proof that the seller has the right to sell the home to you.

◆ Make certain that your agreement covers all of the particulars of the loan—interest rate, grace period, etc. And make sure you know who is responsible for paying the property taxes. This part of the contract is negotiable and should be established up front. You are living in the house, but technically the seller is the legal owner of the property. Because the tax bills are based on ownership, they will still be mailed to the seller. If you and the seller agree that it's your responsibility to pay them, make sure you pay them when they are due so no issue arises later regarding a lien for unpaid taxes.

If you and the seller have agreed that it's the seller who is paying the taxes, the only way you can make sure that the seller paid the bill is to get a copy of the cancelled check from the seller. You can also ask that the seller obtain a copy of a paid receipt for the tax bills from the taxing authority and provide it to you.

♦ Ask your Realtor for his advice on the financing before you commit to an agreement with the seller. He should be able to guide you. Consider asking a mortgage broker for advice as well. You may have to pay a small fee for this, or she may assist in the interest of getting your future business.

♦ Do not proceed without having an attorney draft and review all documents. Have your attorney draft your offer for installment purchases as well as any financing documents. If the seller responds with documents of his own, immediately bring them to your attorney for her approval or changes. This is very important, probably more so than in the case of making a purchase with pre-drawn document forms that your agent supplies. Those very likely have been already vetted by counsel at some point.

Making a Decision

So what do you do? Let's say a seller offers you a five-year loan—do you take it, do you try to get your mortgage from a more traditional lender, or, if you can't qualify for a traditional loan, do you just wait? First, compare the terms that the seller is offering against your bank's or mortgage broker's terms, if you qualify. Who has the lower interest rate?

Then consider how long you plan to own the home. If you feel that this home is one you'll stay in for up to five years before you move, the seller's offer of a five-year loan may be ideal. On the other hand, if you are planning to live in the house for more than five years, the seller's loan may not work for you. Although we cite a five-year term here, and most seller financing is for a shorter term than what institutional lenders usually offer, there is no time limit on the term of a seller-financed loan.

Consider whether you want to deal with only one person for your home loan or whether you want the convenience of a bank and want to have access to other services it can offer to you. Once you consider all of these factors, you'll know whether seller financing is right for you.

> **Warning!**
>
> Have an attorney look at the loan agreement, no matter what type of financing method you finally decide on, to protect yourself from any conditions that may be difficult for you to abide by. Consider researching the seller through the county courthouse to see if he is timely with his tax payments or if there are any civil suits against him. If so, pursue a more traditional loan. No one wants the aggravation of ending up in court because the seller didn't hold up his end of the deal.

Saying No

When do you step away from a home if the financing, either traditional or seller, isn't right? No specific rules apply, and every situation is governed by its own circumstances.

Work with your agent when you find any sticking points on the financing with your seller and you cannot seem to reach agreement on it no matter how hard you try. For example, what if the seller's best offer is a high interest rate on a term that is too short for your needs? If you have other lending options, you can tell the seller "Thanks, but no thanks," and pursue the other options, or you may decide to walk away from the purchase entirely.

However, if your credit is a little tarnished—other lenders have turned you down for a loan, and seller financing is your only option—you could say yes to the current terms if it's affordable for you and it gets you into the home. Later, you could always look to refinance with better terms.

Reverse Mortgages for Those Aged 62 and Over

Are you 62 or older and want to buy a home? How about having your new home pay for itself? It's possible in a reverse mortgage. This is when the equity in your home pays for the mortgage. When you sell the home or die, the loan is then repaid from the proceeds of the property sale. Most buyers are mistakenly under the impression that a reverse mortgage can be used only when you actually own the home. In 2008, new regulations were issued that allow reverse mortgages to be used for home purchases up to $625,000 or the appraised value, whichever is lower. It's called a Home Equity Conversion Mortgage (HECM), and it's federally insured. An HECM must be obtained through an approved FHA lender.

Although this concept may seem alien to some due to its uniqueness, it does work. The equity in this case, like in any form of purchase, comes from the down payment the buyer makes as part of the purchase price. Assuming values increase over time, this equity value rises, and the payments for the reverse mortgage come from that equity value.

Since one can never be certain about a possible dip in market values, HECMs also carry insurance that you pay for when you take out your loan. The payment is called a Mortgage Insurance Premium (MIP) and guarantees that you can never owe more than the value of your home. This fee can be included in the loan, so you don't even have to pay this out of pocket. However, if you do so, it lowers the amount of loan principal you have available to buy the home. For more information, talk with your mortgage broker or go to the following website: www.hud.gov/offices/hsg/sfh/hecm/hecmhome.cfm.

Tips and Traps

You can obtain more information on reverse mortgages from your mortgage broker or bank, or online at www.hud.gov.

The Least You Need to Know

◆ You don't have to seal a deal in just one way; you can negotiate with the seller to get what works for you.

◆ If you can't get a traditional loan with a bank, the seller might finance the home for you; just ask what he might be willing to do.

◆ With a seller installment purchase, you make payments to the seller instead of making those payments to a bank.

◆ If financing offered by the seller doesn't meet your financial needs, consider walking away from it.

Chapter 8

Tax Breaks

In This Chapter

◆ Owning a home provides financial benefits

◆ State tax breaks

◆ Improving your home improves your bottom line

◆ Selling your home and the tax benefits from the capital gains exclusion

As you know by now, owning a home has many advantages—you can decorate it the way you want, and it provides stability for you and your family. You also have one more substantial benefit to being a homeowner—your home becomes your own little tax shelter. From the moment you sign the documents and close on your home, it provides you with a number of income tax savings. It's just a matter of knowing where to look for them. For example, did you know that there was an $8,000 tax credit for first-time home buyers in 2009? If it's not extended into 2010, don't worry—there are more tax savings when you buy a home. Some of these apply to every homeowner, and some vary depending on your individual circumstances.

Of course, owning a home costs money—mortgages, taxes, maintenance, and upgrades—but there are financial advantages to owning versus renting. Unfortunately, your tax return may become a little more complicated, but you won't mind once you see the savings and tax breaks you'll get (if it gets too complicated, be sure to talk with a financial or tax professional for guidance). This chapter focuses on exactly what those tax breaks are and how you can take advantage of them.

Mortgage Interest

When you purchase a home, you pay interest on the mortgage loan, just like you would pay interest on a personal or car loan. The difference is that you are permitted to deduct all of the interest that you pay on the first mortgage of any amount—up to a $1 million mortgage—on your income tax return. It's not unusual for those in higher tax brackets to deliberately maintain a mortgage on their home so they can claim the interest paid on their taxes. Remember, though, this savings is a deduction from your taxable income, not a credit against your taxes.

> **Quotes and Facts**
>
> A tax deduction is an expense incurred by you, the taxpayer, that you can subtract, or deduct, from your gross pretax income. However, a tax credit is a direct reduction in your tax liability. For example, if you owe $5,000 in taxes, a tax credit of, say, $500 would reduce that to $4,500.

> **Tips and Traps**
>
> Want to know what tax bracket you're in? Look at last year's 1040 tax return. On line 43, find your taxable income. Then look at the government tax tables to see what rate this number falls under. You can find tax tables on the Internet at www.irs.gov.

Here's how it works: you deduct the mortgage interest from your income. You are then taxed on what is left after any other deductions you may have. For example, if you are in the 15 percent income tax bracket and pay $13,000 in deductible interest on your mortgage, you'll deduct that amount of interest from your income and have a tax savings of 15 percent of that, or $1,950. Not too shabby!

What's just as good is that you don't have to be in any particular tax bracket to be eligible for this tax deduction. Obviously, it is probably more valuable to you if you are in a higher tax bracket because you have more income to try to shelter from taxation, but the rule applies to every taxpaying homeowner who has a mortgage.

Points

Points, discussed in Chapter 5, are a form of fee income that the lender can make on the mortgage loan at the time it is given to the homeowner. Each point is equal to 1 percent of the principal amount of the loan.

The amount you pay the lender in points is deductible on your income taxes. You can claim points on your tax return in two ways. You can either deduct the entire amount you paid for points in the year you paid for them, or you can deduct the amount over the life of the loan. The choice is yours, but there are limits to both choices as established by regulations published by the Internal Revenue Service. To be sure of which way is best for you, discuss this with your tax advisor.

To claim the entire deduction in the year the points were paid, you must meet the following criteria:

♦ The underlying loan must be collateralized by your home.

♦ You must be in an area where the payment of points is accepted. Your mortgage broker can tell you if this is common.

♦ You must not have paid more points than is the norm for your area. Your broker can also tell you this, and your accountant likely has some insights.

♦ You must be on a cash method of accounting (most individuals are).

♦ You must not have paid the points in lieu of some other closing or loan fees.

♦ You must use your loan to buy or construct your home.

♦ The points must have been computed as a percentage of the mortgage's principal amount.

♦ The points paid must have been shown on the *Settlement Statement* (*HUD-1*) specifically as points.

Tips and Traps

Cash accounting means you account for everything—receipts and payments—as you actually pay or receive them. This relates to your tax situation, not your mortgage.

def•i•ni•tion

The **Settlement Statement (HUD-1)** is a form used by the closing agent that itemizes all the charges imposed upon you and the seller for a real estate transaction.

On the other hand, if you want to deduct the points over the life of the loan, you must conform to a different set of rules. You must meet the following criteria:

♦ You must be on the cash accounting method (as with the previous rules).

♦ Your loan must be secured by your home.

♦ The term of the loan must be no longer than 30 years.

◆ If your loan term is 10 or more years, it must be made with terms similar to others in your geographic area of the same term. You can find this out by talking with your mortgage broker or lender.

◆ The principal loan cannot exceed $250,000, or the number of points charged cannot be more than 4 if the term is 15 years or less, or no more than 6 points if the loan exceeds 15 years in length.

Real Estate Taxes

You'll love this one! You actually save on taxes by paying your taxes! It may sound confusing when you first hear it, but it's really quite simple. Your local or county government makes you pay taxes on any real property you own in its jurisdiction—known as property, real property, or real estate taxes. Each jurisdiction has its own method of calculating the tax and when it is due. For example, in California, real estate taxes are due twice a year, on April 10 and December 10, with each payment being half of your annual property tax bill. Once they are paid, you can deduct them from your federal income tax.

In some cases, the state where you live also allows you the same type of property tax deduction from any state income tax you pay. This varies from state to state, so your tax advisor can give you more detail on your exact savings. Some states, such as New Hampshire, have no income tax, so this doesn't apply in those states.

Just as with mortgage interest, real estate taxes are a deduction on your taxes, not a credit. As a deduction, you get to deduct the amount you paid in property taxes from your gross taxable income. Again, this reduces the amount of income you pay taxes on. For example, if you are in the 28 percent tax bracket and pay $5,000 annually in real estate taxes, you have just reduced your federally taxable income by $5,000 and in doing so have saved 28 percent of that figure, or $1,400, in income taxes come April 15.

Special Real Estate Tax Savings

Separately, some of the citizen-based tax "revolts" of the late 1970s and 1980s have resulted in special real estate tax savings opportunities in certain states. A good example is a law passed in California that requires that property tax be assessed based on 1 percent of the purchase price, with additional local bond issues added in based on voter approval. Due to likely inflation increases, the law also allows minor adjustments in the tax obligation annually.

It makes no difference how long you've owned your home. The tax on your home cannot increase by any more than 1 percent of the tax amount you had assessed on purchasing it. Because of this, it's fairly common for two homes that exist side-by-side to have dramatically different tax bills, based entirely on their respective dates of purchase.

Although California was the leader in this tax revolt, other states took a cue from this and restructured their laws. Massachusetts is one. In that state, the law was changed by Proposition 2½. Also, in the state of Washington, tax rates are limited to 1 percent of assessed value, while property tax levies are limited by Initiative-747.

State Savings

Does the state where you live or are planning to buy have real estate tax savings? For example, in California, Proposition 90 is a law that allows a homeowner to take his tax basis to the next home where he lives. It's a godsend to those nearing retirement who would be most disadvantaged by drastic increases in their property tax bills. However, it does have some limitations, including a once-in-a-lifetime use. The other major limitation to this privilege is that it is usable only if the county where you plan to buy your next home accepts it. In other words, if you move from one county to another and the new location is in a county that rejects this benefit, your tax on the new home will be based on its new purchase price. However, if the county you move to accepts this benefit, then your real estate tax on your new home will be based on your tax basis from your former home—very likely a huge savings for you.

As your accountant can tell you, your tax basis is the original amount you paid plus any expenses you have had in improving the property. Also, if you paid the commission to your Realtor, that is included. For example, if you paid $500,000 for a home five years ago and have since redone the kitchen at a cost of $25,000 and the master bath for $15,000, your basis is $540,000.

Check with the state tax authorities in the state where you are considering purchasing your next home. Additionally, ask your tax advisor.

IRA Withdrawals

In Chapter 5, you read how IRAs can be used to fund your down payment and that there are typically tax penalties for early withdrawals. Just as a reminder, you are exempt from these penalties if you use the money to purchase your home.

> **Tips and Traps** _____
>
> If you're making home improvements, go green to save green! In 2005, President George W. Bush signed the Energy Policy Act, a national law that provides federal tax credits for those who make energy-efficient upgrades to their homes. For example, you can add solar water heaters and electric systems and receive a 30 percent credit on your tax returns. Check into other federal and state credits. The Database of State Incentives for Renewables & Efficiency (DSIRE) is a searchable website for state credits (www.dsireusa.org), and you can find out about federal credits at www.energystar.gov.

Refinancing

So far, everything sounds pretty simple, doesn't it? Well, nothing is ever that simple! Things can get complicated when you refinance your home after having partially paid down the mortgage. Let's say you take out a $200,000 mortgage when you buy your home. Fifteen years later, you've paid it down to $100,000. You decide to refinance and take out a larger loan at the same time so you can borrow cash for a vacation, your daughter's college education, or your home improvement projects. As a result, you increase your debt to $225,000.

> **Tips and Traps** _____
>
> If you need additional money for a college education or home improvement and don't want to refinance, tap into your home equity instead. A home equity line of credit (HELOC) has floating interest, usually based on the prime rate, while a new first mortgage will have a specific fixed rate of interest or, if it is an ARM, will be adjusted on a less frequent basis than one based on prime. While most HELOCs are floating rates, they are sometimes available with fixed rates.

When you paid down the original loan, the remaining balance of $100,000 became your acquisition indebtedness amount when refinancing, which allows you to deduct interest on only $100,000 over that new amount of $100,000. Thus, having refinanced to a new total of $225,000, you are over the excess of $100,000 principal over purchase money debt allowed for interest deductions. All you'll be able to do is deduct the interest on the first $200,000 of the refinanced loan, not the interest on the entire new principal. Put another way, the interest on the last $25,000 of your new principal will not be deductible.

The reason for the difference is that your original first and second mortgages were borrowed to purchase and physically improve your home. The refinance of the mortgage has the limitation cited because the Congress recognized that it may very well be used to pay for things other than the physical acquisition or improvement of the home.

This rule does have exceptions, however. If your refinance was done to remodel, that money is looked at as if it were spent on an acquisition of your personal residence; thus, the interest you pay for this loan will be fully deductible. However, you must be able to trace the funds you borrowed directly to the remodeling projects so you can claim these funds as acquisition money and receive the interest deduction. Again, if this sounds confusing, and it can be, consult with your tax advisor.

Selling and Saving

Although this book is about buying a home, a chapter on the tax advantages of home ownership wouldn't be complete without mentioning the tax savings you may receive when you sell your home. In terms of federal income taxes, there are at least two of them.

The first of these is the *capital gains* exclusion rule. Under the federal tax code, if you sell your home, you may be able to exclude up to $500,000 in increased value from being subject to capital gains tax on the home if you meet certain conditions. You must have lived in the home at least two out of the previous five years, and it must have been your primary residence. It's just that easy.

For example, let's say that three years ago you bought your home for $125,000, and it is now worth $200,000. That's a gain of $75,000. Without this rule, you'd expect to pay what's called capital gains tax on that $75,000. Currently, the capital gains tax rate is 15 percent, so you'd have to fork over $11,250 to the federal government, along with whatever capital gains tax your state may require.

But under the capital gains exclusion rule, you may be able to exclude from taxation the first $500,000 of any gain. Thus, you would have no taxable capital gain at all. It's as if the gain never existed! The $500,000 is for married couples only; if you're single, your exclusion can max out at $250,000. Still, it's a nice deal!

def•i•ni•tion

Capital gains are the increase in value of any asset that you purchase over the time you own it. If you own a home (that does not meet the criteria for exclusion from capital gains) for a year or more when you sell it, those capital gains are taxed at special capital gains tax rates, which usually are lower than many regular income tax rates.

Improvement Value

When you put money into your home for remodeling and upgrades, you often get that money back when you sell. Improving your home adds to the value of your home. For example, let's say you bought a home five years ago for $200,000. Two years ago, you added a master bath ($20,000) and attached a small addition for a home office/studio ($45,000). The total cost of your work so far is $65,000. Therefore, your current basis of your home is $265,000, not $200,000. Any potential capital gain on the home has been reduced by that increased $65,000 in basis. Along with it, your tax liability has also been reduced. You've improved the value of your home.

Tips and Traps

Keep all of your receipts on any remodeling or addition you do, in case you get audited. Without them, the IRS may reduce your claimed basis amount, resulting in an increase in your tax liability.

Let's say you buy your home for $600,000 and live in it for 12 years. Over that period of time, it increases in value to $1,200,000. That would be a hefty capital gain to pay taxes on, even at only 15 percent. But hold on a minute—part of that increase in value comes from the in-ground Olympic-sized swimming pool you added five years ago and the second-story master suite that was added seven years ago. The cost of those two items is $125,000 combined.

So now your basis has grown to $725,000 ($600,000 + $125,000). But now you have a gain of $475,000 to pay capital gains tax on. Not yet. Remember the $500,000 exclusion? When you deduct the $500,000 gain from the $475,000, you have suddenly wiped out any possible capital gains tax because you no longer have any taxable gain.

If you're single, your exclusion would be $250,000, so you'd have a taxable gain of $225,000. In this case, you would have to pay capital gains tax, but only on that remaining $225,000, not on the whole increased value of $475,000. With capital gains rates of 15 percent, the difference in tax liability is $37,500 less than you'd otherwise have to pay. That's still fairly impressive.

Depreciation

While your tax breaks are generally limited to what we've already discussed, one potential additional break is available in certain cases: the duplex. In this case, you, the owner, would live in one of the two units and lease out the second. This second unit becomes an investment property and comes with additional tax advantages.

One of these is depreciation, an accounting fiction by which the value of an asset—the second duplex unit, in this case—is reduced by a regular amount each year. This on-paper reduction in value helps create a paper loss for your investment for the year, and you can deduct that loss from your taxable income. Because of this, your income is lower and so are your taxes.

In addition to depreciation, you also deduct your maintenance and repair costs from the unit's operating income. This further reduces your own income, and thus again lowers your income tax. Check with your tax advisor for details in each specific case.

As you can see, you have many possible ways to use your purchase to reduce the amount you will pay in income tax every year. This varies based on the specifics of income and mortgage, but you definitely gain valuable tax benefits from owning a home.

The Least You Need to Know

◆ Owning a home comes with many tax advantages, both during and after you own your home.

◆ If you're planning to do upgrades or remodeling, go green—you can get many tax breaks for installing energy-efficient appliances and home systems.

◆ You may have additional tax breaks that apply in your state only, so check with your accountant when it's tax time.

◆ Consider the money you used for improvements and upgrades an investment, since you'll get back much of it when you sell the home.

Part

Finding Your Home

You'll be eagerly looking forward to this part since we discuss all the ways you can search for a home, from surfing the web to attending open houses.

You'll learn how to determine whether a home meets your wants and needs, or whether circumstances may not make it the perfect home for you. You'll also learn what questions to ask the sellers about the home you're interested in.

Finally, when you find a home you like, this part takes you step-by-step through making an offer—deciding on the price, determining what contingencies to ask for, selecting your intended occupancy date, and understanding various other terms designed to protect you.

Chapter 9

Learn the Market

In This Chapter

- Finding information on the real estate market
- Checking out the local economy
- Understanding what a buyer's market is and how it can work for you
- Understanding a seller's market and how you can still find your dream home
- Playing the numbers—understanding selling and listing prices

The current real estate market can tell you a lot about buying a home. For example, if the economy is doing poorly, home prices may be dropping, making it a perfect time to buy your home. If the stock market is soaring, home prices might be, too, and you might have to pay top price for the home of your dreams. Knowing the economy and real estate market where you want to buy is important, too. Is it a growing town where homes will be in demand, or is it a struggling town where home prices are dropping? This information will be helpful for you when it's time to decide where you want to live and whether this is the right time to buy. As with anything else, you can make a better, more informed decision when you have information in hand.

This chapter focuses on where you can find this real estate information. We discuss how to cull relevant information from real estate and business websites, newspapers, and more. In addition, you will learn the difference between a buyer's market and a seller's market—the way the market is swinging can make a big difference in the final price of your home! And real estate statistics are nothing if you don't understand them, so part of the chapter is dedicated to understanding those numbers and how they can work for or against you.

Collecting Information from Multiple Sources

The best way to start increasing your market knowledge is to read as much as you can and start asking questions. You can read info on the local and national real estate market on the Internet and in the business and real estate sections of the local and national newspapers, and see it on the local and national business newscasts. Some great sources include *The Wall Street Journal*, *The New York Times*, *RealtyTimes* (www. realtytimes.com), *Money* magazine, and CNN, to name just a few.

Tips and Traps _____

Stay on top of any announcements from the Federal Reserve (the Fed). This is the governmental department that controls interest rates for loans. If suddenly, due to other factors in the economy, the Fed drops interest rates, you can work with your mortgage broker to get a mortgage that has a lower interest rate and therefore saves you more money.

You can also tap into the expertise of mortgage brokerages and other financial firms, as well as your own real estate agent. To find out about your local real estate market, you can visit the local government office or website where you want to live and get some information on what's going on. National real estate organizations also can provide current market information.

In some cases, just driving around the neighborhood you're interested in can be helpful to your decision. Let's say that you like a split-level home and want to make an offer. Hop in the car and take a drive around the neighborhood. The neighborhood seems attractive enough, but the more you drive the more you realize that many of the surrounding homes have for sale signs on the front lawn. This should be a red flag for you. Has something suddenly changed or even deteriorated in the neighborhood, or do all the for sale signs just mean it's a seller's market? A simple drive around the neighborhood can be valuable in your decision-making process.

Tips and Traps _____

Check out the U.S. Census Bureau (www.census.gov) website. The housing information section is a good foundation of helpful details on housing costs, market trends, and the quality of housing in different regions. The census is based on surveys and includes numbers and types of modern appliances in a typical home, and availability of utilities and public services such as water and sewer. It takes time to interpret the info, though.

Local Governments

The local and state government offices, such as city hall or the statehouse, are valuable resources of local market information. Visit their websites and ask for any printed housing reports to be mailed to you, or ask your agent to track down this info for you. The reports are usually free, but some offices charge a nominal fee.

The National Association of Realtors

You already know that the National Association of Realtors (NAR) has a website that lists homes for sale all across the nation. What you may not know is that they have another website, www.realtor.org, which is typically geared to NAR members, but most sections are accessible to anyone. On this site, you can learn about trends in regional and national sales volume and pricing.

The site includes statistics on pending home sales, where a contract for the purchase of the home has been signed but the buyer and seller have yet to close. Knowing about these pending home sales can provide more detail on the direction the local real estate market may be taking.

For example, let's assume the NAR statistics in the area you're interested in show that there has been a slow real estate market sales year. This slow year has caused sellers to lower their prices, so you're thinking that it's a good opportunity to get a great deal on a home.

Tips and Traps _____

Sign up for Google Alerts to receive regular news and website updates on areas or property-related subjects you are interested in. For example, if you are moving to Oshkosh, Wisconsin, you can visit www.google.com/alerts and sign up for a "real estate, Oshkosh, Wisconsin" alert. You can choose to receive the information as it happens or once a day, you can sign up for more than one, and you can cancel at any time. It's a great way to stay current.

Other Websites

In addition to the websites mentioned earlier, other websites provide housing and real estate market information for free or for a nominal fee:

♦ **DataQuick** (DQNews.com)—One of the best private sites is run by DataQuick, a major statistics provider of the housing market. It is a free news site that can also provide detailed custom reports or monthly charts for a fee, ranging from $50 to $250.

♦ **Alto Research** (Altosresearch.com)—You can get basic city-by-city, statewide, or national sales information about single-family home and condo markets for free. If you subscribe, you can get more in-depth information, including sales figures that will help you make your decision. Depending on the degree of detail you seek, a subscription costs anywhere from $19 to $149 a month.

♦ **Inman** (Inman.com)—Named for its founder, who was a very successful former Realtor and broker, Inman is an excellent real estate news source. It has stories about all aspects of the housing market, which are free on its site. It also includes a blog on the real estate market, www.inman.com/blog. Reading this blog is a good way to keep up-to-date on changes or activities in the real estate market.

Television News

Another source of real estate information is the traditional news outlets—national and local print or electronic media, television, and radio stations. In some cases, the local news will only whet your appetite for details and you may have to tune in to major news networks, such as CNN, for more in-depth coverage. Other networks that present real estate coverage from time to time are CNBC and Fox News.

Tips and Traps _____

Want to know what other buyers go through when they are deciding on a home? Check out HGTV's popular show *House Hunters,* where you can follow one buyer through three different homes to see which one she chooses to buy. Remember that every market and seller is different, and pricing is unique to each specific area. This show should give you an idea of the process, but you should still talk to your Realtor about the specific trends in your area.

Multiple Listing Service

The local Multiple Listing Service (MLS) is a great source of local sales and market trends. Depending on how much your agent makes available to you from the MLS on his website, you may be able to access a web page of market statistics. If not, you will at least be able to research prices on a home-by-home comparative basis in the neighborhoods you like. You can see how much a home was listed for, how much it sold for, and, in some areas, the number of days on market (DOM) a given property had. This process can be a bit tedious, so it's best to use the MLS to just narrow your search to a specific neighborhood, or a few specific houses, and then ask your Realtor to provide comps of previous sales and current homes on the market for that area.

Seller's or Buyer's Market

Homes are a commodity, whether they are single-family homes or condos, and the traditional rules of supply and demand apply, just as they do with other items, such as food or gasoline. What's in demand can determine whether the market is a buyer's market or a seller's market. Which market it is depends on buyers' demand for properties.

A Seller's Market

You've probably heard "it's a seller's market" or "it's a buyer's market" while reading articles on the real estate market or watching news broadcasts, but what do these phrases mean? Typically, a seller's market starts when there are far fewer homes and condos on the market than normal. At the same time, there are a high number of buyers competing for these homes. As a result, sellers have the advantage and will start to raise their prices, knowing that some buyers will pay the price to get the home they want, possibly even going into a bidding frenzy and paying over the asking price.

The real estate market also can become a seller's market because of the mortgage money that is available to buyers and relaxed lending rules in the industry. When more money is available to lenders to make mortgages and there are many buyers, home prices begin to rise. How fast they rise depends on how many buyers there are and how many homes are available. The state of the economy in general is also an important factor—a robust economy pushes prices up because more people are employed, often at higher salaries and with more cash to spend on houses.

This brings up a point. How do you handle buying a home in this type of market? Again, there is no automatic right or wrong answer. If you have the funds, can afford the cost of a mortgage, and think that prices will continue appreciating, then purchasing a home now may be the best decision for you. You can then reap the benefits of a steady increase in value of the home.

A Buyer's Market

Conversely, a buyer's market occurs when there is an overabundance of homes for sale and a lack of buyers. This reduces the demand for the homes, and sellers become anxious to sell and begin to reduce prices. If the conditions are extreme, the drop in prices will accelerate. This is when buyers can often find a bargain home.

One example of a buyer's market began in 2006, when the mortgage market collapsed. The market's downturn continued for a year, and buyers stayed out of the real estate market as they watched prices collapse. In many areas, a record number of homes remained unsold, and some sellers worried that they might lose their homes as conditions worsened. It got so bad that by late 2008, in some areas of the nation, sellers stopped putting their homes on the market. They decided to wait and see how the market would play out. This slowed the drop in prices, but at the same time, buyers stayed away in droves—a continuation of a buyer's market. However, in late 2009, in a few areas, there were very subtle signs that this trend may be beginning a slow reversal. More than ever, it is becoming a factor of location.

When to Buy

Clearly, you are better off buying your home when it's a buyer's market. Prices, and possibly interest rates, will be lower and sellers will be forced to be more reasonable in their negotiations with you—and you can benefit when the value of homes begins to rise again. But of course, circumstances might not allow you that opportunity. You may have to buy when it's a seller's market if you need a home at that time. If you find the house you want but it's a seller's market, remember that you may have to negotiate a bit harder and may possibly have to spend more than you want to.

Open Houses

Open houses are public showings of homes that are for sale. There are two types of open houses: brokers' open houses and public open houses. Brokers' opens are for real estate professionals only so they can have an opportunity to see what new properties are on the market. This allows brokers to gather information on a new property and properly advise their clients, because they can match a particular client to a specific home they have personally seen. As a buyer, you can have full access to these open houses, too. To do so, either accompany your Realtor or visit the brokers' opens and leave your Realtor's business card, noting that she sent you. To find out when these events are taking place, ask your Realtor to keep you in the loop. In most cases, these events aren't in the Sunday real estate section with other open house listings.

If your agent is with you, he can ask the proper questions and get a great deal more information. By "proper questions," I'm referring to finding out things such as the size of the living area, any known problems, and other information that wouldn't be obvious from a simple viewing of the home. Additionally, if any remodeling or repair work has been done on the home, the agent would ask about the details of the work, to be certain that it was professionally done and up to current building codes. The listing agent will be happy to provide you with the information, since your agent has expressed interest.

A public open house is most commonly held on a Saturday or Sunday, and is open to anyone who wants to see that home. Attending an open house provides you with an opportunity to walk around and check out the place. You can ask the agent questions at that time (the seller is usually not at an open house) and take a flyer or brochure to remember what you saw.

A suggestion: if you are already working with an agent and decide to attend a public open house, tell the agent that is holding the open house that you already have an agent. If you are interested in that home, tell her who your agent is. The agent that is hosting the open house will appreciate this information, as she can contact your agent to offer any additional pertinent information.

If you're not interested in a particular home, you can also attend a public open house just for background information. You

Warning!

If work has been done by the seller that requires permits, make certain that they have been "finaled." This means that the permitting authority has approved them in a post-work inspection.

Tips and Traps

Take a small notebook or mini tape recorder and a digital camera along to open houses to make notes or take pictures. This will help you to recall things that you liked or disliked about each home you visit. Although there's no legal prohibition, as a courtesy ask the agent for the seller's permission before snapping any pictures.

can get an idea of what the inside of the homes in the neighborhood look like and how much they are selling for.

You can access open house information—date, time, listing agent, and more—through listings on an agent's site or through a link from the site to the local MLS. Open house information is also available in the real estate section of the local newspaper and its accompanying website, and on public bulletin board type sites such as Craigslist.

Keep in mind that there is a disadvantage to attending weekend public open houses. Depending on the home or neighborhood, an open house can be deluged by hundreds of viewers on the weekend. Some viewers are like you, potential buyers, but others are either neighbors who want to take a peek into the home now that it's for sale, or "lookie-loo's" who have nothing better to do than attend open houses. Crowds like these make it difficult for a serious buyer to see everything in the home and makes it very hard to talk to a busy agent who is talking to everyone who attends. Of course, you can still go and follow up with the agent afterward.

What to Look For

When you tour a home you are interested in, you're there to accomplish two things. First, you want to decide if the house meets your wants and needs (if you haven't written this out by now, go back to the earlier chapters and start making your lists). Second, you want to get a look at the condition of the house to see if looks as if it's been kept up-to-date or has problems that might need fixing. Keep in mind that even if you don't see anything wrong with the home, some problems may not be visible; you'll still need an inspector to check things out if you end up working out a purchase agreement.

As you walk through the home, don't rush. Take your time, whether you're with your agent or you're attending an open house. Your real estate agent may have more homes for you to see, but take whatever time you need to get a solid impression of the home. Fifteen minutes to a half-hour is usually enough time to decide if you're interested.

> **Warning!**
>
> If you walk through the door and the home is obviously not suitable for you and you don't want to go any farther, there's nothing wrong with immediately turning around and leaving.

If you have children, think about whether or not you should bring them along when you view houses. There are no hard-and-fast rules about this. If your children are well behaved, then you can bring them. If they are at the age when staying quiet for more than a few moments is an effort, or if they can't resist touching things, it might be best to leave them at home. If you are attending an open house with your spouse or significant other, an option is to take turns viewing the home, leaving the kids in the car with the other parent.

Have a Look-See

When you are with your Realtor, she should give you a basic listing printout of each home ahead of time. Once you get inside the house, you have the right to investigate a little further. For example, you knew the home had the number of bedrooms and bathrooms that you needed, but are they big enough? Is the layout good for your furniture? If you need a home office, is it where you want it to be? Is the kitchen open and airy so your guests can mingle, or is it a separate room closed off from the rest of the home?

When you are looking around, feel free to open closet doors and look into storage areas. Don't look at the backyard from a back window—go outside and get a close-up view. Walk into the garage and see if it is large enough for your cars, trucks, motorcycles, and storage.

Conditionally Speaking

Inside, take note of how modern the kitchen is and the condition of the fixtures. Is the bathroom perfectly sized but needs to be modernized? Will that add to your bill later? Note it. The same goes for the rest of the rooms in the house.

If the home needs work, is it just cosmetic work or does the home shriek "major remodel"? Can you afford to do either? (Remember that a home shouldn't max out your budget, and you should have extra money put aside for at least small repairs and some cosmetic changes.) Some people are happy to do minor repairs and remodels when they first move in, because it not only allows them to make the home theirs, but also because a home that needs work done is often lower priced. Of course, you may want a home in move-in condition.

While you're taking note of things that need to be changed, also make a note to check with a contractor or other tradesman to get a price on the work you would want done. If you do not know a local contractor, ask your agent for a recommendation.

Add the costs of this work to the purchase price to determine whether your home's total cost is still within your budget. For example, if the home is already at the top of your budget at $250,000, but you still need $50,000 for repairs and remodeling, can you afford to pay for both? If you can, great—you can go ahead and place the offer if you want. If the house has now become too expensive for you, you have two options—forget about the house and keep looking, or decide whether the repairs or upgrades need to done now or can be delayed until you can budget them in later. If waiting until later makes the home affordable, you can proceed with your offer.

Amenity and Privacy

Check out the home's amenities. Is there a pool or hot tub, if you wanted one? What kind of condition is it in? If there isn't one, is there room for one? Does the home have a patio with a barbecue area like you wanted or is there enough space to put one in if you'd like? While you're outside, look next door at the neighbor's house. Do you have privacy, or is there an open view from their home into your backyard? Are there any trees and shrubs that can provide the privacy, or can you add some?

Tips and Traps

As silly as it may seem, look at the sun when you are in the backyard. Is there any protection on your property, or will the sun be beating down on your backyard during the day? One homeowner loved the home but was discouraged to find out how hot the backyard got during the summer because it lacked shade. Although he installed some awnings, it limited his entertaining.

Talk It Out

After you've seen the homes that your agent has for you, let her know your impressions, both good and bad. She might have noticed things that you didn't. Ask her how long a home has been on the market, both in total days and at its present price. In fact, ask if there have been any price reductions and, if so, how many. Also ask her how it compares to others in its price range. Does she feel, as a professional, that its price is reasonable, given its condition and time on the market?

It's also perfectly acceptable to ask for a return visit. If your significant other couldn't make the first tour, he can accompany you to the next one. Or maybe you want to examine something more in depth (take your notebook and camera again). This is also the time you can cross some of the homes off your list for whatever reason.

It is generally safe to say that you will know by the second or third visit if a particular home gets your interest to the level that you want to consider making an offer to the seller. Assuming that you do, we cover this process in Chapter 13.

Ask Questions

When you visit a home, the seller is not generally present, but you might have follow-up questions after your tour. You can submit these questions to your agent.

If you haven't already, ask if there are any problems, past or present, with the house or the lot. Just because the structure is fine doesn't mean that the ground it sits on is necessarily in the same condition. If the answer is yes, ask about the status of the problem. Did the seller deal with it already, or is it something they are leaving for the buyer? Ask for proof—receipts, warranties, and permits—when required. If the problem hasn't been rectified, you may submit a lower offer to cover the cost of repairs.

 Warning!

Do not return to the home without the real estate agent to ask more questions of the seller. Everything should be done through your agent.

It's also okay to ask about the seller about the neighbors and the neighborhood. You can also ask why they're selling at this time and where they are moving to, although not all sellers answer these questions.

Disclosures

If you like the home, ask your agent to see if any disclosures are available. Most states have home disclosure laws that require the seller to tell you any material defects in the home. If information is not disclosed and you find out about it later, some states allow you to sue the seller for failure to disclose it to you. This lawsuit must be done within a year of closing. Disclosures can include inspection reports, building reports, permits, warranties, and so on. Disclosures are discussed in more detail in Chapter 14.

Tips and Traps

If the seller has added onto the home or added a pool or other amenity, make sure they show you a Certificate of Occupancy (CO), if it's required. A CO is a document issued by a local government agency or building department certifying that the addition, pool, or whatever is in compliance with building codes and other laws. In some cases, buyers have had to remove items from a property that didn't have a CO, or apply for the CO after the fact.

So there you have the basics about how to educate yourself on the real estate market before buying a home. Not every buyer goes through this process, but as you can see, educating yourself on the markets will have great benefits for you when you finally find your dream home. You will know whether it's the right time to buy a home or whether you should wait until prices drop. This information can save you thousands of dollars or more when it's time to place an offer.

The Least You Need to Know

- ◆ Education is key to becoming a smart home buyer, so learn the market and know what homes are selling for in the area you are interested in.

- ◆ Visiting open houses can be a great way to learn about other houses in the market, ask the agent questions, and get to know what you do and don't like.

- ◆ Check out the Multiple Listing Service before making your bid so you know what the area market is doing and what homes are selling for.

- ◆ Markets change frequently, especially in local areas, so don't make an offer on a home without checking out other listing and selling prices.

Surfing the Web

In This Chapter

◆ Surfin' the 'net for a new home

◆ Learn about home-buying sites

◆ Research a new community

◆ Narrow your search

◆ Sit back and take a tour

One of the most valuable tools you have at your disposal when looking for a home is the Internet. Just about everyone is familiar to some degree with the web and its potential. You can find virtually everything on the web, including your new home. Just be careful about how accepting you are with the information you find on the Internet. Not everyone is totally honest and straightforward about everything, and websites can be the same.

There's no end to the number of websites that focus on residential property sales—from Google listings, to mass home buyer websites, to individual agent sites and more. You can find everything from a small one-bedroom condo to a mansion and anything in between. Even if you wanted to buy a cave, for whatever reason, you could probably find it somewhere on the web (one cave owner sold his cave home on eBay).

According to the National Association of Realtors, more than 85 percent of all home buyers begin their search for a home on the web, even before they've chosen a Realtor. Additionally, many folks use the web not just to find a house, but to learn about prospective neighborhoods. You can use the web to find a home right in your own neighborhood, in another city or state, or even in another country!

Interestingly, some people have found a home on the web and even bought it without seeing it in person first. One colleague sold a $3 million northern California house to a man from Scotland without the buyer ever leaving his location. He saw it on the web, e-mailed the agent, and purchased the house long distance. This is not the norm, but it does illustrate just how much you can do with the web when seeking out your new abode. The possibilities are truly endless.

In this chapter, you'll learn how to work the web from the comfort of your home or office. In fact, if you have a wireless laptop computer or a cell phone with Internet access, you can update your search for a home from your car, while sipping a cappuccino at a local cafe, or while relaxing on a flight 35,000 feet in the air.

Finding Information

Let's say you live in Portland, Maine, but have just been transferred to your company's office in Chicago—you've never been to Chicago, though, except to change planes at O'Hare International Airport. You know nothing about the city other than it's in the middle of the country and it has two baseball teams (the Cubs and the White Sox). Or maybe you are looking for a home just a few towns away, but, again, you've never been there. How do you start your home search from far away when you don't even know one neighborhood from another? Grab your mouse and log on to the Internet.

Warning!

Not everything you read on the Internet is true, so be sure to check it all out before you sign any papers.

You want to break down your initial search into two components. First, you need information about the new town—say, Chicago. Second, you need to know what homes are for sale and how much they cost.

So let's get information on the area first. If you already have a Realtor in Chicago, that agent should be sending you information, as well as information on homes for sale. But if you still want to find information on your home, you can start at your local government websites.

Most local city, county, and state municipal governments have websites. For example, Chicago has a site (www.cityofchicago.org) that provides information on affordable housing, property tax information, homeowner tips such as scam information, maps, things to do, and more. The site also has sections on fair housing, lead laws, and so on, although it doesn't have a section where you can search for homes for sale. You can search for a government site for the town you are moving to by typing in "(Your new town) and government." These government sites can also tell you about the area's public utilities, shopping, Chambers of Commerce, taxes, and cultural activities, to start. Knowing this information about your new city can help you decide if you really want to live there.

Something else to look into via the web when considering homes in an unfamiliar area is cost-of-living information. This information can give you an idea of what the cost of living is in a given area and where trends show it's heading. Visit www.coli.org, www.bls.gov/cpi/, and www.money.cnn.com/tools/costofliving/costofliving.html.

Public Utilities

Public utilities are your electricity, gas, water, and sewer services. Sometimes trash collection is considered a public utility as well, but not in all cities. These services are normally handled either by private corporations or by a government or quasi-government agency. In some areas, you have multiple options for choosing a utility company. In Portland, Oregon, for example, consumers have two electric companies to choose from. Some areas are limited to one choice. Some companies handle just one utility, such as electricity, while others handle more. Find out what your options are.

Remember, when you buy a home, your utility bills can eat a huge chunk out of your monthly budget, so it's best to know what your options are ahead of time. You don't want to be shocked to find out that your utility budget is triple what you were paying in your previous home. You can ask your agent to find out what the seller's average utility bills are. You can also ask the utility companies about reduced rates for energy- or water-conserving methods you may wish to install later. If the area has more than one utility company to choose from, check them all out and see if different rates are available and what the other differences are. Once you have this information, you can determine how it will affect your monthly budget. Your agent can get this information for you, too, and, once you've purchased your home, even have the service started for you.

Tax Information

Government sites can also provide information on taxes—for example, real estate, income, and sales. All states levy real estate taxes, but of the other two, some have both, some have only one, and only one state, New Hampshire, has neither. Remember to ask what the tax situation is in the area you're moving to—every state and city is different, and some may have special taxes if you live there.

The best advice I can offer to cover all of the many different possible tax rates and laws you may have to deal with is to go online and research the towns and areas you're specifically interested in. Visit the local websites of the town, county, and state that you are considering. Many will provide basic tax information, or at least contact information for those responsible for tax policy in a particular locale.

Shopping

Government websites can also provide information on local shopping, including shopping malls and grocery stores in the area. Is enough shopping available in the area where you are going, or do you have to travel to a mall in a nearby town? While you're at it, if you have a favorite store, you can also check its website to see if it has a location in or near your new town.

Chamber of Commerce

The local government sites may also provide information on the local Chamber of Commerce and a link to its website. While a Chamber's chief focus is helping local businesses, it also provides valuable information to visitors and those relocating to the area. Along with information about the Chamber's membership, activities, and local cultural events, the local Chamber's website may include information about local stores and other businesses. Frequently, the Chamber's website also links back to city government websites, so if you can't find the city government site, you might be able to find it through the Chamber site.

Another good service that you may find through the local Chamber of Commerce website is the names and contact information of various contractor and repair firms. If you know that you will need to do upgrades or repair work on your new home, you can find local companies on this site and start asking them about rates. As a result, you can work out your budget with a little more information now that you've talked to local companies. Make sure you do your background checks on the company you choose.

Cultural Attractions

City government sites can also tell you about cultural and social amenities in the area—museums, art galleries, theaters, and so on. If they don't, look for the city's tourism association website. For example, when you type "Chicago Tourism" into your search engine, you will find a link to the Chicago Convention and Tourism Bureau (www.choosechicago.com). Most cities have a convention and tourism bureau, but if it's a small city, search for the convention and tourism bureau of the largest nearby city. Here you can find out if the area has an orchestra, ballet, parks, athletic fields, golf courses, or boat launches available.

School Information

If you have children or are thinking about starting a family, the local government site can provide information on the local school districts. How good are they? Test results can give you an idea of where the schools stand compared to other schools locally as well as nationally. Are the test scores high, average, or low? How do they compare with schools in other nearby communities? Do they offer programs that your children need? If your child is a special-needs child, does the area have services available for him? Will the district provide your children with a good education, or will you be forced to consider private school (another item to add to your budget)? Most of the city websites have links to school districts in the area. You can also search for the actual school district website, and even the individual school websites, for additional information.

School information is also important because, whether you have children or not, one day you may sell that home you're buying. The expression "As go the schools, goes the community" is a fact. Homes in communities with good school systems command higher prices, so buying a home in that community is a great investment.

Warning!

As school budgets get tighter, ask if the district has cut arts, academics, athletics, or any other programs that might be of interest to your family.

If you want to do additional research, you could look at test scores over a longer period of time. You may find that the test scores of some areas are up over a period of a few years and then may drop way down, or vice versa. Other areas may have test scores that maintain a fairly constant level year in and out. The results are often a reflection of the success, or struggles, of the school systems.

Finding a Home

Okay, so now you have your basic information on Chicago, or the town that you're looking in, and its surrounding areas. It's time to look at what houses are for sale. With or without an agent, you can view an incredible number of homes of all styles, prices, and sizes on the Internet. It's now a question of how to search through them all and narrow it to a manageable level.

You could start by doing a Google search for, let's say, "Chicago real estate," but immediately you'll find millions of results on the subject. Google is terrific, but when it comes to buying a home, it can be overwhelming. Even though the computer took only a fraction of a second to find the results, it would take you from now until your retirement to go through them all. What do you do? Narrow your search.

> **Tips and Traps**
>
> Google Earth (http://earth.google.com) lets you see actual property and its surroundings right from your computer. This tool can limit the map to a couple of blocks around the selected house or stretch out to cover a radius of a mile or two. Want to see how close the schools are to the house? Checking on the length of your commute? Google Earth provides you with a view of the entire town, from your place of work to the particular home you're viewing.

You can start by using Google to narrow the search to "Chicago real estate agents," "Chicago homes for sale," or "Chicago property management firms" that have coops, condos, and townhouses for sale. Or you can visit specific websites that help you narrow your search. For example, you can visit your Realtor's site or her brokerage site, or you can use mass home-buying sites, such as Realtor.com.

Builder Sites

A local developer or builder may have a website promoting their latest development. It will list all homes, plans, details, and prices. It very likely also has either photos or artist renderings of at least some of the finished homes and the rooms inside some of them. This is a great place to see if the builder has a spec home for sale, or to see if you might be interested in building a home in the development.

If you are researching builders on the Internet, run the builder's name through a news search on Google or MSN. There may be articles or news stories about a local builder in the paper or on television that can help provide more information. For example, if a builder is in the paper because of a problem, the local residents may know, but if you're just moving into the area this may be the only way you can find out that type of information about the builder.

Mass Sites

A mass site has hundreds, if not thousands, of homes for sale from agents and companies all around the country. These mass sites provide you with the greatest number of homes to look at, as well as contact information for the Realtors who represent the homes. Realtor.com is the largest real estate website in the world and is owned and operated by the National Association of Realtors (NAR). It's a great place to start your search.

Each listing includes basic information about the property features, such as square footage; acreage; number of bedrooms, baths, and other rooms; garage size; school information; information on cooling/heating; interior features; and exterior features. It usually offers photos and may offer a video tour as well. Each listing also has the purchase price and the name and contact information for the listing Realtor.

Realtor.com frequently also provides a link to the listing agent's website. For example, let's say you find a home on Realtor.com at 123 Main Street in Wheresthat, Iowa. The listing agent is Mary Helpubuyit. Realtor.com provides Mary's contact info and a link to her (fictional) website, www.maryhelpsu.com.

Being a very thorough agent, Mary has also linked her Realtor.com listing to the property's own (fictional) website, www.123mainforyou.com. You can expand your search and go to either or both of these additional sites to see if there is additional information on the home or other homes that you may like. You can also obtain further information about the Realtor, Mary, including her background, real estate expertise, and other listings, without having to actually talk to her, if you choose not to. It's all up to you!

Agent and Brokerage Sites

Agent sites, like Mary's, fall into two categories: those that are the agent's and those that belong to the agent's firm or brokerage. On the agent's website, she is responsible for its entire content, oversees what properties are displayed, and adds new listings and removes those that are sold.

For example, my own website is www.comehometomarin.com. It has my listings that are currently on the market, including commercial and *foreclosed* properties, a separate page of listings I have sold in the past, additional pages for items such as school information, and a listing of each town in the county where I sell real estate. It also offers links to two of my *blogs* on real estate market conditions in my area. In each case, the information is accompanied by one or more photos of the properties I represent and the communities where I work.

def•i•ni•tion

A **foreclosed** home is a bank-owned home for sale because the owner has defaulted on paying the mortgage.

A **blog** is an online diary that can include personal thought, information, business information, and so on.

A real estate firm or brokerage website typically has a list of the brokerage's agents and their biographies, real estate listings, and information about the area that the brokerage services. It may also offer information on other professionals that the Realtor has worked with, such as mortgage brokers and insurance agents. Any recommendations such as these, however, should be considered as endorsements only for past performance and not a guarantee or warranty for future performance.

Multiple Listing Service (MLS)

When a Realtor wants to look at what's on the market at any given time, he looks at the local Multiple Listings Service (MLS), which at one time was closed to buyers. Today the service is no longer just for Realtors, and buyers can view properties, too. Now, through your agent's website, you can select MLS Search, input your requirements, and select a property that interests you. Once you find one, call your agent to set up the appointment. Note that the public cannot see any confidential information—for example, lock combinations or other security-related information—that is intended only for agents.

Property Websites

In the last few years, agents have created sites solely to feature one single property and all of its attributes. These sites have the same things the other websites have—in-depth virtual tours, maps, school details, Realtor information, and more. Additionally, some sites allow you to download a flyer of the property listing, as well as condensed copies of the tax records. Many of them also allow you to make an appointment to see the featured home. However, be aware that some Realtors use these location-specific websites only for higher-priced homes.

Craigslist

Craigslist has become a worldwide research tool for people searching for almost anything, including garage sales, items for sale, jobs, dates, and even homes.

Most home listings are placed, for free, by Realtors and by individuals who are selling their properties on their own. The ads are listed only chronologically, so it requires a little more digging, and there is no way to change your search criteria like you can on Realtor.com, for example. However, you can narrow your search by city.

As with all websites, there are good ones and not-so-good ones. Some sites are very informative and leave you feeling incredibly educated about the area and the homes when you leave the site. Others leave you feeling that you haven't gotten any meaningful information. Look through the sites and decide which ones you feel comfortable with.

Narrow Your Search

Once you find a site or sites that you're comfortable with, start narrowing your search to specific wants and needs (except on Craigslist, as we mentioned). For example, you can check boxes on the site to find a townhome with three bedrooms, two baths, a den, and a two-car garage. Some sites may also allow you to narrow by square footage, acreage, and even cost. You can be specific—say, $250,000—but more commonly you can indicate a price range.

For example, let's say you are being transferred to San Francisco. While on a trip to meet your future colleagues, several people have mentioned Mill Valley, a small town about 13 miles north of the city, as a wonderful place to live. Your budget tops out at $600,000. You'd like to know what homes exist between $300,000 and $600,000. You click on the appropriate boxes, fill in the information, and click Search. Immediately, nine listings come up in this locale within your price range.

Take a Tour

Take a tour without leaving the comfort of your own home. Most listings include pictures, and some offer a "virtual tour" of the home. With a simple click, you're "walking" through every room, from kitchen to master bedroom, even though, in reality, you may be sitting 3,000 miles away.

If you decide that you like a particular house, you can request a copy of that virtual tour, a brochure, or other printed information. You can provide your e-mail address and other contact information; depending on the site, you will receive the information by either e-mail or regular mail. It's a great way to figure out if you want to take the time to make a more intimate walkthrough.

Request an Appointment

Once you've narrowed your search to a few homes you like, you can contact the agent and request an appointment through the Internet, too. You can even find a real estate agent who's a relocation expert if you know you're going to be in your new town soon. Let's assume that you know you're going to be visiting the Chicago area on a particular date. You can click on the Request a Showing tab, and a calendar grid will pop up, broken into daily half-hour segments for a week at a time. Pick the one that suits you, and the agent will call you directly by phone to confirm the appointment. Of course, it's best to have your agent go with you, but if you don't have one yet, you can still see a home you're interested in. During this visit, you'll have the opportunity to tell the agent your preferences and, if you wish, arrange to see more homes in your price range.

You can also use this contact form to request other information relative to that particular home, including an insurance quote and mortgage information.

Like everything else, buying a house has moved into the twenty-first century. In addition to all of the other tools and methods we've discussed so far to help you buy just the right house, technology has taken the process a few steps further. The best thing about this is you get all of the benefits and eliminate many of the headaches that once existed.

The Least You Need to Know

- Don't let the Internet intimidate you; take your time and narrow your search using different real estate websites.

- The Internet helps you weed out some properties and areas before you invest the time and money visiting.

- Your Internet search, plus your hard-working real estate agent, provides the perfect partnership to find you a new home.

- Once you're ready to find a home, you can use the Internet to schedule a tour of the area with an agent and a tour of several homes for sale.

Foreclosures, Auctions, and Short Sales

In This Chapter

♦ Finding a deal on a home

♦ Foreclosure listings

♦ Buying from the bank

♦ Going once, twice, sold—buying from an auction house

♦ The pros and cons of short sales

When you buy clothes, do you visit a luxury retailer and plunk down mounds of your hard-earned cash for a great suit or a perfect dress? Or are you the type of person who shops discount racks at the local department store? Maybe you're even the type of person who visits vintage thrift shops hoping to find a great article of clothing for a fraction of the cost.

You can compare buying a home to buying clothes. You can pay full price at the luxury retail store, or you can look for that same dress on the rack at the thrift shop. The thrift shop purchase is a special steal that could net you a nice hefty savings. When you buy a home, you can pay full price—or even custom-build exactly what you want—negotiate a lower price, or look for a special property that may net you a bigger savings.

Yes, you can buy homes cheap. And buying a home cheap doesn't have to mean that you're buying a cheap home. Thanks to some of the practices in this chapter, you can find a great home in a beautiful neighborhood for a fraction of the cost. You just have to know where to look.

In this chapter, we show you where to look. You'll learn about foreclosures, public auctions, and short sales. Each has its own unique characteristics, special benefits, and disadvantages. Depending on the type of sale, you could be dealing with a traditional homeowner, or a bank or other lending institution that has taken over ownership through a foreclosure of the property. This chapter tells how to handle buying a home through one of these nontraditional methods.

Foreclosure Facts

A foreclosed property is a home that the lender has taken ownership of because the homeowner has defaulted on the mortgage for whatever reason—usually nonpayment of the mortgage or property taxes. It has been said that 1 percent of all mortgage loans go into foreclosure. For buyers, these foreclosures are of interest because you can typically, but not always, buy a home for less than what other comparable homes are selling for. Why? Because once a bank forecloses on a property, it wants to sell it and get its money back as quickly as possible; this is how you, the buyer, might find a bargain home. There's no guarantee that you will find a bargain, though. Some foreclosed homes are actually priced higher than their actual value, since the foreclosing bank wants to reclaim their previously lost loan amounts. When all is said and done, however, no home, regardless of its status, will sell for more than the market value. So if a bank has overpriced a home in hopes of regaining all of its lost funds, it is more likely to find it sitting on the market unsold until the bank decides to be more realistic about the price.

Also, buying a foreclosure may take longer than buying a home the traditional way. Let's discuss a few other things you need to know about foreclosures.

> **Tips and Traps**
>
> The U.S. Department of Housing and Urban Development (HUD) offers many foreclosed homes for sale. This is because HUD previously guaranteed the mortgages that banks made on them, and took them over after foreclosure. Often HUD sells them at exceptionally good prices. You can find these homes at www.hud.gov/homes/index.cfm.

Sold "As Is"

One of the most important things you need to know is that *REOs* are always sold "as is," which means that what you see is what you get. This means that the bank that owns the home either has never been inside the home or, in some cases, has never even seen any pictures of it before the foreclosure. As a result, they take no responsibility for the condition of the house.

This could mean that the property was well maintained by its previous owners or that it needs serious upgrades and repairs. Unfortunately, a common occurrence, even in homes that were well maintained before, is that previous owners have trashed the home before they moved out, or stolen appliances and plumbing fixtures because

def•i•ni•tion

REO is bank-speak for "real estate owned," and represents foreclosed properties owned by banks.

they were mad at the bank for foreclosing. As a result, you'll be stuck cleaning up the mess if you buy it. Depending on how you are buying the property (we talk more about that in a little bit), you may or may not get to view the property ahead of time, so it can be a crap shoot for whether your house is in good condition or needs work.

As examples of the aforementioned, I have seen situations where range exhaust hoods, stoves, refrigerators, plumbing, garbage disposals, light fixtures, electrical generators, carpet, toilets, custom cabinets, granite countertops, built-in shelving, and (this one is my favorite) colored gravel in the front entryway have been removed by the former owner.

Depending on the type of sale (more on that later in the chapter), you may be able to arrange an inspection on the home—but you may be limited on time, and disclosures aren't readily available on certain homes. It's a risk you'll have to decide whether you want to take. Do you want to roll the dice?

Paying for Repairs/Upgrades

Keep in mind that if you are interested in a foreclosure property that needs a lot of repairs or upgrades, the bank will not make those repairs. You can ask for a price reduction just as you would with a traditional sale, but you may not get it. Figure carefully the projected cost of those repairs so that your "bargain home" doesn't become more expensive than you planned on.

Just because it's a bank-owned home doesn't mean you shouldn't complete your full range of inspections. You should plan on completing your inspections to be sure of exactly what you're buying. In fact, most lenders that are selling foreclosed properties, while clearly stating that they have no knowledge of the condition of the property having never lived there, want you to have as many inspections as you feel necessary so that you have full knowledge of its condition when you close. The only limit most banks place on foreclosure inspections is that they keep the time period for inspections a bit shorter than a private seller might allow.

How Long It Takes

Depending on the home, the foreclosure process itself can take one day, a few weeks, a few months, or much longer. Some banks reply to your offer within one or two days, while others can take days or weeks to respond. Do you have time to wait for this process to be completed, or do you need to buy a home more quickly?

Paying for It

How you pay for a foreclosure depends on how you purchase it. For example, if you find a foreclosure through an agent's or bank's listings, you may be expected to put down a deposit, similar to buying a traditional resale home. Like a traditional sale, this earnest money deposit has no specific required amount, but is at least $1,000.

To pay the balance of the purchase price, you can pay cash, which many people do, or take out a mortgage. If you pay cash, some banks will require proof of your funds beforehand—copies of your bank or brokerage accounts, for example.

To finance the balance, you'll likely need a prequalification letter when you submit your offer. If you are taking out a mortgage, the application process is the same as for a standard resale home. You can either use a bank of your choice or the bank that owns the foreclosure, if it offers financing options. Some banks that handle foreclosures are more than happy to provide a loan for a buyer if you qualify, while others feel they have had more than enough to do with the specific property and want nothing further to do with it once it's sold.

No matter which bank is providing you with a mortgage, you have the same options available to you as you would in a nonforeclosed home, including an FHA or VA loan. However, be aware that a bank that is selling a foreclosure, like any homeowner, has the right to specify what type of financing it is willing to accept as a part of the purchase contract. Such limits vary from institution to institution.

If you decide that the risks of buying a foreclosed home are worth it, it's time to learn how to find these potential treasures.

Finding a Foreclosed Property

You can find lists of foreclosed properties in several ways:

◆ Ask your agent. She should be familiar with the foreclosed properties in the area.

◆ Visit foreclosure websites. Some websites specialize in foreclosures, such as www. realtytrac.com and www.foreclosureradar.com. Both sites require a subscription and nominal fee, but they contain fairly thorough information. The former offers a free one-week trial, while the latter's free trial is for three days.

◆ Visit bank websites. Banks that own foreclosures may post them on their websites.

◆ Attend police auctions. Police auctions sell homes, cars, planes, boats, jewelry, and other items that officers have seized during arrests. One reason a home would be seized is if the owner was involved in illegal drug trafficking. To learn of these sales, contact the law enforcement agency in the area you're interested in buying, or check out online sites, such as www.policeauctions.com.

◆ Look for "for sale" signs. Some "for sale" signs on a home's property are actually labeled as foreclosures, so you might spot one as you drive around (although this is a little more time consuming).

◆ Visit the Fannie Mae website, http://reosearch.fanniemae.com/reosearch/.

◆ Visit the Internal Revenue Service website, www.treas.gov/auctions/irs/.

◆ Read the real estate or public notice section of the local newspapers.

◆ Visit www.homesales.gov/homesales/mainAction.do, which includes information on FHA and VA homes that have gone to foreclosure.

◆ Attend regular public auctions. A public auction is a meeting in an announced public location to sell property to repay a mortgage that is in default. Once the seller's foreclosure paperwork has been completed, the foreclosing entity provides a Notice of Sale—a formal notice sent to the owner and published in a newspaper as public information—that includes a date, time, and location for the foreclosure sale, always by public auction.

You can also buy a foreclosure directly from the bank, at a foreclosure auction, or at a post-foreclosure auction. We explain each of these methods in the following sections.

Buying from a Bank

When you find a listed foreclosure property that you want to buy, you proceed in the same way you would with a traditional purchase (which we go over in much more detail in Chapter 13). Your agent will write up an offer to the bank to buy the home at a specific price, closing at a certain time, and so on. You include all of the same contingencies in your offer, such as loan approval and inspections, and you attach a check for earnest money. Then you wait for the bank's response to your offer.

Be aware that it often takes a selling bank a bit longer to respond to an offer than it does for a traditional seller. This is due to sheer volume of their REO portfolio. You can typically expect to hear from the bank at least three or four days from when you make your offer, but it may sometimes be a longer period of time. Have your agent ask the listing agent for some guidance in this area when writing the contract.

Tips and Traps

When you are buying a foreclosure from a bank, the lender frequently won't sign the contract until you have agreed to all the terms in a seller's addendum (an additional list of terms and conditions to the sale). Read carefully! Often it severely limits the time for buyer inspections. Many reject the reliance on mediation and arbitration, and often carry a per-diem penalty payable by you if you fail to close on time. The daily per diem varies from $50 to as much as 1 percent of the purchase price.

Buying at Auction

Both types of public auctions—the foreclosure auction and the post-foreclosure auction—have different purposes, but with both, the property goes to the highest bidder. The foreclosure auction is used to foreclose on a property where the owner defaulted on the loan. The purpose of a foreclosure auction is to either sell the home and use the proceeds to pay off the bank, or for the bank to take over ownership so it can sell the property at a later date and recoup its funds. A post-foreclosure auction involves only homes that the bank has already taken over as a foreclosure but has, to date, been unable to sell by traditional means.

Whether you can view the home before buying depends on the owner. In the public auction that forecloses the home, it is entirely up to the owner if he wants to let you see the home. Thus, there is a very good chance you'll buy sight unseen, at least as far as the interior is concerned.

In a post-foreclosure auction, the owning bank usually arranges through its Realtor to have at least two or three open houses to allow you a chance to not only view the home, but also have your inspections done. Other than this, there may be a lockbox on the home so you can arrange to have inspections completed before the auction date.

As with any auction you attend, if you like a specific home, you get the auctioneer's attention and shout out your bid. If yours is the final and highest bid, you have just bought a home. Congratulations! Technically, though, your actual ownership occurs once the money has been paid to the foreclosing bank and the title is recorded in your name.

> **Warning!**
>
> Foreclosures are sold at auction to the highest bidder, but if the bank's representative isn't happy with the highest bid, he can make a final bid so that the bank's bid is the highest and the bank then owns the property.

Public Auction

At the so-called "auction on the courthouse steps," an auctioneer appointed by the foreclosing institution gets everyone's attention and briefly describes the property by address and foreclosing bank. He may have previously met individually with potential bidders at the auction site to ensure that the bidders do have adequate cash or a cashier's check to pay for their maximum bid. This is because, in most cases, the whole purchase price must be paid at the time of auction.

The auctioneer will announce a starting bid and throw it open to bids from the attendants. Highest bidder gets the property, but often if the highest bid isn't equal to, or in some cases even close to, the amount the bank is owed, a person representing the bank will put in a bid. Initially, that bank bid is merely to keep the bidding going and possibly spur other bidders to bid higher so that the final winning bid reaches what the bank is owed. Sometimes the bank bid will be the final bid because no one else is there or no one else cares to go any higher. In that case, the bank ends up owning the property and will sell it later through a Realtor or at a post-foreclosure auction.

If the winning bid is someone other than the bank's representative, that person then owns the home. The auction has ended and the home has been foreclosed. Note that your real estate agent doesn't earn a commission with a foreclosure auction (unless you agree to pay it yourself).

Tips and Traps

Figuratively speaking, a public auction is called a "sale on the courthouse steps," because in the past this is where such sales most often took place. In most cases, they still do today.

Post-Foreclosure Auctions

A post-foreclosure auction is staged by a professional auction house that lumps together hundreds, sometimes thousands, of previously foreclosed homes and auctions them off one at a time to the highest bidder. The pace is very rapid, with a home turning over every 60 to 90 seconds. The lender that owns these foreclosed homes arranges the auction, hires the auction company, and reaps the proceeds of the sale after the homes are sold—minus the auctioneer commission and buyers' Realtor commissions.

Frequently, the winning bid comes in at as much as one third to one half of the home's former appraised value, but after having had no success selling the home by traditional means, the lender recoups whatever money it can. Clearly, buying a home at a post-foreclosure auction is a buyer's opportunity, since you'll be getting a great price on a home. Your real estate agent also benefits from this type of auction because she will earn a commission (although usually less than with a traditional sale), as opposed to the foreclosure auction, where she receives no commission for your winning bid. As in the case of the courthouse steps auction, actual ownership takes place once the title has been transferred to you and your funds have been transferred to the selling bank.

Finding Out About Auctions

These auctions are usually advertised in newspapers, on the radio and TV, and by direct mail. Ads begin running weeks, sometimes months, in advance to get as many people to attend as possible. Also, Realtors who have listed properties are asked to circulate flyers for the auctions and post auction signs at and near the locations of the properties that are being auctioned. Your Realtor will know about these events through this advertising, just as you can. If she has signed up with the major property auction firms, she may receive e-mails announcing any coming auctions.

Financing an Auction Purchase

Auction financing is pretty straightforward. As in a traditional sale, if you are financing the purchase, you usually need an earnest deposit of $5,000 to $10,000, with the balance financed by a lender. In addition, when you make your offer on the home, you may have a contingency that states if, for any legitimate reason, you cannot obtain financing, you can cancel your contract without putting your deposit at risk. This contingency may be allowed only if you apply for financing from a lender at an auction. If you choose not to use that lender, you may be denied a financing contingency. Finally, the deposit won't change hands until you release your contingency and proceed with the purchase under the contract's terms. This deposit will be held in escrow for your protection.

If you plan to pay with cash at the auction, it must be held in escrow for an agreed-upon period of time. Once the closing takes place, it changes hands.

Inspections

As you already know, inspections are a vital process to buying a home that is structurally sound. However, when it comes to inspections on foreclosures, you are not likely to get much in the way of disclosure about the foreclosed property, because the lender that owns it most likely hasn't lived in the property—and, in many cases, has never even physically been in it. So inspections become even more important with foreclosures, but the process is a bit different.

First, banks that own foreclosure properties allow you to have as many inspections of the property as you want. The only negative is that REO-owning banks usually don't allow as much time for doing your inspections compared to a traditional sale.

For example, in a traditional sale, you might get about two weeks to complete your inspections, but you may find that you have only a week when you're buying a foreclosure from the bank. This is because the bank wants to get rid of the home as quickly as possible. As with any contract, you and the seller can negotiate inspection time frames. Furthermore, if you find serious issues during inspections, you can cancel your offer before going to closing.

When it comes to auction purchases, inspections are not permitted after the auction is concluded because the banks want to prevent the sale from falling apart. However, to avoid this, the bank and their auction company will provide about a month's worth of pre-auction open houses. At this time, you can have your inspectors complete their full inspections. If you find serious issues during your inspections that make you reconsider buying the property, you can also cancel your contract within the terms of the agreement.

So you must decide early on if you want to spend the money necessary—several hundreds and possibly thousands of dollars—on inspections on a home you may never get to own. However, if you think about it, this is not very different from a regular purchase. You would get into a contract and then do your inspections, not knowing whether they'd reveal something way too expensive to repair, with the result that you cancel the sale. One thing I would remind you, though, is that it is very unwise to buy a house anywhere, an auction included, without doing inspections at some point in the process.

Warning!

Be careful! In a courthouse sale, you could end up as the winning bidder on a foreclosing mortgage that is not the first mortgage. For example, Mrs. Smith owned the home before you but took out more than one mortgage. If the lender foreclosing is the one from the first mortgage, you're fine; but if the foreclosing lender is from the second or third mortgage, you will own the house and owe any other loans that Mrs. Smith had—and you must pay them. To prevent this, do a title search to reveal which mortgage is foreclosing. This won't be disclosed at the auction.

In order to avoid the unhappy circumstance of buying a home at a courthouse steps sale only to find that you also owe the former owner's other mortgages, spend a few hundred dollars and have a title search completed. That way you won't find out that you now own the house, but the auctioning bank held the second (or even more subordinate) mortgage. Now, in addition to owning the house, you also own the "right" and legal obligation to pay the previously existing first mortgage.

Short Sales

As another option, you buy a home *before* it's in foreclosure through what's called a short sale. Typically, when a home sells, the seller uses the proceeds of the sale to pay any outstanding balance of the mortgage owed. The seller then receives what's left, or his equity, in the property. In a short sale, the homeowner owes more to the bank than what his home is worth. To avoid a foreclosure, the homeowner and his bank agree to sell the home for a minimum specific price that is lower than what the seller owes, allowing the bank to cut its losses and come up "short," per se. Again, it's another way to possibly get a great deal on a home.

For example, assume in the current market the house is worth $350,000. Unfortunately, the owner/seller owes the bank $450,000 on the home. When the sale closes, the bank expects to receive full payment for its loan, but in this market and with the seller's financial situation, that cannot happen. So even if the house sells for $350,000, the bank will receive less than it is owed. As a result, it has to agree to accept this "short" amount as payment in full for the debt in order for the sale to close.

The fact that the bank and the seller agree to a minimum amount that the bank won't go below in accepting a short sale does not prohibit you from negotiating the best price you can at or above that level. Typically, you make the best offer you can, and if the seller accepts, then it's submitted to the bank for its blessing.

Before you put in an offer on a short sale, ask your agent if she works on these sales. A lender may put limits on the agents' commission because they reason they're going to lose money and the seller will get nothing, so why should the agents get a full commission? If your agent will work on a short sale, she may ask you to sign a buyer-broker agreement, which contractually requires you to pay her commission if the seller won't or can't.

One thing about buying a property by short sale can be terribly frustrating. It often takes longer for a lender to approve the terms of a short sale than it does to have the entire foreclosure process run to foreclosure sale. While this issue makes little sense, because it is a choice by the lender to lose a portion of the loan principal instead of losing all of it, lenders frequently seem unable to make a decision on a short sale in a timely manner.

Warning!

Sellers usually face various income tax obligations with a short sale. This is not a concern of yours, as the buyer, except that it may affect how low the seller is willing to go on the sales price.

If time is of the essence for you, decide to forego this option unless the seller already has an approval for a short sale from his lender. Otherwise, it can literally take several months for the lender to make a decision. By then, you may have lost other opportunities or the bank may have foreclosed and the home is not available at the same price any longer.

The most important thing to remember about short sales as a buyer is that you can sometimes get a really good deal on a home. However, it will likely take longer than the process you'll follow on any other type of purchase transaction. If you're very lucky, once the seller has accepted your offer, you may get an answer from the bank in one to two weeks, or you may have to wait months. How long are you willing to wait?

Keep all of these facts in mind when deciding whether foreclosures and short sales are for you, and act accordingly.

The Least You Need to Know

- ◆ You don't need to pay full price when you buy a home—there are always deals to be made and ways to purchase homes at a bargain, including foreclosures and short sales.

- ◆ Read any fine print on any documents, such as seller addendums, that you receive so you know what you're getting yourself into.

- ◆ If you buy a foreclosure, be aware that many selling banks enforce the time frames by charging a per-diem penalty to the buyer for any buyer-caused closing delays.

- ◆ Remember that what you see is what you get; although you can get inspections on some, if you want time to look at the property, these methods of buying a home might not be for you.

Part 4

Getting Closer

Ah, here we are, the main course! Here, we show you what should happen between the time the seller accepts your offer and the time you close. You'll learn the importance of inspections, and how to use results to either reduce the price of the home or require the seller to make repairs. We also go over the various documents, such as disclosures from the owner, in detail so you will be able to successfully navigate your way through them.

While we're at it, we explain what seller financing is and discuss seller concessions, which can significantly cut your closing costs.

Is It Your Dream Home?

In This Chapter

- ◆ First impressions count
- ◆ What you want versus what you need
- ◆ Looking at possibilities
- ◆ Flood zones can wash away your dreams
- ◆ Getting the disclosures

If you've been following the guidelines in the book, you've been doing your homework about the real estate market you're looking in. You've made a list of wants and needs, and you've figured out your budget. You've researched and found a real estate agent and a mortgage broker, who has preapproved or prequalified you. You've searched the Internet and looked for homes for sale, and your agent has taken you to see several that have attracted your attention. You might have even attended some open houses and found a home that you think is "the one."

But how do you know it's "the one"? This chapter helps you figure that out. We discuss how you can decide whether a home is the right one for you and highlight some issues—such as flood zones—that might make you reconsider a home right away. By the end of this chapter, you'll be able to pull out your list of wants and needs and compare it to the home you want to put an offer on. The house that you want to make a bid on should have much of what's on that list.

Connecting Emotionally

Of course, home buying should be a logical decision because it is probably the biggest purchase you'll ever make. However, there's an emotional side to buying a home, too. Often you'll hear buyers say they walked into a home and just knew it was "the one."

Think about whether you made an emotional connection to the home when you drove up to the property or walked through the front door. Did you feel a sense of "I'm home," or did it make you cringe and think, "Ew"? That first impression is everything. If you connected with the home before even walking through the door, that's a great start.

Did you feel that same emotion as you toured the whole house? Could you see yourself living there? Could you envision the extra bedroom as a future nursery? Could you imagine the kids playing in the backyard or you and your spouse cuddling by the fireplace? If the house instantly has you picturing your family already moved in, you might be in the house that is "the one."

Be careful, though! You're not ready to make an offer strictly because the home meets your emotional needs, so don't make your decision solely on this. You still need to think about the logical side of a home-buying decision. That means you need to make sure the home fits your budget, that it's structurally sound, and that its layout, features, and neighborhood are what you're looking for.

Compromising

When you go looking for a new home, you are probably told to "look for what you want." The reality is, you don't always find exactly what you want, and it's rare to find a home that has every specific feature you need or desire. So when do you compromise and buy a home that doesn't quite have everything you want, but comes close? Honestly, it depends.

For example, Matt and Erica are a young New Jersey couple with two school-aged children. The couple wanted to find a home with at least three bedrooms and 2,000 square feet of living space. After searching diligently with the assistance of a good Realtor, the closest home they found to what they were looking for was an 1,800-square-foot home that had four bedrooms. It met their wants and needs in several other ways, but it was a bit small.

After giving it some thought, Matt and Erica put an offer on the 1,800-square-foot home and it was accepted. They decided to compromise on the square footage because the home had an extra bedroom, which they could utilize, and it met several other needs, too. They love their new home! Every buyer is different, though. Another couple might have said that they didn't necessarily need a fourth bedroom, but the 2,000 square feet of living space was non-negotiable. That's okay. Everybody has to make their own decisions according to what feels right for them.

In another example, Nicole wanted to buy a home that definitely included a garage and large plot of land, since she likes to garden. She found one home that had a perfect plot of land for her garden, but it didn't have a garage. As a result, Nicole decided that even though the plot of land was perfect, she really needed to find a house with a large garage, so she kept looking for her dream home.

It's not likely that you will find a home that has every little detail of what you want or feel you need, unless you have it custom built. So the way you decide what you are willing to accept, while also deciding what is non-negotiable, is to use the following two-step process.

Remember your wants and needs list? Now it's time to prioritize it from most to least important. Next, visit the house again, and examine it room by room. How many of the items on the list does this home have? Are you checking off many of the things you want? Does the dining room have the easy kitchen access that you wanted, and is it spacious enough for get-togethers? Does the kitchen have the cabinet space that you need? Are the bedrooms the right sizes? Keep asking yourself these questions for each room.

At the same time, look at the negatives of buying the home—after all, even if the home has everything you want, it can still have more negatives than positives. For example, it may have four bedrooms, but the home isn't structurally sound. After you've completed this process, look at the results. You should now have a much clearer picture of whether this home will work for you. Alternatively, the four bedrooms you insist on may be so small they are almost useless for your needs.

Are there absolute must-have items on your list that aren't checked off? Are any of these deal breakers for you? Maybe what you're missing is something you can add later—for example, an outdoor deck. Would you be able to buy the home the way it is now and add the deck later? If so, also think about whether you can live with the home the way it is until you add the deck. If you don't like the results of your analysis, it might be prudent to walk away from the home and look for what you want in another home.

Location

When buyers tour a home, often they go straight to the home, tour the inside, get back inside their car, and leave. Some buyers don't take the time to drive around the neighborhood and see what it's like, too.

It's easy to get excited about a great new home, but don't forget that you're not only buying a home—in a sense you're buying into a neighborhood, too, so it's really important to like what's around you. However, don't limit yourself to a single drive around the neighborhood. Maybe today is a nice day, but on another drive at a different time, you might see situations or circumstances that become red flags to you.

Tips and Traps

When you're taking a home tour, don't forget to look out the windows! Remember, you want to know what the view is and what you'll see day in and day out for the entire time you'll own your home. For example, do you have trees in your backyard, or do you look right into your neighbor's yard? Also keep in mind that a great view is a huge plus for the resale value of your home. And open a window! You might hear traffic noise that you didn't notice before.

Industrial Areas

What if you find out when you're driving around that the home is located in an industrial zone? The word *industrial* pretty much tells you all you need to know. Most people don't want to live near a manufacturing plant or an industrial zone. These areas are prone to being extremely noisy and, depending on the type of industry, not very pretty. There's also the potential to be exposed to air and water pollution, as well as toxic ground contamination. Over the years, toxic contamination has been shown to cause cancer, birth defects, and miscarriages in nearby homeowners.

In some older developed areas, you may not even have to be in an area designated as industrial to be near a plant. Sometimes a single manufacturing or other form of industrial plant was established in a particular locale long before anything else was built. The industrial operation never expanded beyond the original plant, but due to the fairly large amount of unused open land surrounding it, at some point one or more developers put in a residential subdivision, or three. Once again, this is a situation in which a careful on-site exploration or two of the area around your possible home may save you a great deal of upset and aggravation later. Additionally, ask your agent and carefully peruse the disclosures provided to you by the seller.

If it's an entire industrial area, not just one plant, these negatives are multiplied. Even what might seem like a good deal in an industrial zone is probably not a good home-buying deal overall, especially when it comes time to sell. Some folks live in these areas, of course, perhaps because of budget reasons or other factors, but given the option to locate elsewhere, most certainly would do so.

Quotes and Facts

In the mid-1950s, an industrial plant in Niagara Falls, New York, was closed and the chemical wastes were buried. The lot was turned into a housing development for approximately 900 families, and a new school was built. In the 1970s, many cases of severe physical problems and diseases arose among the citizens, although it was never proven that these problems were caused by the buried chemicals. Federal funding was used to clean up the area, and homes were abandoned and the school was torn down. About 90 percent of the families moved away at government expense, and the company successor paid millions to settle lawsuits.

Highways and Parkways

Ah, you found a beautiful home with a fenced-in backyard and a lush lawn with a surrounding garden, and you can imagine the sights and sounds on a warm spring morning of ... thousands of eighteen-wheelers and cars zooming along each morning spewing exhaust fumes as they pass by. Some buyers—especially commuters or frequent travelers—might prefer a home located near the highway, but in most cases, the only benefit to living very close to a highway is a lower-priced home. When you ultimately go to sell, the nearby highway can become a liability. Unless you have a really good reason to live there, it's best to pass up a home that's backed right up to the freeway and buy elsewhere. However, there's usually nothing wrong with a home that has convenient access to the highway but is located several blocks away from the road itself.

Tips and Traps

If you just can't avoid where the house is located, you may be able to minimize the noise, including adding a fountain in the yard. The noise of the water can mask traffic noise amazingly well. Obviously, the degree of success you have with this will depend on both the volume of traffic and the size of the fountain.

Flood Zones

If the neighborhood is near a river, lake, pond, or other waterway, you have more to consider than just the view. If you're looking at homes along one of the major rivers in the country, there's a good chance that you may be buying in a designated flood zone. A formal designation of flood zones is a result from a study done by the U.S. Army Corps of Engineers. The group analyzes an area and the likelihood that it will be flooded from nearby rivers or streams, and how many times. The mere fact that an area has flooded in the past doesn't make it an officially designated flood zone.

Most of the major rivers in the nation—the Missouri, Mississippi, Ohio, Snake, and Red, to name a few—have flooded on occasion, but often and severely enough to make living nearby them riskier than living elsewhere. However, sometimes a flood can even occur from smaller streams if there is enough concentrated or continuous rainfall in a short period of time.

> **Tips and Traps**
>
> Flood zones are designated by studies performed by the U.S. Army Corps of Engineers (www.usace.army.mil) and are regularly updated. These studies predict the likelihood of an area being flooded by any waterway in the area. However, there is no specific schedule for updating these studies. Any changes in zones include not only the work of the Corps of Engineers, but also input from the local community involved and the U.S. Federal Emergency Management Agency (FEMA).

Floodsmart.gov is a website dedicated to creating awareness about the dangers of flooding areas. For example, the website tells the story of one young man who lived near a small creek that hadn't flooded in 40 years. He closed on the house in December and purchased flood insurance; 18 days later, the home was flooded. The home shifted off its foundation, and the owner needed to take a boat to the house to look at the damage. Scary stuff, but it's something to think about if you want to buy in one of these areas.

If the home is in a declared flood zone, the seller must disclose this fact to you. If you still want it, consider the fact that you must buy flood insurance as a condition of your mortgage.

It's important to note, however, that flood zones do change; some areas may be removed from an officially declared zone, while others may be added. When this occurs, FEMA sends formal letters to homeowners in the affected areas so they can either obtain flood insurance if they are now in a flood zone, or have the option of canceling theirs if the area's designation was removed.

Tips and Traps _____

Two inches of water can cost you $7,500, according to Floodsmart.gov. In 2007, flood insurance claims were nearly $600 million, with an average paid claim of $33,000. In 1968, Congress created the National Flood Insurance Program (NFIP) to help provide a means for property owners to financially protect themselves. The NFIP offers flood insurance to homeowners, renters, and business owners if their community participates in the NFIP. Participating communities agree to adopt and enforce ordinances that meet or exceed FEMA requirements, to reduce the risk of flooding.

If a neighborhood is statistically likely to flood once every 100 years, as the most severe flood zones are at risk to do, but everything else there is to your liking, you will have to decide which factor outweighs the other. Flood insurance costs about $1,500 annually for coverage of $250,000. This is an approximate figure, and varies with the value and location of your home, as well as the insurance company that's providing the coverage. For more information, visit www.fema.gov/business/nfip/cover. shtm.

Warning! _____

Regular homeowner's insurance does not cover flood damage. Don't find this out the hard way. Flood insurance is specifically designed to cover damage from flooding. It is provided by major insurance companies and further backed by support from the federal government.

Airports

Is the neighborhood you're interested in located close to an airport, small or large? Homes close to an airport or under its prevailing flight patterns can be subject to plenty of noise (especially at night). You have to decide if you can tolerate airport noise, no matter how much the house meets your wants and needs. Another concern about living near an airport is that it will most likely always be there, and, assuming normal growth in travel in or near the city, the noise will get worse with the passage of time. This can affect the future marketability when you decide to sell the home down the road.

Mixed Blessings: Golf Courses, Parks, and Playgrounds

Driving around on your neighborhood tour, you might find that the home is located near (or maybe even on) a golf course, park, or playground. These amenities can be mixed blessings. The good thing about living close to a golf course, park, or playground is that you can use the facility. Also, all of that open expanse of lush grass looks very nice from your home. It can almost be like a visual extension of your yard.

The negatives of living close to one of these facilities could include the traffic, noise, and debris from the people regularly using them. Let's break each down a little more.

Golf Courses

Those who love playing the game might dream of buying a home on, or close to, a golf course. Step out your door, and in minutes you could be teeing off. You have all this lush, well-maintained land right around the corner from your backyard and, best of all, you'll never miss a tee time if you're part of the membership (no, you don't need to join, but keep in mind that you may have to join to play there and it can be pricey). That's the good side of things.

> **Tips and Traps**
>
> If you buy a home or a condo in a golf community, add in the cost of homeowners' association fees to your budget. This is to help keep up the golf course property and any other buildings or properties that are part of the golf course. The seller should disclose this information to you.

On the negative side, there are the weekend crowds and traffic to contend with, coupled with the possibility of golf balls ricocheting off your home or occasionally shattering windows. And that view will cost you, as homes located on golf courses tend to be priced a bit higher than other types of homes.

If you find a home you absolutely love and it lies close to a golf course, take a few moments and carefully consider all the pros and cons before making an offer.

Playgrounds

If you have children, a neighborhood playground is a wonderful nearby amenity. In most cases, a playground provides a safe area for your children to play and make new friends, and for you to meet other neighborhood parents. A nearby playground is also a great amenity if the home you're interested in doesn't have much yard space. However, while that's a plus, a playground can also mean increased car and pedestrian traffic and noise, especially if community events are held there.

Parks

A park is a large area of land preserved in its natural state as public property. If you find a home that borders a park, it's almost like having a second yard without having to handle the maintenance. It also guarantees that no construction will be taking place there, since it's legally protected.

As nice as this sounds, parks have the same negative that playgrounds do. Everyone else—neighbors and tourists—are attracted to the park, too. So on a nice day, your peace and tranquility may be put to the test by hundreds of people and their kids and dogs making noise. Whatever privacy you thought you had may be a memory once you see the people rolling in to use the park. Again, it's all about personal choices.

Another thing to think about when considering the beauty of nature is some of the things that come along with it. Depending on the part of the country you live in, bodies of water or open parkland can provide you with a variety of insects, frogs, snakes, or land animals to annoy you or damage landscaping. Of course deer are beautiful, but they love snacking on attractive home landscaping. Raccoons can be fascinating creatures, but they also damage shrubs and rummage through garbage cans looking for food. You don't have to ignore homes with beautiful natural surroundings. Just be aware that there are tradeoffs.

Think About the Future

Now that you've checked out the inside and outside of your home trying to decide whether this house is "the one," it's time to put on your magic hat and look into your crystal ball. What will the future of the neighborhood be?

All kidding aside, you really need to think about the future of the neighborhood. Will there be future development? Is it possible that your wonderful view will be blocked by another home or building a few years down the road?

For example, one couple searched for a weekend getaway ski cottage several years ago and were quite taken with a relatively new two-story vacation home that more than matched their needs, especially its bargain-basement asking price. The couple wanted to place an offer but found out during their due diligence that the beautiful redwood-studded empty parcel across the narrow access road was available for building and had no restrictions, which meant there could be a small ranch-style home built on the property or a 40-story apartment building. Either one would have interfered with their view. Although it wasn't a guarantee that any construction would ever take place, the couple didn't like the uncertainty, so they decided to keep looking.

What does your crystal ball tell you?

Disclosures

Now that you have that feeling that a certain home is "the one," it's important to make sure you have all your ducks in a row. In this case, you need to make sure you've been given all the necessary disclosures. Every state has laws that require sellers to disclose certain information to buyers about their home. Laws about disclosures are designed to protect buyers so that by the time you take title, there are no secrets. Failure to provide any disclosure documents can lead to costly litigation against the seller. What you see in these disclosures can tell you what you need to know about your home to make that final decision.

Health and Safety Disclosures

Some disclosures are mandatory inspections of the property by government inspectors for compliance with health, safety, and building code and permit regulations. In California, for example, the seller must provide confirmation that the hot water heater is strapped to the wall to prevent tipping in case of an earthquake. This is because a water heater's pilot light can cause a fire after the heater has tipped. Several states require verification that there are smoke detectors in place and operating in a residence. These disclosures are completed by the sellers, although it is likely that violation of one of these required items will be noted by an inspector you hire.

Washington's King County requires underground fuel oil storage tanks to be removed or filled in, and the buyer given a disclosure that this has been done. In Texas, sellers with septic systems must provide buyers with an On-Site Separate Sewer Disclosure document that details everything about the system. In Maryland, a variety of special disclosure documents are needed, covering such things as *latent defects* and proximity to airports. Each is county specific.

def•i•ni•tion

> **Latent defects** are those defects that would not be likely to be noticed by a purchaser in a careful visual inspection, but could be potentially harmful to occupants of the building. A professional inspection might find them, and a seller is bound to reveal them to a buyer if they're known to her. Failure to do so could subject her to serious civil liability.

In New Jersey, sellers must provide a health and safety disclosure for homes with well water. Want to hear an odd one? California mandates that any death—not the method or cause—on the property within the past three years be disclosed. The buyer can ask if the deceased died in a certain way or from a certain specific disease. If asked, the seller must answer. Alaska's law requires that sellers disclose any deaths by murder or suicide on the property within the last three years.

Another health disclosure regards mold, which has become an extremely important issue over the last decade. In several states, the seller must provide a mold disclosure to you if she has personal knowledge of mold in the home, past or present, or if there have ever been any water leaks. If you are buying a foreclosure, some banks include a mold disclosure that notifies you to check for mold in your inspections. This is to avoid liability for any mold issues down the road that the bank was not aware of.

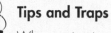

Tips and Traps _____

When reviewing seller disclosure documents, pay attention to special disclosures that are unique to the location of the property. They frequently cover items that you may not be used to if you're coming from another area. Examples of these can be obtained from a Realtor or from your state's Association of Realtors.

Structural Disclosures

Many states also require a real estate agent's visual inspection disclosure. Although the seller is required to reveal what she knows about her property, the agent is also required to inspect and reveal what he noticed about the property. These are also disclosures about any past or existing defects of the home's structure and outbuildings.

Tips and Traps _____

Ask the seller if he has any inspection reports from when he purchased the home. Some states mandate this as part of the disclosure requirements if the seller still has them. Other states do not. Also ask the seller for copies of architectural and building plans. Similarly, if the seller has remodeled at any point, he should make those remodel plans available to you, too.

What's important about past defects? Perhaps the previous problem was severe enough that you'd like to have an inspector examine the problem again. This disclosure can run at least three pages, sometimes coupled with lengthy explanations. Also, it will give you a clue to look for remedial work on the old problem.

> **Warning!**
>
> If the seller discloses any water intrusion or plumbing leaks, make sure to have a professional inspector evaluate the situation. You should know how severe the problem is before signing on the dotted line.

Special Disclosures

As society changes, so do its laws. Megan's Law is named after Megan Kanka, a seven-year-old girl who was kidnapped, raped, and murdered by a neighbor who had a sexual criminal history that the family did not know about. Named after her, Megan's Law mandates that you must be told before closing if there are sexual offenders in the neighborhood. You should also be told about any state database of sexual offenders that you can view privately. The particulars vary in each state, but the intent is the same—to help you avoid the potential risk of a sexual predator who may live nearby. Who tells you this information depends on the state. It is usually the seller's responsibility to tell you, but some states mandate that the agent provide the information. Ask your Realtor if this concerns you.

Other Disclosures

The notifications don't stop here. There are a wide variety of disclosure requirements around the country. Some areas are required to have low-flow toilets, while in other locales you must receive a hazardous zone report that tells you if the property is located in an official earthquake zone, flood zone, wildfire area, former military munitions disposal area, toxic waste zone, and so on.

However, the firms producing these reports don't visit the property every time to assess its disaster potential. Rather, they check into massive computer databases maintained by the states and federal government on all of these dangers, and then provide the information on whether the specific property actually lies within one or more of these zones. The costs of these disclosures run from approximately $50 to $150 per property. The seller usually foots the bill for these.

There is also a drug lab site disclosure, which would be needed if the seller knew that the property had previously been used to manufacture illegal drugs. The reason for such disclosure is that some of the chemicals used in making illicit drugs can be highly toxic. This is a good thing to know because of the toxicity of the chemicals involved and the relatively high cost of remediation of these chemicals.

Real Estate Tax Disclosure

You know that you have to pay property taxes, but what may be interesting for you is how they are broken down. For example, the real estate tax disclosure may show that a certain percentage goes to schools, some for bond issues, some for water and sewer maintenance, some for highways, and so on. It's just a disclosure that's informative in nature. If you see something you don't like, you could cancel the contract, but this is rare. Check with your agent and your attorney before making this decision. Usually, this information is available from either the local taxing authorities or from the title company. In the latter case in California, it often accompanies the preliminary title report produced as part of the escrow process.

Dealing With the Fear

Let's say that you found a home, connected with it emotionally, and love its location—and it doesn't have any outstanding deal breakers. Now you're moving closer to putting an offer on the home, but you're scared. Don't worry—this fear is normal, and many buyers experience it. Perhaps you are about to go from renting an apartment, living at college, or living with your parents to moving into a place you own. Before now, your parents or your landlords took care of the property, and now you're going to have to pay for and maintain the property on your own. This can all become very overwhelming.

The fear can be so taxing that some buyers might even decide not to place an offer on their dream home because they let their fears overtake them. Try to work out your fears and move forward. The best way to do this is to list all of the pluses and minuses of buying that home. For example, consider the tax breaks you'll get and the equity you'll build. If your fears still don't subside, however, perhaps stepping out of the transaction is the right thing for you. Hopefully, though, after this reevaluation, you will feel comfortable enough to put in an offer.

Warning!

If you do decide that buying the home is not the right thing to do at this time, but you have already released your buyer contingencies before you decide to cancel the deal, you could face costly damages for breaching your contract with the seller.

The Least You Need to Know

- ◆ Listen to your gut—if a home doesn't seem right for you, walk away.

- ◆ You really will know what home is perfect for you—compare it to your list of wants and needs, and picture yourself living there for 30 years.

- ◆ Buying a home on a golf course, near a park, or by a playground might sound idyllic, but weigh the pros and cons of living near something that's open to the public.

- ◆ Home buying is an exciting—albeit scary—time; getting cold feet is a normal part of the process.

- ◆ Pay careful attention to disclosures—they may save you a lot of money or heart-ache.

Making an Offer

If the home you like has most, or all, of the things you have on the checklist that you made in the earlier chapters, you're ready to make an offer. If it's currently a buyer's market, you may need to act quickly—get the offer in and close the sale. If you don't, you may lose the house to someone who gets their bid in before you.

Knowing not just how to make an offer, but how to make the "right" offer, is very important. Just because someone is asking $275,000 for a three-bedroom raised ranch home doesn't mean that it's worth that much. It's possible that the seller has an inflated idea of what her home is worth, or the Realtor gave her inaccurate information on its value. Maybe her friends have convinced her that $275,000 would be considered "a steal" by a buyer, when in fact it's highway robbery. Conversely, you might find out that the home is really worth more—but you'll wonder why it is priced for less than it's probably worth. Maybe it's deliberately underpriced because the owner has to sell it quickly and is willing to accept a bit less than its true value as a way of enticing a buyer to make an offer and close quickly.

However accurately the home is priced, how do you know what your offer should be? Pricing is not an exact science. If it were, there would never be any debate over the selling price of a home. The seller and his agent would put a price on a home and a buyer would just offer that amount—but it's a bit more complicated than that.

This chapter gives you the tools necessary to evaluate the market, price the home, and craft your offer. Of course, not all negotiations end with a handshake and a signed contract, so this chapter also discusses when you should walk away and what to do if things go seriously wrong during the bidding process.

Comparing Comps

To properly bid on a home, you first need to compare it to other homes that are for sale in the neighborhood. You wouldn't want to submit a $500,000 bid if the rest of the comparable homes in the neighborhood are selling for between $200,000 and $250,000. Ask your agent for a list of all recently sold comparable homes, or comps, in the area, as well as a list of other homes that are currently for sale.

First, compare each home on these lists to your candidate home so you're comparing apples and apples. For example, was each home built at approximately the same time? Do they have similar numbers and sizes of bedrooms and baths; living, dining, or family rooms; and garage? Do they have the same amount of living space or lot size?

In some cases, comparing price per square foot may be helpful, but this is more valuable in neighborhoods where the homes resemble each other than in areas where the homes are individually unique in design and style. However, even in locations where homes are each uniquely designed, the information can still be of use.

You may want to visit the comps in person to make notes of the similarities and differences and get a firsthand opportunity to see exactly what a certain amount of money will buy you at a particular time in a given market. You should do this within a day or two after you find a house you're interested in. Keep in mind, however, that even taking a day or two to do this research could cost you the home—your agent will know how fast you need to move on your offer.

Once you are done comparing the physical structure of the home and the land, compare the prices. Is a similar home selling for much less or about the same as the home you want to buy? Ask your agent what she thinks you should offer for the home based on the comps, and the reason for her decision.

As a general rule, if the market is a hot seller's market with lots of competition, seriously consider offering at least the asking price, sometimes a bit more. However, if the market is slow, one that favors buyers, consider coming in below the asking price. If the seller doesn't like your offer, you can always raise it later. To determine the status of the market, ask your Realtor how reasonably priced the home is in relation to the current market, and then make your offer accordingly.

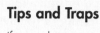

Tips and Traps

If you choose to visit comps before making an offer, take along a camera. If something strikes you about a comp, take a picture and then visually compare it with your own candidate home—but ask first. Since you're considering buying another similar home and the pictures are for personal use only, permission to do so is usually not required.

Crafting Your Offer

When you like a home and want to buy it, you present an offer to the seller. This offer is a written proposal that tells the seller the terms and conditions of your purchase, such as the price you're offering and the length of time the offer is good for. The offer includes contingencies for inspections and the mortgage, and how much time there will be between your offer and the closing. The offer will also include a list of any fixtures and attachments, such as removable lights that you want to stay, as well as any items such as *creditbacks* or payments of locally mandated fees and taxes. The latter are funds that may be mandated by a particular loan program you're using. Taxes may be the property taxes due from previous years, usually paid by the seller, but possibly contracted for buyer payment as part of the deal.

Writing this much detail in the offer minimizes the chances for misunderstandings or disagreements between you and the seller. You're making certain that any particular items you want remain with the house, and having everything in writing helps to avoid having your purchase become a lawsuit,

def•i•ni•tion

Creditbacks are amounts credited back to you at closing by the seller, usually in lieu of the seller doing repairs before closing.

now or at some time after you take possession. Your Realtor can carefully craft the proper terminology of your offer and detail exactly what you want from the seller and what you are willing to pay to get it.

Remember that the house you are interested in buying has been someone else's home for a period of time. You may think of it as a palace or you may see it as a dump that you're planning to totally gut and remodel, but to the seller, it's his home until he hands you the keys. Therefore, when you make your offer, show him some respect. Act like you know that it's an important place to him—because it is! Even if you're going to make a very low offer, let him know, through your Realtor, that you're doing so for a reason and you're not trying to steal the home. This could, in some cases, make a difference in whether the seller even continues to deal with you at all. Believe it or not, some sellers get offended when lowball offers come in, and then they won't work with you again. Smooth things out as you go along.

Breaking Down the Offer

In the offer, the property is usually identified by the address and the *parcel number.* (This may seem over the top, but you'd be amazed how often a buyer and seller think they are talking about the same piece of real estate but find out they were mistaken.) Typically an offer is at least five pages long, although longer forms are certainly common and there can also be a few additional forms appended to the basic contract.

Preprinted forms are available and simplify the process, but these aren't required. Your Realtor supplies these forms for you.

The offer form you use may depend on where you live and take into account local laws, while other forms are just preferred by a particular real estate agent, for whatever reason. All are legally binding when accepted and signed by both parties. Let's discuss some of the basic parts of the offer—price, closing, loan, and inspections and other contingencies.

def•i•ni•tion

A **parcel number** is not your street number. It's a number given to each individual piece of real property, usually by the local county assessor, that specifically identifies that property.

Price/Finance Terms

This part of the offer itemizes and then sums up the financials of the purchase. It includes the price you are willing to pay for the house, which is, in most contracts, broken down into the good faith or earnest money deposit, the amount of your mortgage loan, and the down payment balance, which is the amount you still owe from your own funds after you've paid your initial deposit. When you add your deposit with your mortgage amount, it totals the purchase price. In most offers, the purchase price is shown in both figures and words to ensure that the amount is clearly understood.

This section also addresses liquidated damages. Liquidated damages is a sum of money that you and the seller agreed to in the offer that you will forfeit to the seller if you breach the contract once it's signed by canceling it after releasing all of your contingencies. The seller agrees to accept this amount of money instead of going through a lawsuit against you. The amount can vary from contract to contract, but it usually is equal to no more than 2 to 5 percent of the contract purchase price.

Warning!

When you are reviewing the offer, make sure all the numbers are correct. Don't just assume that since one is right, they are all right. Look at every one and make sure it's correct. Then add them up to be sure they equal the correct total, your intended price.

Seller Concessions

A seller concession is when a seller provides the money for closing costs. For example, in your offer you ask the seller for a concession of 3 percent of the purchase price of the home. That additional money, $3,000 for each $100,000 of the price, is returned to you by the seller at the closing for your use in paying closing costs.

Tips and Traps

If your seller has agreed to a concession, do not increase the loan amount by the amount of the concession and then receive it back from the seller, as this is considered lender fraud and is illegal. For example, if the purchase price is $100,000 and the seller has agreed to a concession of $3,000, you don't raise the purchase price to $103,000.

Deciding whether to ask for a seller concession depends on local custom and practice. Just remember—whatever you borrow, you have to repay, along with interest.

The Closing

The next portion of the offer deals with the closing. Although the closing happens at the end of this whole process, it appears early in the offer because the seller wants to know two things before he considers everything else—how much he is receiving for his home and when he will get it. This part of the contract either stipulates that the closing will be held within a certain number of days after you and the seller have a signed contract, or states a specific date for the closing. Either way is fine—it's just a matter of choice for you and the seller.

This part of the offer might also include information on exactly when you will take possession of the property and when the *deed* will be *recorded*. For example, the contract might say that the buyer will take possession at "noon on the day of the closing," or "midnight on July 1," and you're closing on June 30. This is done to specify exactly when the title changes hands. Basically, you can't receive the keys or move in until you're actually on title, which means the deed is recorded, unless you have made special arrangements through your agent to get early access to the house from the buyer. This is something I strongly recommend against doing because if anything goes wrong and the deed doesn't record, you could be liable to the seller.

def•i•ni•tion

The **deed** is the document that legally transfers title to the property from the seller to the buyer.

Recorded means that the local county recorder has placed the deed and related documents transferring legal title to you on record in the county's records. This is called being "on title" or "on record." You'll know for certain that you're on title when the recorder's office notifies your escrow company or closing attorney. After the title is recorded, depending on your state, the escrow company or closing attorney either calls your agent or you'll receive your deed by mail. In these cases, the funds have already been transferred and you take possession even though the recordation may be a day or two later.

Some forms provide the option of taking possession a specific number of days after closing. This is when you and the seller agree, for whatever reason, that he can have this extra amount of time to move out after you have received the title. However, some forms do not specify recordation; it varies from state to state. Your Realtor will guide you.

Loan

The loan section of the offer specifies the amount of your financing and frequently includes a description of the type of loan you plan to use, including the maximum interest rate and number of points you're planning to pay, if any. This section also includes other loan particulars, including the term and a description of any loan contingencies. A loan contingency means that if you are unable to obtain a specified acceptable loan to use in the purchase of the home within a specific period of time, you are free to cancel the contract without penalty. If your loan terms have changed between the time your offer was made and the time you receive a loan, you still have the option of going forward with the new loan if you wish to do so.

Many contract forms also have a section for what is referred to as "additional financing" or "secondary financing" terms. This covers whether your financing also includes a home equity line of credit (HELOC), partial financing from the seller of the home, or assumption of an existing loan that the seller already has on the home.

This section also includes a place for cash transactions and a section where you can mention that there are no loan contingencies. Since the majority of purchases include a loan contingency, having a box on the offer form to cover all cash deals where no loan contingency exists can eliminate any possible confusion.

Inspections

The section of the offer that refers to inspections covers your right to have the property inspected as you feel necessary before you complete the purchase. However, a typical form mentions many inspections, which may be more than you will arrange. For example, some cities and counties require health and safety inspections to be performed, such as for smoke detectors or septic tanks. In other areas, the local municipality requires the seller to have a *resale inspection*, which is an inspection that covers both health and safety issues, and ensures that any prior work done by the seller is permitted and up to code.

In areas of the country where there is an increased risk of earthquakes, special safety inspections are required to ensure that gas

def•i•ni•tion

A **resale inspection,** where required by the municipality, is to ensure that health and safety codes have been adhered to in the home. It also allows the buyer to verify that any work done by the seller was completed with permits or is up to code and therefore not a violation of local law. As with other disclosures, the results of this inspection must be provided to you.

water heaters are metal-strapped to the wall, to prevent them from toppling in an earthquake and starting a fire. In some cases, these safety inspections are included in the resale inspections as a part of the overall inspection.

In most cases, inspections such as pest, contractor, mold, structural, and others relating to the condition of the home are paid for by the buyer. However, most legally mandated inspections, such as a resale inspection, are paid for by the seller.

Mediation/Arbitration

As the cost and time involved in litigation continue to grow, more and more disputes are resolved through other means of dispute resolution. The two most common of these are mediation and arbitration, which are defined and discussed later in this chapter.

Tips and Traps _____

The American Arbitration Association is an excellent source of information and assistance on both mediation and arbitration. Visit their website at www.adr.org/arb_med.

The sections in the offer regarding mediation and arbitration usually require that both you and the seller specifically agree to their inclusion in the final contract terms. There are usually places next to these clauses for each of you to initial as acceptances or refusals to have them as part of the contract. In some contracts, they are automatically accepted and you do not have the option of opting out.

Rent Back

In some instances, it is not convenient for the seller to move out on the date when you decide to close. However, at that point, the seller no longer owns the home—you do. If you and the seller agree, part of the offer can allow the seller to "rent back" the property from you. This is different than the seller taking an extra day or two to move out. It is a rental period and is covered in the contract. A subsequent lease for the rent back is created and agreed to.

Warning! _____

If you agree to a rent back with the seller, make sure your possessions, wherever they are, are covered by your insurance policy during the rental period. If not, get a rider for this from your insurance broker.

Usually the rent back is mentioned in the purchase contract, but the specific terms are spelled out in a separate lease between both parties. The separate lease agreement defines the term, the amount of rent to be paid, and any security deposit that the seller must provide to you for the duration of the rent back. Most commonly, the rent usually is whatever the buyer's daily PITI would be for the time the rent back covers. PITI is the buyer's daily **P**rincipal, **I**nterest, **T**axes, and **I**nsurance.

Disclosures

Many purchase offer forms include a place to discuss all disclosure information that the seller must provide to you on the condition of the home. This may include federally mandated disclosures, such as the Lead Paint Disclosure, or state-mandated disclosures, such as California's Natural Hazard Zone Disclosure. For more discussion of disclosures, check Chapter 12, where this is discussed in more detail.

Contract Contingencies

Another important part of the offer is the contingencies section. Contingencies are terms inserted into the offer, usually by the buyer, that say you are making a specific offer to the seller, but your offer is subject to you being satisfied with the overall transaction and the condition of the property. Occasionally, the seller may demand contingencies, but these occur far less frequently. The most common contingencies are loan, inspection, and appraisal, but there are also others, such as spousal approval and release.

There's no limit to how many contingencies you can have in one offer. However, there is a stipulated period of time for the contingency to be satisfied and released by whoever is requesting it. When a contingency is released, it means that you have done whatever the contingency calls for and no longer need it as a way of getting out of the contract. For example, let's say you had an inspection contingency in the contract, and you have completed all the inspections on the home that you wanted, reviewed the inspection reports, and are satisfied on the condition of the home. Now, in writing, you release that contingency. You are telling the seller that this is no longer a contingency for the transaction.

If you, as the buyer, fail to release any of the contingencies within the agreed-upon time, you are said to be "out-of-contract." The contract terms require that the seller notify you that you are out-of-contract and provide you with an additional one or two days to release the contingency. If you don't release the contingency by then, the seller can cancel the contract. If the contract is cancelled, the seller cannot keep the earnest money, nor can he sue you for damages.

In some locations, contract forms require that you notify the seller of any issues his inspections turn up by the deadline for contingency release. Failure to do so can constitute waiver of this contingency, just as if the buyer had formally released it. Check with your Realtor on the method used in your area, as contingencies and their releases can be a major issue in a contract.

Loan Contingency

One of the most common contingencies is the loan contingency, which stipulates the amount of time you are permitted to obtain financing. If you cannot obtain the loan within that period of time, you have the option of canceling the contract without risking your good-faith deposit. You can even include in the contingency a maximum interest rate and number of points that you will accept on the loan.

As mortgage lending has become more stringent, more buyers are also including a clause that requires that the loan actually be funded before they have to release it. This is due to the fact that some buyers are receiving commitments from banks and then releasing the loan contingency only to find out that, for some reason, the banks are refusing to move forward and fund the loan. The buyer would now be legally bound to proceed with the purchase even after finding out he has no loan. This could subject him to breach-of-contract damages in a lawsuit by the seller.

Many lenders are taking an additional step before funding, which sometimes causes the lender to back out of the loan. Even though the lender may have already had an appraisal done, they sometimes order an "audit" or "review" appraisal at the last second by a different appraiser, to be certain of the value of the property before they fund the loan. If this final appraisal comes in too low, they frequently refuse to fund, often killing the deal.

Inspection Contingency

An inspection contingency provides a time period—ranging from a few days to almost a month—during which you can have any number and type of inspections done on the home to be certain that it has nothing materially defective. If inspection reports come back with defects, this contingency provides you the opportunity to either back out of the contract with no risk or request that the seller either remedy the problem or reduce the agreed-upon selling price accordingly.

Appraisal Contingency

Your financing depends on the results of your appraisal. As a result, you should have an appraisal contingency. Let's say you're offering $400,000, 80 percent of which will be financed by a bank. If you had only inspection and loan contingencies, you might release them during the due diligence period and then find out that the home failed to appraise to the agreed price of $400,000. You could be left to purchase a home for more that it's currently worth, or walk away and risk being sued for breach of contract. An appraisal contingency prevents this because it allows you to cancel the contract if the home fails to appraise at the agreed price.

Appraisals play a huge part in deals not working out. If an appraisal comes in low, you are going to have a difficult time with your financing and will probably be required to come up with more of a down payment if you still wish to move forward.

Spousal Approval Contingency

A spousal approval contingency makes an offer contingent on the spouse who has yet to view the property. For example, let's say you are buying a home in Texas and you live in New York. You fly out to see a home without your spouse and fall in love with it. You decide to put in an offer on the house, but you're worried that your spouse might not like it. With a spousal approval contingency, if your spouse doesn't like it when he or she does see it, you can cancel the contract.

Permit Satisfaction Contingency

Let's say you want to buy a home that you plan to remodel or add to the property after taking title. For this type of purchase, you can add a permit satisfaction contingency, which allows you time to go before the relevant authorities—such as a town or zoning board—and make sure you'll receive approval for these changes. This process will add time to the whole contract process. However, without their approval, you have the right to cancel the contract, since you won't be allowed to do the planned work on the home.

Release Contingency

If you own a home that you need to sell before you can buy a new one, you use the contingent-release contingency. This is released either when you sell your own home or when the seller of the home you want to buy receives another offer from someone who does not have this contingency. If that happens, the seller will give you notice—it depends on your state, but it could be three days or some other period you've agreed to in the contract to release the contingency, or you'll be out-of-contract and no longer the buyer. That three-day period is negotiable at the time the contingency is originally agreed to.

Insurance Contingency

In some instances, you may add a contingency that allows you to cancel if you cannot obtain homeowner's insurance. This is not a general rule, but arises only in unusual circumstances. It is usually an issue only if obtaining insurance in an area is difficult, as was briefly the case after California's Loma Prieta earthquake in the 1990s, and also in some areas after a series of major wildfires devastated the areas and their insurance companies.

Extension Contingency

If you are having difficulty meeting your contingency release date through no fault of your own, you could ask the seller for an extension. For example, let's say a home inspection has revealed questions about the foundation, and the inspector recommends another inspection by a structural engineer. The engineer's inspection can't take place for another week, and then there's an additional two days' wait for the engineer to write and send you his report. This wait now pushes you over the contingency period date.

Your agent will send an extension request, signed by you, to the seller's agent to extend this date. If the seller agrees, you have extra time. If the seller doesn't agree, you are considered out-of-contract and at the mercy of the seller as to whether he'll cancel the contract. What action the seller takes may depend on how hot the market is. Contingency extensions are not to be used frivolously; they should be requested only when conditions beyond your control force you to request an extension.

Fixtures: What Stays and What Goes

Another part of the offer lists what fixtures you want to keep that the seller might otherwise take with him. A fixture is something in a home that is firmly affixed to the structure and considered a part of the structure, such as faucets, shower heads, and certain lighting fixtures. The general rule is that anything considered a fixture stays when the owner leaves, unless otherwise stated beforehand. For example, the seller may own a magnificent antique, and expensive, bathroom faucet that he is taking. You have taken a liking to it and want it, but the final decision comes down to whether the seller or his agent told you he was taking it.

If you just won't be able to live without some item in the house, make sure you specifically mention it in the offer. Once the seller accepts your offer, he's legally bound to let it remain with the house when you become the owner.

If there was a mention in the listing that the seller was taking the faucet, it's hers. If there was no mention, the seller may have to part with the fixture. Similar situations have been known to arise with sconces, custom-sculpted wash basins, and custom-cast spigots.

When it comes to appliances, a built-in dishwasher, trash compactor, and refrigerator with wood paneling to match the cabinets are clearly meant to stay with the house. The same applies to garbage disposals, kitchen or bath exhaust fans, cooktops, an instant hot faucet, and various built-in small appliances such as ice crushers, blenders, and fold-out toasters.

However, a free-standing dishwasher, the washer and dryer, a standard refrigerator, and a deep-freezer aren't built in, but they don't move easily, either—so who do they go with? In most cases, the seller leaves these appliances behind, but occasionally, the seller may want one. This part of the contract outlines what appliances you want to keep. It doesn't mean the seller will agree, but it doesn't hurt to ask. The more clearly you detail your wishes, the less room there is for misunderstanding in such a situation. No matter what exactly you want to stay with the house, spell it out. You can simply state "all appliances" or itemize them if you feel more comfortable. If unsure, ask your agent for guidance.

Window Treatments

Do you like the custom draperies and their hangings? Since they're custom for the home, there is probably no reason for the seller to take them along when he leaves, but you should still spell it out in the offer if you want some or all of the window treatments.

"Special" Requests

While buying a home and agreeing on terms of a purchase contract are pretty standard, occasionally you will have special requests. The number of possible requests is limited only by your imagination when crafting the offer. These special requests can include a home warranty, closing costs, early access to the home, and seller financing, which was covered in Chapter 7.

Home Warranty

One of the most common buyer requests is asking the seller to pay for a home warranty at closing. Usually good for an initial period of a year, a home warranty is like an insurance policy on the home systems—plumbing, heating, and electrical.

Since service calls can run hundreds of dollars, this can save you in the long run. If your seller won't agree to a warranty, ask your agent if he will foot the bill. You may be surprised that often the answer is yes because the agent will likely show goodwill or provide this as a closing present to you. Also, it removes a minor item from possibly becoming a sticking point in moving forward to closing.

Tips and Traps

If you do not obtain a home warranty before you move in, many warranty companies will be more than happy to sell you one. These generally have the same coverage and terms as the one you would buy when purchasing an appliance.

These are not expensive, but they are worth their weight in gold. Usually costing between $200 and $400, it's money well invested. There are a number of them in various parts of the country, some better than others, so check with your Realtor for advice on who should underwrite the warranty.

Closing Costs

Buyers also commonly ask sellers to pay some or all of the closing costs. Closing costs can run into thousands of dollars, so this is a substantial request that the seller may not eagerly receive. However, if you offered him the price he requested, it isn't an unreasonable request. In fact, even if your offer was a little below the asking price, it may not be unreasonable if the home's been on the market for a long time, or if your offer is close to the asking price. With FHA loans, the seller commonly is requested to pay an amount equal to 3 or 4 percent of the purchase price toward buyers' closing costs.

Early Access

Another common request in an offer is for the buyer to ask to move in before closing if the house is already vacant, or to store some possessions in the garage or in the house before closing. You may also want to ask the seller if you can start painting or remodeling before the papers are even signed at the closing. These are somewhat touchy requests. If it appears the transaction will close on time as planned, there is nothing wrong with making the requests. However, a good agent—especially the seller's agent—will usually frown upon these requests, because if something crops up and you don't close, either you are living in their house already or you have painted or remodeled and those changes will need to be repaired.

Signatures

An unsigned offer is not a valid offer, so there is a place for you to sign and date the offer. There's another place for the seller to sign and date it if it's accepted. If the seller rejects your offer, she'll note that it's rejected and send it back to you. If she's rejecting it because of one or two items, however, she'll probably counter your offer by noting that on the contract and attaching the counteroffer to your original offer. There are even occasional instances when the seller will not even respond to your offer and it goes unanswered at its expiration date shown in the offer.

This counteroffer is sent back to you for your response. No matter what items she is countering on, the balance of your offer will remain as it was originally written. If you agree to the counteroffer, it will become part of the original contract.

Expiration of Your Offer

When you submit your offer, put a time limit on it. You don't want to leave it open-ended, because that would allow the seller too much time to try to use it to entice other potential buyers to make an offer. It carries the risk that another buyer might make a better offer than yours, and your chances to buy this home would be gone. It's recommended that the offer expiration be no longer than 24 hours after it's presented, but some buyers go to a maximum of 72 hours.

However, if the seller's agent has informed you through your agent that the seller is either away for a few days or just unable to receive it for a few days, you may want to allow the seller extra time. Let your agent guide you on this.

In addition to these basic parts of an offer, any number of other items can be included. It all depends on your particular purchase.

Counteroffers

If your offer is accepted exactly as you presented it, your offer becomes a "real estate purchase contract" and you and the seller proceed to closing. But the offer isn't always accepted the first time it's presented. Most likely, you submit your first offer and the seller responds with another offer, called a counteroffer. In this case, you do not have a contract just yet. In contract law, a contract exists only when you and the seller have agreed to everything in the offer.

For example, let's say that the seller receives your offer and agrees to the price you've offered and everything else, except the closing date. Legally, he has rejected your offer. He then provides a new offer to you with a new closing date. If you accept his counteroffer, you have a contract. If not, you may respond again with your counteroffer, and so the process goes until either you reach an agreement on a contract or one of you finally says that you're not going any further and the proposed transaction is dead.

There's no rule to how many times an offer can be changed or by how much. One line can change or the entire thing can change. Keep in mind, however, that while all real estate transactions must be in writing, agents can negotiate the offer back and forth over the phone or in person until you reach agreement. It must then be put in writing.

Potential Contract Problems

Not all contract negotiations go smoothly. Problems can crop up, and being prepared can help minimize the stress of sorting them out. Nobody wants to go to court to settle their differences, but sometimes it happens. How these problems are to be solved, if necessary, is outlined and agreed to in the offer. Here are some options that will help solve possible problems between you and the seller and reduce the risk of litigation.

Tips and Traps _____

If you don't already know an attorney to handle possible litigation, you can get a free referral from your local or state bar association. Alternatively, if cost is an issue, check with your local Legal Aid. This is an organization set up to give basic free legal advice to those unable to pay for it.

Liquidated Damages

Liquidated damages are a commonly used device by both parties in purchase contracts to avoid potential litigation between the buyer and seller. Normally, if you or the seller breaches a contract and no agreement to remedy the situation is possible, the damaged party sues for damages. The trouble with this is that it is very time-consuming and costly to both parties, and is often unnecessary.

Instead, you and the seller can agree to have your liability for breach-of-contract limited to the amount of the deposit you have put down toward the purchase (the earnest money). In California, for instance, liquidated damages are limited to 3 percent of the purchase price unless the parties to the contract agree on another figure.

Mediation

If a problem arises as you are going through the process to purchase the house, mediation and arbitration are also commonly used to avoid the extreme costs of going through a lawsuit while obtaining a settlement of issues agreeable to both parties. This isn't written in the contract, but in some states, it's the law to proceed through these methods first before going to court.

During mediation, a professional mediator, who is agreed to by both sides, hears the dispute, weighs the strength of the conflicting claims, and then renders a decision. Usually, the decision is a payment from one party to the other. There is no specific time limit to a mediation hearing, but they usually last only a week at most, unlike the weeks, months, or years that a lawsuit may last.

Mediation is not binding to either party, and if after a decision is rendered one of the parties is not satisfied, that party may proceed to either arbitration or full-scale litigation, if necessary. Once an award had been made by the mediator and agreed to by both parties, failure to make the payment is actionable by lawsuit.

Arbitration

Arbitration is similar to mediation, but it is binding. This means that, with very few exceptions, it is not possible to litigate an issue that has been decided through arbitration. An arbitrator is selected by both parties, usually from a list of local arbitrators, who hears the claims and evidence of both parties. After weighing the information and strength of the claims, she renders a decision that is usually monetary in form.

Arbitration usually takes a bit more time than mediation but is less time-consuming and less costly than litigation. If one or both parties did not originally agree to arbitration as a dispute-resolution method in the contract, they can still, at such later date as they choose and agree, avail themselves of the process. Once a decision has been rendered through arbitration and an award made, failure to pay that award can be litigated.

An Example

For example, let's say you buy a home in a nice area of town. It has the number of bedrooms and baths you wanted, and a spacious backyard bordered by lush flower-beds and fruit trees. It has open space on two of three sides of the yard. The junior high school is located three blocks away from your backyard, but the yard size and open space provide a nice buffer from the hustle and bustle of kids going to and from school.

What you weren't told, however, was that kids use your open space to cut across and save time to and from school. Your cherished flower beds and vegetables have been destroyed. Because the seller failed to mention this, you take the issue to mediation. You want the seller to pay for the cost of an 8-foot fence along the perimeter of your rear yard, a shielding hedge, and an irrigation system. The cost for this is estimated at $2,500 to $5,000.

The mediator reviews and analyzes both parties' information and decides that the damage is serious enough to rule in your favor. However, she feels that a 6-foot fence is sufficient to handle the problem and awards you $2,200. The seller can accept the decision and pay you $2,200, reject it and agree to arbitration, or force you to sue for damages. Chances are, given the relatively low award amount, he will likely just pay, and the issue then is resolved. This is especially likely to be the case if he is liable for only part of the award, with the balance coming from his Realtor.

The issues we've discussed in this chapter certainly do not cover every possible eventuality, nor can we attempt to do so. Disagreements are a common occurrence in any contract negotiations, so it's important to know how to rectify potential situations before things get out of hand. It might sound repetitive, but work closely with your Realtor in crafting your offer and working through the responses you may receive from the seller.

Sample Purchase Contract

Now that you know all the parts of an offer and how you can handle any potential problems that arise, check out Appendix E, where you can see an actual real estate purchase contract. Keep in mind that the purchase contract you use might be different where you are located, or depending on your particular purchase.

The Least You Need to Know

- ◆ Everything in a contract is up for negotiation.

- ◆ Negotiations don't need to last forever; decide what your walking-away point is and then stick to it.

- ◆ Go with your gut instinct—if something doesn't seem right about a negotiation, it probably isn't.

- ◆ Take advantage of your support systems—such as mediation and arbitration—that are there to help you work through problems with sellers.

Chapter 14

Home Inspections

In This Chapter

- Finding a home inspector
- Inspecting the home for problems
- Pest inspections—looking for little buggers
- Testing the house for mold
- Testing the home for release of radon
- Understanding inspection results

Would you buy a car without taking it for a test run? Would you buy an expensive pair of Jimmy Choo shoes without trying them on first? Most likely, you would try out any major purchase before investing the money. Although you can't live in the home before buying it (although it is possible to do a rent-to-own arrangement in which you buy a home you have rented for some time first), you can do the next best thing—have the home inspected. Home inspections are a vital part of buying a home. This is not only for older homes, but also for brand-new ones, as builders do make mistakes or forget things. You've seen the inside of your home when you visited, but a home inspection tells you about the stuff you didn't see or notice—cracks, leaks, potential hazards—so you can make an informed decision about buying that home.

Unless your state requires specific additional inspections, the only inspections you really should have done on your potential home are a complete home inspection and a pest, or termite, inspection. Each one looks for different problems in the home.

A home inspection is a comprehensive inspection that covers every part of the home, from the roof to the foundation. A pest inspector checks for active, past, or potential infestations of termites, wood-boring beetles, and dry rot. Insects and rodents can cause significant damage to your home, so a pest inspection is extremely important. You don't want to move in only to find out that a family of termites has also moved in and eaten away a large part of your home's structure.

After both of these inspections have been completed, you should have a fairly good idea of the overall condition of the home. Ideally, you want a report free and clear of any problems, but some issues may require even more specialized inspections to put your mind at ease.

This chapter focuses on the details of each inspection, how to read the inspection reports that you get back, and, most important, how you can use the results of these reports to your advantage when it comes to renegotiating your offer.

Finding an Inspector

Your real estate agent most likely has an extensive list of different inspectors that she has used often and knows to be reliable. She can make the necessary appointments for the inspections, get price quotes, and attend the inspections.

Once you have an inspector(s) in mind, the Department of Housing and Urban Development (HUD) suggests that you ask him the following questions:

- **What does your inspection cover?** The inspection must meet all applicable requirements in your state and comply with a well-recognized standard of practice and code of ethics. You should be able to request and see a copy of these requirements ahead of time and ask any questions. If you want to make sure that certain areas are inspected, be sure to identify them up front.

- **How long have you been practicing in the home inspection profession, and how many inspections have you completed?** The inspector should be able to share his professional history with you and provide you with a few references.

- **Are you specifically experienced in residential inspection?** Related experience is helpful but is no substitute for training and experience in home inspection.

◆ **Do you offer to do repairs or improvements based on the inspection?** Some inspector associations and state regulations allow the inspector to perform repair work on problems uncovered in the inspection. Other associations and regulations strictly forbid this as a conflict of interest.

◆ **How long will the inspection take?** The average on-site inspection time for a single inspector is two to three hours for a typical single-family house, although it can be significantly longer; anything significantly less may not be enough time to perform a thorough inspection. Additional inspectors may be brought in for very large properties and buildings.

◆ **What type of inspection report do you provide, and how long will it take to receive the report?** Ask to see samples, and determine whether you can understand the inspector's reporting style and whether the time parameters fulfill your needs. Most inspectors provide their full report within 24 hours of the inspection.

◆ **Do you maintain membership in a professional home inspector association?** There are many state and national associations for home inspectors. Request to see his membership ID, and perform whatever due diligence you deem appropriate.

◆ **Do you participate in continuing education programs to keep your expertise up-to-date?** One can never know it all, and the inspector's commitment to continuing education is a good measure of his professionalism and service to the consumer. This is especially important when the home is much older or includes unique elements requiring additional or updated training.

> **Quotes and Facts**
>
> The National Association of Home Inspectors, Inc. (NAHI), was established in 1987 as a nonprofit association to promote and develop certified and licensed home inspectors in the professional home inspection industry. Visit their website at www.nahi.org to search for a home inspector.

Attending Your Inspections

You don't have to be at the inspections (your Realtor will be there and can handle it for you, if necessary), but it's strongly recommended that you go and walk through with the inspector. An inspector should not refuse to allow you to come along—this is a major red flag. The inspector can then explain exactly what he has found and how severe the problem really is, and you can ask follow-up questions.

Also, to avoid liability, inspectors may comment on an issue and make it sound more severe in the written report than it really is. They'll tell you that it may not be as bad as the written explanation makes it sound, pointing out exactly what the issue is and its likely remedy.

Costs

According to HUD, the typical range of inspection costs is $300 to $500, but this depends on the size of the home and the scope of the inspection. In some regions, basic inspections can cost several thousand dollars and more if you want or need a specialized inspection. These fees are usually paid at the time of inspection, at least in part because the inspector might not get paid at all if he waited until closing and no closing took place.

It's worth the money—after all, this isn't a suit you can return to the store if there's a problem. Whether you proceed to closing or cancel a deal due to a negative report, consider it cheap insurance. Better to spend a few hundred, or thousand, dollars on an inspection and not buy the home, than not to invest in inspections and find yourself owning a home that already needs a major repair or two. Also, unless your agent is picking your inspector for you, don't make your choice based solely on cost. Some inspectors charge an arm and a leg and aren't worth it, while others are less expensive and fabulous. This is one time to definitely follow your Realtor's recommendation.

Home Inspections

Home inspections cover the entire structure, from roof to foundation. The inspector will check that all construction was done correctly and according to code, even on resales. He will also carefully examine all the operating systems of the home— electrical and plumbing and heating, ventilating, and air-conditioning, sometimes referred to as HVAC. Basic home inspection costs vary based on the home's size—the bigger the home, the more it costs to inspect.

During the course of an inspection, the inspector will check all mechanicals, including flicking on light switches and checking sockets to be certain they work and are grounded properly. He'll also carefully examine the electrical panel and any subpanels that exist, as they are the central controls for any given circuit in the home.

During a plumbing inspection, he'll examine piping and any appliances or receptacles where water flows, including the washer, dishwasher, toilets, and sinks, as well as related fixtures. He'll even run the appliances to ensure that they work properly.

Similarly, he'll check out the heating and air-conditioning systems. This is particularly important with the heating system because a malfunctioning furnace can produce carbon monoxide gas, which, even in small quantities, is lethal. Outside your home, he will examine such things as external drainage from your water heater, clothes dryer external venting, all drainage piping leading away from your home, and sidewalks and driveway pavement, to be sure there are no dangerous cracks or uneven surfaces that could cause falls.

Roof, Chimney, and Fireplace

A roof inspection is not necessarily when your inspector climbs to the top of the house and pulls the roof apart to see how old it is and how much time it has left, but he usually will "walk" the roof or at least climb up to where he can look at it. After all, do you really want to buy a home where the inspector has torn the roof apart? Nah. The inspectors have special procedures and equipment—including infrared equipment— that tell them about the roof, including hot spots that show temperature differences. These temperature differences can be a sign of potential problems with the roof that will need to be repaired later—a decision that might factor into your purchase decision.

All chimneys—brick, concrete, stone, and so on—are visibly inspected and their conditions evaluated. The inspector will note any cracking around or in the chimney or its foundation, and will note if any pieces are broken and need to be replaced. He will also tell you if the chimney is pulling away from the house and needs to be secured better. If the chimney was already secured, the inspector will find out what the problem was before and what that might mean to you now.

Outbuildings

The inspector will also inspect the outbuildings on the property, although the cost will be a bit higher, as it takes more work and more time. Outbuildings include structures such as separate studios, guest cottages, gazebos, sheds, and detached garages.

Mold Inspections

Most species of mold are relatively harmless. In fact, some standard medicines, such as antibiotics, are made from mold. Unfortunately, a few types of mold are very harmful and can even be lethal when humans are exposed to them. Technically, molds produce chemicals called mycotoxins, which can cause illness in people who are particularly sensitive to them or who are exposed to them in large amounts or over a long period of time. The most common symptoms of mycotoxin exposure are runny nose, eye irritation, cough, congestion, and aggravation of asthma. *Stachybotrys chartarum*, otherwise known as black mold, has been the subject of many building-related illness investigations.

Signs of mold include standing water in the basement, water marks on walls, and musty smells—especially in bathrooms or other areas you use water. Remember, sellers or real estate agents are required to disclose information about any mold that has already happened in a house. If your state is not one of the required ones, you can ask for the information and the seller must tell you.

> **Warning!**
>
> Take mold very seriously. Homeowner's insurance policies now include a clause that excludes or limits payments for mold-related issues. While mold is a problem, in most instances, its growth can be prevented or stopped before it causes excessive damage.

If the inspector finds mold, he will gather samples and have them tested. If the results show that the mold is black, this is a serious issue. We recommend that you *not* buy a home that currently has a black mold issue. A regular mold problem can always be eradicated, but the decision will be yours about deciding whether to buy it. Some buyers just don't feel comfortable buying a home that has already had any sort of a mold problem.

Radon

Radon is a commonly occurring radioactive gas that results from the decay of radium or uranium. It is released into the atmosphere as the gas reaches Earth's surface. When a building is constructed, radon can accumulate in the building, particularly in basements and other enclosed areas. Radon is dangerous and is the second-leading cause of lung cancer in the United States, causing 21,000 lung cancer deaths annually, according to the Environmental Protection Agency (EPA).

The highest concentrations in the country are in Iowa and southeastern Pennsylvania. There is some radon-inhibiting construction possible, although the level of its efficacy varies with the home and amount of radon there.

Short- and long-term tests for the presence of radon are available. A short-term radon test lasts for just a few days and requires that the windows and doors of the home be closed, as well as any fans turned off. The kit is placed in the lowest regularly lived-in room and left there. After a few days, it's resealed and sent to a lab for analysis. The results are returned anywhere from a few days to a few weeks. During a long-term test, the test stays in the room for more than 90 days. Obviously, for the purpose of buying a home, you will use the short-term test.

The amount of radon in the air is measured in picoCuries per liter of air (pCi/L). The EPA estimates that 1 in 15 houses has a radon level of 4 pCi/L or more, which is considered high. There are ways to fix the problem—for example, a venting system can be installed—but you should discuss the situation with a radon professional. Each state has someone appointed by the EPA who specializes in radon issues; you can find yours at www.epa.gov/iaq/whereyoulive.html.

Lead Paint

Lead-based paint has been illegal in the United States in housing since 1978. So if you buy a home built since then, you don't have to worry about it. Lead paint is common in homes older than that, however. The danger is that small children or pets may eat chips of the dried paint and get lead poisoning, which, aside from being potentially lethal over a long period of time, can lead to permanent brain damage. Your disclosures from a seller must include a federal lead paint disclosure document on whether the seller knows of the presence of lead in the home, or if there is a possibility that lead paint is present because of the age of the home.

Your sales contract must include time (up to 10 days) for you to check for lead hazards. Home buyers aren't required by law to test for lead—but you must be given the opportunity to do so. You may be concerned about lead in the home, especially if any young children will be living in the home, or if you are about to remodel, renovate, or repaint your home after you move in.

The lead-based paint inspection is a surface inspection of all painted surfaces, including the outside and inside of the home. "Painted surfaces" include all surfaces coated with paint, shellac, varnish, stain, coating, or even paint covered by wallpaper. A risk assessment is an on-site investigation to determine the presence, type, severity, and location of lead-based paint hazards.

A certified inspector or certified risk assessor should perform the testing. If results show lead in the home, the inspectors might suggest that you repair or remove the lead from the areas, or you might have to replace entire windows or doors. Obviously, the latter may seem a bit extreme, but it may be more effective and not much more costly. Consult a good contractor as to what the best remedy is.

Tips and Traps

You can find out more information about testing for and dealing with lead paint in a house by calling the National Lead Information clearinghouse, at 1-800-424-LEAD (1-800-424-5323)

Asbestos

Asbestos is a fireproof mineral that was used extensively in fireproofing and insulation of homes well into the 1960s. According to the Consumer Product Safety Commission (www.cpsc.gov), asbestos has also been found in the following:

◆ Steam pipes, boilers, and furnace ducts insulated with an asbestos blanket or asbestos paper tape

◆ Resilient floor tiles (vinyl asbestos, asphalt, and rubber), the backing on vinyl sheet flooring, and adhesives used for installing floor tile

◆ Cement sheet, millboard paper used as insulation around furnaces and wood-burning stoves

◆ Door gaskets in furnaces, wood stoves, and coal stoves

◆ Soundproofing or decorative material sprayed on walls and ceilings

◆ Patching and joint compounds for walls and ceilings, and textured paints

◆ Asbestos cement roofing, shingles, and siding

Asbestos is not used much anymore. If it is disturbed and particles get into the air, it can cause a nearly incurable form of lung cancer, mesothelioma. Newer homes use other, safer forms of insulation. If you suspect asbestos in your home, make sure that the inspection includes a complete visual examination and the careful collection and lab analysis of samples. If asbestos is present, the inspector should provide a written evaluation describing its location and extent of damage, and give recommendations for correction or prevention.

Warning! _____

According to the U.S. Consumer Product Safety Commission, do not dust, sweep, or vacuum debris that may contain asbestos. These steps will disturb tiny asbestos fibers and may release them into the air. Remove dust by wet mopping or with a special HEPA vacuum cleaner used by trained asbestos contractors. Asbestos should be removed only by a professional.

Indoor Air Quality

Indoor air quality involves the existence of any number of air pollutants in indoor air, and ways of alleviating these pollutants. Information is available from the EPA on its website, www.epa.gov. Indoor pollutants can include cigarette or cigar smoke, fumes from natural gas or heating oil, paint, and solvents or household chemicals, to name a few. How "bad" the indoor air quality gets depends on how many of these pollutants exist in your home and in what amounts, balanced against what filtering or ventilation systems are employed to limit their effects.

Again, this isn't required by law, but if you are concerned about the air quality or if you are sensitive to certain chemicals, you may want to have a qualified inspector come to the home. The home may be improved by adding ventilation systems, but these will add to the cost of your home.

Pest Inspections

Many home inspectors can actually perform both the pest inspections and the actual home inspections. In addition, if they find an active pest infestation, most are licensed to eradicate the infestation. Pest inspectors are an exception to the general rule that your inspector shouldn't be doing the repairs to avoid conflict of interest, since they may also be licensed to apply insecticides. The inspectors examine all accessible areas of the home and look for signs of an active pest infestation or conditions that could lead to one at a later time. They also report if they find inactive infestations.

Wood-Destroying Insects

Several insects can destroy the wood in your home, depending on where you live. Termites, carpenter ants, and powderpost beetles are the most common. Termites, both the flying and crawling kind, can get into your floors, foundation, and walls, and literally eat away your structure.

The infestation signs the inspector looks for vary with the type of pest involved. According to Orkin Pest Control, there are several signs that there may be a termite infestation in the home:

> ### Quotes and Facts
> Termites cause more than $5 billion in damage every year in the United States.

- ◆ The swarm present inside the home or in the soil outside
- ◆ Cracked or bubbling paint or frass (termite droppings)
- ◆ Wood that sounds hollow when tapped
- ◆ Mud tubes on exterior walls, wooden beams, or in crawlspaces
- ◆ Discarded wings from swarmers

Wood-boring beetles also chew through wood and can come into the home on the lumber or even the flooring when the home is being built or remodeled. What kind of damage has been done depends on the type of wood that's been infested, how much moisture has been involved, and the local climate. Many types of beetles can cause damage in a home, and the pest inspection report will outline exactly what the home may have.

Rodents

Any indication of rodents is also reported. Aside from being an unpleasant thing to think about, rats and mice carry disease that is dangerous to you, your family, and your pets. There are usually two or three signs of rodent infestation in a home. There will usually be frequent evidence of droppings wherever they have been. Also, you may notice an unpleasant odor, caused by either an excess of droppings or by one or more rodents that have died in the home and begun to decay. Another sign of rodent activity is chewed wood or wiring. The latter presents another danger to you. This is because when a rodent chews away the insulation on electric wire, it can leave exposed wiring in contact with wood or other flammable material and can cause a fire.

Dry Rot

Dry rot, sometimes referred to as fungus damage, is contrary to what its name suggests. Dry rot is caused by moisture that comes in contact with wood. The constant moisture aids in the growth of a wood-ingesting fungus that causes the wood to get soft and rot away. This is evident as a soft-feeling or "mushy" area of wood.

The most common causes of the moisture are leaks from plumbing, toilets, roofs, or gutter flashing along the edge of a roof. Sometimes it can also come from condensation on single-pane windows that allow moisture to constantly come in contact with window frames and sills.

Dry rot can be a serious matter because, left unremedied, it can destroy large wood sections of a home just as severely as termites or beetles. This can even be quite dangerous in the case of wood decks. If dry rot ruins the supporting members, they can collapse under even the slightest amount of weight. If anyone is on them when this occurs, serious injury or death can occur.

Future Infestations

An inspector will also point out any evidence of potential future infestations. For example, two possibilities that may cause potential problems later are earth-to-wood contact and wood debris. Earth-to-wood contact occurs when some of the wood in the home's structure is in direct contact with the ground. Think of this as a highway for every underground pest in the neighborhood that will burrow directly from their nests into the wood of your home. Wood debris results when contractors, who performed work on the home before, failed to pick up their residue, such as wood scraps or sawdust. During construction, a floor gets placed across the foundation, obscuring the sawdust-scrap wood pile. This residue is a natural attraction for such problem insects as termites; once there, they usually don't stop at this appetizer—they go on to their main course, your home.

In some older homes, there's an additional problem. When some homes are first built, the builder must remove trees to make room for the home. All too often, the stumps are left behind. The builder, not wanting to spend the time and money necessary to remove the stumps, figured that they would die and, since they were beneath the floor of the home, wouldn't be of concern to anyone. However, although the stump died, it's still wood and an invitation to termites to come and feed just inches below the lower floor of your new home. Sometimes the termites never make the connection about how close they are to your home. If they do, however, you'll have major issues because you can't even see them doing the damage on your home. Usually this situation turns up only when an inspector crawls under the home and finds the infested stumps.

> **Warning!**
>
> A home inspector is usually a licensed general contractor, fully qualified to do any work on a structure. As a general rule, however, inspectors don't handle the work on whatever they discover, to avoid a conflict of interest.

Other Inspections

You may have as many different inspections on a property as you wish, within the allotted time stated in your contract. In some situations, a pest or home inspector may come across something beyond their level of expertise and will recommend that you retain another inspector who is an expert in that specific subject. Or you may want another specialized inspection even though there is no indication of a particular problem. That is your right. For example, there are specialized inspections for roofs and gutters, mold, electrical, plumbing, fireplace and chimney, structural, drainage, and soil analysis.

For example, let's say there is evidence of a water leak coming from the roof, but the attic wasn't damp during the inspection. You would be well advised to have a roof inspector check out the whole roof. Or maybe the home inspector found efflorescence under the subflooring, evidence of moisture that could lead to dry rot or mold. Efflorescence is a light-reflecting whitish surface substance that is frequently found in areas where there is moisture-caused mold. You could hire mold and drainage inspectors to look further into the situation and recommend what it would take to repair the situation. These recommendations can then be used as a basis for requests for seller repairs or a reduction in price, just as any other issue from inspections can.

No Access

If, during the inspection, the inspector is unable to access any part of a home for whatever reason, he may recommend a specialist who can access it. For example, if the inspector has concerns about the home's foundation, he'll likely recommend an inspection by a structural engineer who has special tools and equipment to determine whether there is a problem.

Tips and Traps

If you're checking a foundation or walls and need to drill holes to access a point in the home, ask the seller first. If the seller denies permission, you need to decide whether you want to buy the home with this uncertainty.

Homes with stucco exteriors are a common problem in California, especially for pest inspectors. Modern-day stucco is usually layered over a wood-and-wire frame, effectively hiding the wood framing from accessibility to the inspector's examination. The wood could be a banquet for termites or could be dry-rotted to the point of near collapse. The only way to detect this is to bore through the stucco surface to the wood underlayment and check for pest damage.

The Reports Are In

After the inspection, you will receive a written report within a few days. The home inspection will be a detailed room-by-room, feature-by-feature discussion of everything that was reviewed, along with photos. A pest or termite report will cover the entire house structure only as applies to the presence of some form of pest.

The inspection reports are your proof of the defects that are in the home you want to buy. The results of these inspection reports will help you decide whether to go forward with the purchase of the home, cancel your offer, or negotiate a better deal for the home.

Going Forward

Ideally, your inspection reports have resulted in no major defects that need repair, and you can move forward to closing. There may be only minor defects, and you can negotiate these with the seller (more on that later in the chapter). In other cases, your report may list extensive and costly repairs that need to be done. For example, let's say you've already offered $300,000, contingent on the inspections. The report states there are significant problems that need to be fixed, totaling $25,000. You like the home so much that you still want to move forward. What are your options?

- ◆ You can reduce your price offer to $275,000 so that you have the extra $25,000 for the repairs. This means you're back to negotiating over the purchase price. If you reach an agreement, the purchase proceeds, but if you don't, the sale falls through and you move on.

- ◆ You can have the seller repair the damage and show proof when it is completed, with permits and by a licensed contractor. However, the seller may be willing to repair only some, but not all, of the problems. Decide exactly what you must have and what you'll negotiate.

- ◆ You can ask for a seller credit of $25,000 at closing in lieu of making the repairs. Remember, where money is concerned, you and the seller have opposite goals. Your goal is to get the property for as little as possible,

Tips and Traps _____

If the seller refuses to reach an agreement with you, your inspection reports become additional disclosure that he must provide to future buyers. They almost certainly will refuse to pay his original asking price, given the nature of this new information, so it behooves him to try to reach an agreement with you.

Warning! _____

Make certain that you have proof of payment for any repairs that the seller makes. If the work is done but the seller has not paid for it, the contractor doing the work can place a mechanic's lien on the property, endangering your title and possible possession of it.

while the seller's is to sell it to you for as much money as possible. The seller may decide to offer you only a portion of the $25,000. You then need to decide whether you still want this house.

♦ You can buy the property as is and not ask for any compensation while you move forward. Speaking of "as is," remember that homes labeled as such mean that you get the home, problems and all. Inspections on these properties are good to find out exactly what you're dealing with.

Time Is of the Essence

If time is of the essence when buying a home, you may find that no matter how bad you'd like to have the seller remedy the problems, it may be best to agree to a reduction in price and finish the transaction without any delay. On the other hand, if time is not as important, you may decide that, even though your seller's tradesmen are an unknown entity, you'll agree to have the seller handle the problems with people he's familiar with, just providing you with proof that everything was done to code and with permits.

Get It in Writing

Whatever you and your seller agree to after the inspections are done should be in writing. Whether the seller agrees to a reduced price or he's fixing the problem at his expense, or he is crediting the money to you, it should all be in writing. Because none of this was in the original contract terms, it must be done as an amendment to the contract. This is usually done in a simple document signed by the buyer and seller that states the changes being made. When you fill in this document, be as specific as necessary, to be sure that your seller fully understands exactly what you are requesting of him. Your agent will likely draw up the document for you to sign, but have a thorough conversation with him about what you want it to say.

> **Tips and Traps**
>
> Be very specific when asking the seller to make any repairs. State exactly what you want done in clear, concise language so there is no confusion or disagreement. Rely on the experience of your agent to craft an appropriately worded request.

Saying No

Not all inspection reports end with good results. If you're not truly happy with the home and see more problems than positives, you can simply forget this home and resume your search. Consider the inspection reports carefully and ask your agent for advice.

Amendment to the contract.

In addition to this document, a document will probably stipulate that you are releasing the inspection contingency in exchange for whatever terms the seller has agreed to with you. This document, which follows, is called a Release of Contingency. In some areas of the country, the two documents are merged into a single document.

Release of contingency.

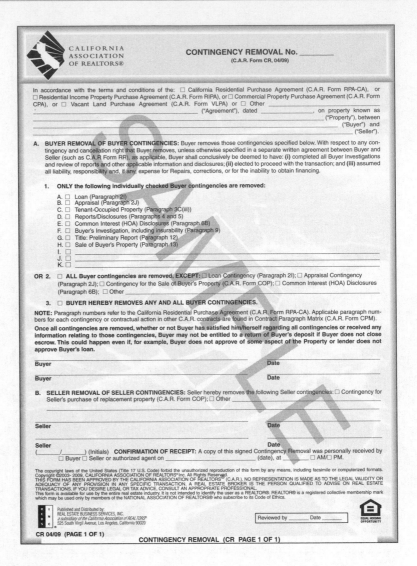

The Least You Need to Know

◆ Don't buy a home without doing one or more home inspections; you don't need costly surprises later.

◆ You can have many inspections done, but unless your state requires more, the most important are pest and home inspections.

◆ If there are problems with the home, decide if it's worth negotiating or if you need to find another home.

◆ If the seller agrees to either fix the problems with the home, provide you with a credit, or lower the purchase price, get it all in writing.

Part 5

Taking Possession and Moving In

Ah, the sweetest part of the meal: you're going to own your home! In this part, we illustrate how closing works, talk about closing costs, and explain the different types of insurance you should secure to protect yourself from major catastrophes.

We also provide guidance on dealing with the unexpected—issues that show up *after* you own the home. Once you own the home, you'll be moving in. We cover all the aspects of moving to your new home, whether from across town or across the country. We cover the differences in hiring a moving company to handle your possessions and doing it yourself.

Chapter

15

Warranty and Additional Insurance Protection

In This Chapter

◆ Conducting a final walkthrough

◆ Using home warranties to protect against surprises

◆ Getting the insurance you need

Once you've bought a home, you want to move in and already know what works and what needs to be repaired. Unfortunately, it doesn't always work that way. Worst-case scenario: you move in and—surprise—you have unforeseen plumbing problems or appliance breakdowns.

The information in this chapter helps you deal with problems if you find yourself with them after you close on the house. You'll learn about a final buyer's walkthrough, during which you should make sure the home looks the way you expect it to when you move in and that nothing has changed since the last time you saw it.

Next, we examine the home warranty, an insurance policy that protects you from major problems once you move in that the seller didn't know about. And of course, we cover your typical homeowner's insurance policy that you are required to have to obtain your mortgage loan. This chapter helps you make sure your new home is insured against all possible scenarios before you move in!

Buyer's Walkthrough

A walkthrough before the closing provides you with a final opportunity to view your soon-to-be new home, and to make sure that the condition of the property hasn't changed since you released your contingencies or that any repairs that you negotiated are done. For example, be sure that the seller hasn't removed any fixtures beyond what you have agreed to and that nothing in the house has been damaged. Everything should still be as it was when you were last there.

When to Conduct the Walkthrough

You should conduct the final walkthrough with your agent. This can be done a few days before the closing or even just a few hours before the papers are signed. The sellers may or may not be home when you conduct the walkthrough. Don't skip the final walkthrough simply because you're pressed for time to get it done or because the homeowners are home and you think you are imposing on their time. This is your right—take advantage of it to protect yourself. If you'll feel uncomfortable having the sellers present, have your agent schedule a time through the sellers' agent when the sellers won't be present.

Warning!

If you find anything amiss during the walkthrough, take careful notes and, if possible, photos. You can use these to support any claim you will make after closing.

If the sellers are still living in the home when you are conducting the walkthrough, remember that damage can occur when they are moving out—furniture bangs against walls, or movers bump into light fixtures, and so on—so it's always preferable to schedule it for after they move out.

If the sellers happen to damage anything, whether during their move or during any brief period of post-close occupancy, they are liable for the damage. You should immediately bring it to their attention and to your agent's attention. If they do not agree to cover the damage, you can always litigate.

What to Check

During the walkthrough, check to make sure everything works properly. Here's a list of standard items you should check (don't forget that there will probably be some unique items to check at your particular house that we haven't mentioned here):

- ◆ Turn the lights on and off.

- ◆ Test the appliances (stove, built-in microwave, and so on).

- ◆ Flush the toilets.

- ◆ Run the heating and air-conditioning units.

- ◆ Run all faucets and check for leaks.

- ◆ Close and open the windows and doors.

- ◆ Turn on the gas fireplace.

- ◆ Open and close the garage doors.

- ◆ Operate the poolsweep.

Don't be shy! You're buying the house and are entitled to know what you are buying.

What If Something Is Wrong?

Final walkthroughs are not a time to conduct additional negotiations with the seller if you discover something that you didn't notice before that you'd now like repaired. If you find something that was fine before but is amiss or just plain missing, chances are you will still have to complete the purchase. This is because your contract doesn't provide for canceling after you release your contingencies, the seller has completed any agreed-upon repairs, and the seller has provided you with the disclosures you're required to receive.

However, don't lose heart. Something that shows up during your walkthrough can be solved by simply asking the seller to fix the problem. It's a straightforward way to get things squared away and head to closing. However, if the seller refuses, you can continue to other nonjudicial methods, such as arbitration, or by suing the seller to get him to make things right. Admittedly, it's not the greatest way to finish the transaction, but at least it provides you some post-closing way to get compensated for the problem.

Often, a buyer will find the seller left trash behind or stained the carpet or walls during the move. Assuming a reasonable seller, this can usually be resolved without too much trouble between the parties.

Quotes and Facts

When the sellers were moving items out of the attic of the home we were buying, someone put their foot through the garage ceiling and left a gaping hole. This happened after the purchase contract was signed, but before the inspection. They agreed to fix it on their own, but when we did the walkthrough, we saw that the repair job was shoddy. To appease all parties, they cut us a check to fix it on our own. We were okay with that and proceeded to closing.

—Jennifer

Home Warranty

Don't confuse a warranty with homeowner's insurance. The latter is a policy that covers damage to your home from fires, explosions, storms, falling trees, slides, and the like. It covers the house and its structural integrity. It can have riders adding earthquake damage, and you can get separate flood insurance coverage if you live in a declared flood zone.

A home warranty, on the other hand, is a type of insurance policy that covers failures or defects of a home's systems and some appliances after you have closed.

A *rider* can be attached to the home warranty, which can include coverage on most home appliances. If any covered item breaks down during the warranty period, the buyer pays a nominal fee (usually less than $50), and the appliance will be either repaired or replaced at no further cost.

def•i•ni•tion

A home warranty **rider** is simply an expansion of the warranty's coverage. Usually, appliances that fall outside the basic warranty coverage are added in the rider. Riders can also cover a swimming pool or hot tub equipment.

If the seller agrees to the warranty, you can extend it beyond the initial period for just a few hundred dollars.

Let's say you move in to your beautiful new home and two weeks later a weakened pipe gives way and sends hundreds of gallons of water all over your basement. You now have a basement full of water and a repair bill that will cost you thousands of dollars. Or you finally get settled into your new home, fill the refrigerator with groceries, and are ready to throw your first dinner party, only to find out that your state-of-the-art oven doesn't work.

In both cases, a home warranty can protect you. It's like an insurance policy for your home and its systems. If something goes awry once you take ownership, the warranty should take care of it. All you have to do is call the warranty firm and report the problem. They'll send a plumber or repairman, he'll fix the problem, and you'll pay a nominal service call fee, usually under $50.

Now, before you get all excited about the wonders of a warranty, note that it won't cover everything. For example, let's say it's pouring rain and your roof begins leaking. The warranty doesn't cover this repair simply because it's designed to cover *only* the systems of the home and some of the appliances. If the roof leak was caused by the storm, your homeowner's insurance should pay for it. If it already leaked before the storm, you'll foot the bill—just as with any normal repair or maintenance issue.

However, let's say that it's January and you live in Aroostook County, Maine. It's cold there, to put it mildly, and your furnace decides to take a vacation and quits working. The warranty will pay for service to get it running again or, if it's totally toast, buy you a new one.

As we've previously mentioned, agents often give the first year's home warranty to the buyer as a closing gift. Also, some sellers will offer one in the listing as a way to attract buyer attention to their homes. However, if yours doesn't, you can buy one for a few hundred dollars for the first year's coverage. The warranty, like most insurance policies, is renewable on a yearly basis.

Tips and Traps

Many home warranties are available on the market. For more information, check out the following websites: www.ahswarranty.com, www.choicehomewarranty.com, and www.nationwidehomewarranty.com. Also, ask your agent for a recommendation.

What's Covered

Keep in mind that the basic home warranty doesn't automatically cover all appliances. However, for a small additional premium, you can add more appliances to the warranty. Standard appliance coverage usually includes heater/furnace, water heater, central vacuum system, stove/range/cooktop, built-in microwave, garbage disposal, and trash compactor.

Electrical and heating systems are generally covered, including ductwork, although the actual vent registers usually are not. In addition to the basic wiring of your electric system, your doorbell system may well be covered, as well as telephone wires inside the walls. In the latter case, however, such attached items as phone jacks, plugs, and cover plates generally are not covered.

More than a dozen different riders, or additions, are available on a typical warranty, each covering one or more specific appliances or systems in the home. Some warranties offer riders for swimming pools and hot tubs or spas. They won't pay to repair a cracked pool or one that has a leak, but they do cover the pool equipment—the filter system, heating system, or pump mechanism. These systems can be costly to repair or replace, so a rider can be well worth the money.

The list of appliances for which you can buy optional coverage keeps expanding. For example, recently expanded appliance coverage includes wet bar and wine refrigerators, and freestanding ice makers. These new riders have become available partly due to competition in the insurance marketplace for customers, as well as the fact that these appliances are becoming much more common in homes today.

A few other riders you can purchase include coverage on a home well pump and coverage for pumping a septic tank or repairing or replacing a sewage ejector pump.

Many plans exclude solar-related systems or equipment from their protection. That might change down the road, though, as green building becomes more popular and as more solar technology is added to homes.

Weigh the Plan

Carefully go over the prospective home warranty item by item to see what you are obtaining coverage for. Carefully consider all of the ones that may apply to you, and then add on the extras you feel are truly necessary. Given that many appliances already come with warranties, and many of these can be extended, you may find it advisable to not get too many extra riders if most of your appliances are new and still under factory warranty. Instead, if you must add riders, limit them to older, out-of-warranty items. You'll save a lot of money that way. Also, find out the annual cost of the rider in comparison to the cost of replacing the appliance. For less expensive appliances, it may be better to avoid the rider and just buy a new appliance when the old one breaks.

Look at many items closely. For example, while a home warranty offers coverage on leaks caused by rain, the roof leak coverage has numerous exclusions; examine them carefully to see if the extra cost is worth it.

The other item that needs your careful attention is a warranty about pests. In this case, we're not talking about termites, wood-boring beetles, rats, or dry rot (which are checked for during your pest inspection). We're talking about bugs such as black widow and brown recluse spiders, roaches, some types of ants (not including fire ants), and centipedes, to name just a few. The pest list is usually found in the warranty brochure. If you live in a particular area that is known for a specific pest that wasn't tested for during the pest inspection, you might want to make sure it's covered under the pest part of the warranty.

Another area that has gained inclusion in the warranty recently is limited coverage for repairs due to mismatched systems—for example, if you buy an appliance that is too big for the capacity of your home's electrical or plumbing system. Because of this, the appliance either doesn't function properly or fails after installation. This may be covered under a home warranty, as may coverage for repairing improper or incorrect installation of an appliance. At the same time, the permit fees charged by local governments for some of the necessary work can be covered as well.

> **Tips and Traps**
>
> Carefully compare warranties from at least two or more providers to determine which plan best suits your needs at the best price for you.

Homeowner's Insurance

Most mortgages require that you purchase homeowner's insurance, or they won't give you the loan. It's also a smart move to have it, since a homeowner's insurance policy is designed to protect you against something that happens to your home—damage from storms, robbery, and so on. A policy comes with a deductible, and those amounts are determined by the policy you purchase. However, just because you're covered, don't make a claim for every little thing that comes up. If you nickel and dime the insurance company, you'll find that your premiums will rise dramatically or, worse, you'll be considered a bad risk and cancelled. Save your claims for major damage situations. For example, if a storm blows a few dozen shingles off your roof and the cost to repair is $200, pay that yourself. However, if the storm knocks a tree over and it destroys your roof, the cost to repair may be well over $10,000. For that amount, file a claim.

The typical homeowner's insurance policy includes two parts—liability protection and property protection.

Liability protection covers you in case a member of your household damages someone else's property or causes injury or death to someone else on or off your property. In a situation like this, you could be liable to pay financial compensation that could cost into the millions.

Property protection covers your home; any structures such as garages, gazebos, pool houses, and detached studios; built-in appliances; plumbing; heating; central air-conditioning systems; and electrical wiring. It also covers garages, storage sheds, fences, driveways, sidewalks, patios, and retaining walls. Your personal property coverage covers what's inside your home and what is owned by anyone else you live with. Although it won't cover appliance failure, it will cover destruction of the same appliances if they're ruined in a fire, storm, or other covered event.

Tips and Traps

Some policies cover your living expenses if you need to move out of your home while repairs are being made to it because of a claim.

Homeowner's insurance policies can cover a wide variety of things, but it depends on your insurance company and what you want to choose. For example, your policy can cover credit card theft, and you can add any endorsements to your policies. Endorsements are things that your standard policy doesn't cover but that you can pay extra for to get the coverage. These include the following:

♦ **Guaranteed replacement cost coverage**—The cost to rebuild your home. Some policies have this as standard, but charge a higher basic premium than policies that don't provide it.

♦ **Extended replacement cost coverage**—A percentage over and above the cost of rebuilding your home.

♦ **Scheduled personal property coverage**—Coverage for personal items, such as your engagement ring or stamp collection. There are limitations, though, so check with your insurance agent about this endorsement.

♦ **Inflation guard**—Automatically raises your homeowner insurance coverage to cover inflation.

Credit, Life, and Disability Insurance

Another way to protect yourself financially after you buy a home is listed on a statement you should have received at closing from the title company. This statement gives you an option to elect credit, life, and/or disability insurance. These insurances are designed to pay off the mortgage in case you die or become physically incapacitated after you own the home.

The lender cannot require that you purchase these insurance products as conditions of the loan, but if you want them, you can check the appropriate box. You will be told how much each will cost, and you'll sign for it. Ask your agent about these items. This will give you time to do research or have your Realtor get you the appropriate information so that you can make an informed decision. However, as I note later, think about this before committing.

These insurance products were once required of all borrowers, but they were found often to be needless extra expenses for the borrower and really served only to enrich the lender. In my opinion, they are not necessary. You can put the money required for them to better use elsewhere.

Title Insurance

Title insurance is another protection from claims made against your title after you own the home.

For example, let's say your property has a garage with an attached artist studio. You were informed by the title search company that this garage/studio lies against the boundary you share with your neighbor. Ten months after you take title, the neighbor decides to survey his property and finds out that the garage/studio actually intrudes about a foot onto his property. He demands compensation from you for this intrusion. Your title insurance policy covers this type of situation and will pay him compensation. If you didn't have title insurance, it could become a serious issue.

Equally important, if you're financing your purchase, lenders require this insurance because they don't want their collateral at risk from a claim against the title that suddenly pops up.

The Least You Need to Know

- Take your time on the buyer's walkthrough; examine every room closely to make sure the home is still in the same condition as the last time you saw it.

- The buyer's walkthrough is not a time for negotiation, nor can it be used as a contingency.

- Don't skip the walkthrough—your schedule may be crazy right now, but make time for this very important step.

- Go over your homeowner's warranty to make sure that it covers what you need.

Chapter 16

The Closing

In This Chapter

- Escrow closings
- Attorney closings
- What to bring to your closing
- Closing cost information
- Other fees you need to pay

Getting to the closing is what you've been working toward throughout this whole book. This is when all the documents and contracts are signed, the purchase is complete, and the title passes from the seller to you. In other words, after the closing, you own the home!

There are two types of closings—an escrow closing and an attorney closing. You will be attending one or the other. Think of an escrow closing as a third party who holds the money until the deal is complete. The money stays in an escrow account, and you and the seller work out the details of the purchase. Once all the details have been agreed upon and all the contingencies have been met, all documents signed and title passed to you, all of the money will be released from escrow and paid to the seller. Depending on where you live, the funds may change hands either by wire transfer or check to the seller's account (and, if there's a mortgage being paid off, to his lender). However, in most cases, a wire transfer is used because there is no delay waiting for a check to clear. If a check is used, it must arrive early enough to clear before closing. Other states use an attorney for closing. The attorney examines the title records to ensure that clear title, one with no liens or other clouds on it, passes to the buyer. He may be involved in drawing some closing documents as well, depending on local custom. In New York, for example, closings are frequently held at the offices of either the buyer's or seller's attorney. Typically, both the seller's agent and the buyer's agent are also present.

In the case of escrow closing states—California, Arizona, and Oregon to name a few—the closing happens through the escrow company's office, but the parties don't usually get together. Instead, each party comes in to sign their documents a few days prior to closing. Then funds are wired into the escrow's account and transferred to the seller. Finally, the deed goes to the recorder for recordation.

This chapter provides information on both escrow and attorney closings, including what to bring to a closing and what you can expect once you get there.

Escrow Closings

In an escrow closing, all of your payments toward the purchase price and any funds from your mortgage are deposited into the escrow that was created for your purchase. In the case of the mortgage funds, they are deposited into escrow just a day or two before closing, and your existing deposits remain there until closing. Once all the paperwork has been completed, the funds are paid to the seller. The escrow holder will not transfer any funds to the seller until all conditions of your purchase are met, all relevant documents are signed, and you're at the closing.

def•i•ni•tion

A **fiduciary** is one who acts on behalf of another in any matter that requires a high level of trust. It is a very serious level of trust and, if violated, is dealt with very harshly by the courts.

Similarly, the escrow holder will not refund any monies to you that you deposited until the seller agrees in writing that the purchase has been canceled for any number of reasons that we've already discussed. Though the escrow is usually opened in your behalf, once it is opened, the escrow company has *fiduciary* responsibilities to both you and the seller.

Opening an Escrow

An escrow account is opened as soon as the seller accepts your offer and your deposit has to be put into the account. In most cases, the buyer's agent chooses the escrow company, opens the escrow account, and deposits the check. The only exception is in the purchase of REO property; the selling bank often chooses the escrow holder because it usually uses the same company for all of its sales and therefore gets a cheaper fee. Usually a buyer pays this escrow fee, but with REOs the selling bank pays for it as part of choosing the company to do the escrow.

Your agent will provide the escrow company with all of the relevant information about the transaction—the address of the property you are purchasing; the purchase price; your name, address, e-mail, and other contact information; and the same information for the seller, your agent, and your seller's agent. The company appoints an escrow officer, also called a title officer, to handle your account, and assigns an escrow account number for identification purposes.

If the funds have not arrived to the escrow company by wire transfer, you will need to provide a cashier's or certified check. These checks clear more quickly and easily than personal checks. Your earnest money check might have been submitted by a personal check, but that was early in the home-buying process, so there was plenty of time for it to clear. Now, you'll need a check that clears faster.

The funds may not all arrive at once at the time of closing. For example, the original earnest money deposit has been held in escrow since you went into contract. In the contract, you may have a clause that requires you to increase the amount of your deposit once you have released all of your contingencies. You'll receive a receipt from the escrow officer for every deposit you make, including the remainder of your down payment, and a copy will be sent to the seller's agent.

The escrow account officer also receives a copy of the purchase contract and any counteroffers or addenda that you and the seller have signed and dated. This is so the officer knows the total amount that will be deposited into escrow and when it can be expected. The contract will also tell her which contingencies have been agreed to, when they must be released, and any other requirements. The escrow officer has a duty to notify both parties if any deposit dates are missed. She will also check with your agent if she has not received notification that all contingencies have been released by their scheduled release dates.

Title Report

One of the first things the escrow officer will do after the account has been opened and the first check deposited is to order a preliminary title report for the property you are buying. The report is considered preliminary because it gives you and the seller an opportunity to see what turns up. If anything appears erroneous, the seller can tell the escrow firm, who will investigate the claim and, if necessary, arrange for a corrected title report to be created before the closing. In some states, this may be ordered by the listing agent when she first lists a home. It saves time and work for everyone once they receive an offer.

This report covers all the known legal information on the property as of its date of publication. For example, it covers the legal boundaries of the property; any recorded liens, mortgage or other types; judgments or *easements*; and real estate taxes owed. It also notes any exclusions from coverage under a proposed title insurance policy. Exclusions, as the name suggests, are items that the policy specifically does not cover.

def•i•ni•tion

An **easement** is the legal transfer of a right to a nonowner of property that burdens the property. Easements are granted in perpetuity. For example, a landowner could grant an easement to another person for a right of passage across a piece of land, or an owner might grant the right to a nonowner to discharge water across the owner's land.

The report highlights items that a title insurance company would likely refuse coverage on and indicates potential claims or liens against the title (we cover the title insurance in more detail later in this chapter). If you or your agent notices a particularly serious issue, you can question it and, if it is found to be correct, decide whether you still want to buy the home.

Start Your Due Diligence

Once the escrow account is open, start your due diligence—inspections, financing, investigation of homeowners' association documents, and so on. When a release of a contingency is due, you will sign the document and your agent will provide a copy to the seller and to the escrow officer so the file stays up-to-date.

Warning!

Frequently, the only time the buyer doesn't select the escrow company is when the property is a foreclosure. However, in some states it is common practice for the seller to select the escrow firm. With a foreclosure, the bank will have already opened the escrow well in advance of any offers on the property. In exchange for you using this firm, the selling bank will pay all or a part of your title insurance cost.

Attorney Closings

In some states, an attorney closing is also called a settlement of the property. However, it means the same thing. The attorney comes into the closing after all the inspections and other contingencies have been satisfied. In some cases, the attorney draws up all but the loan documents to be recorded, and may have drawn the purchase contract. In other cases, the purchase contract may be drawn by your agent and then sent to the seller and her agent. The attorney steps in once a contract has been established.

For example, in Illinois, an attorney reviews the contract after the parties have agreed to it. The attorney is permitted to make any alterations he feels necessary to protect his clients, but he cannot change the agreed-upon price. Also, any changes an attorney makes have to be agreed to by the parties.

Costs

Everybody knows how expensive attorneys are. However, in attorney closings, they do not get paid unless the property sale actually is completed, much in the same way that the Realtors don't receive their commissions until the sale is completed. Fees vary with the attorney.

Responsibilities

The lawyer either investigates the title or contracts the process out to a title company. He may do the lien search to determine what, if any, liens have been filed against the property. The attorney also draws the HUD-1 statement, which is a document that shows all receipts and disbursements connected to the transaction, and must be approved by both parties. Some states have the Realtors draw up the purchase contract and then turn it over to the attorneys for review before it is signed. This review is limited to a certain number of days. For example, in New Jersey, there is a three-day limit for review. The attorney will contact the bank to find out the exact amount of remaining down payment money the buyer needs to deliver at closing to complete the purchase. The attorney then draws up the *Real Estate Settlement Procedures Act* (*RESPA*) disclosure documents.

def•i•ni•tion

According to HUD, the **Real Estate Settlement Procedures Act (RESPA)** is about closing costs and settlement procedures. RESPA requires that consumers receive disclosures at various times in the transaction and outlaws kickbacks that increase the cost of settlement services. RESPA is a HUD consumer protection statute designed to help home buyers be better shoppers in the home-buying process, and is enforced by HUD.

The RESPA documents are designed to help buyers avoid unnecessary expenses related to closing. They explain the policies of the escrow firm and detail any connections between the escrow company and other companies involved in the process whose fees you pay at closing. The idea is to have an informed buyer who can know if the fees he is being charged are legitimate and reasonable.

Tips and Traps

At this point, if you are having an attorney closing, you should already have an attorney, but if you still need one, choose someone who is experienced in real estate closings. You can contact your local bar association or ask friends or relatives for recommendations. You may wish to talk with more than one attorney before choosing the one who will handle your purchase, but don't wait too long if your closing is rapidly approaching.

Mortgage Papers

If you are mortgaging your purchase, the bank will send the various mortgage documents to the escrow company or attorney for your review and signing. Usually this is one of the last parts of the process because if any part of your purchase does not work out or fails to be completed, there is no reason to go to a closing.

Among the mortgage documents you will sign are the following:

- Loan agreement
- Promissory note, often just called the note
- Mortgage document, referred to in some states as a deed of trust
- Truth-in-lending document
- Closing statement (HUD-1 statement)

◆ Closing instructions

◆ Deed

Likely others will also be involved, depending on where you live, your lender, and the type of transaction, but these cover the most common documents you'll sign.

Tips and Traps _____

Due to the large number of mortgage documents that you will encounter at a closing, it's a good idea to request copies of them from your lender in advance and read them through. Make note of any items that are an issue for you. You can then ask your Realtor and lender any questions you have before the closing. Although you can read the documents at a closing, this can hold things up, so it's better to do so beforehand. As these are generic documents in most cases, it is unlikely you'll find anything that needs changing. Your preview just helps your understanding.

Loan Agreement

The loan agreement is the agreement between you and the lender. It says that the lender is loaning you a specific amount of money to purchase your house. The agreement includes the rate of interest, the term, the frequency and amount of your loan payments, the loan maturity date, and the terms and conditions governing the loan, such as late fees, conditions of default, and any prepayment penalties.

Promissory Note

Lawyers refer to the promissory note as "the proof of the debt." Like the loan agreement, the promissory note shows the amount of the loan, the interest rate, and the final maturity date of the loan.

Mortgage or Deed of Trust

The mortgage or deed of trust gives the lender a security interest in your home as collateral for the loan. This document recognizes the right of the lender to foreclose if you do not make your payments. When recorded in your local recorder's office, this document becomes a lien on the property. Many buyers jokingly say they own their home in partnership with the bank. Strictly speaking, that is incorrect. Even if you have a loan covering all but the tiniest of down payments on your home, you own the entire home. But your ownership is subject to the bank's security interest in the property represented by the mortgage you have agreed to on that property.

Truth-in-Lending

The truth-in-lending document is a federally required document that protects you, the buyer, by disclosing all the key terms of your loan. This includes the principal amount of the loan, rate of interest, and annual percentage rate (APR).

Buyers were once unaware of the true costs of their borrowing—the fees, interest rates, and points—until they got to the closing. Required by the federal Truth in Lending law, this statement is meant to keep you fully informed about the details and costs of your loan. The information is broken down and detailed in easy-to-understand language.

The statement outlines your real rate of interest—the APR and how much the loan will cost over its lifetime. This can be a particularly sobering moment when you first see the total. The reaction usually goes something like, "Oh my! I'm paying all that money just to borrow money to buy a house?" The answer is, yes, but if you didn't borrow it, you likely wouldn't be able to buy the house.

The statement also details the principal amount of the loan, also known as the amount financed. Your payments will then be broken down. For example, if you have a 30-year loan, fully amortized, with monthly payments of principal and interest of $275, you will make 360 payments of $275, for a grand total of $99,000. However, if your loan requires you to make 30 years' worth of payments at $1,800 every month, you will have paid $648,000. Chances are, more than half of that figure is interest alone. Your statement will also include a month-by-month schedule of your individual payments. This will show, payment by payment, the number of each payment: 1, 2, 3, and so on, through the final scheduled payment; the amount of each payment; and when each payment is due. For example, if your payments are due on the first of every month, you'll see an actual date for the payment date for each of the enumerated payments on the schedule.

The Closing Statement

The closing statement, sometimes referred to as the HUD-1, looks like a page out of an accountant's book. It shows every dollar that was paid in or out to both the buyer and seller. It includes all cash deposits into escrow, loan funds, and any closing expenses, such as insurance premiums, title insurance costs, loan fees, escrow fees, and Realtors' commissions. There will be a closing statement for both you and the seller. Examine it closely to be sure there are no errors. Your agent can guide you.

Closing Instructions

Closing instructions are not actual instructions. Instead, they show the names, addresses, and contact information of the parties involved; the details of the purchase price; and its breakdown of loan and down payment, any encumbrances on the property, and your agreement to arrange for homeowner's insurance on the property. It also shows the Realtor's commissions and makes reference to any fees related to the escrow, any homeowners' association obligations that may exist, and local city or county regulations that may apply.

The instructions also include the availability of funds. This refers to the date that your loan funds are actually available from their source, the lender, to be paid out to the seller by the escrow company. The date of availability is not always the same date that the funds are deposited into the escrow. Depending on the day of the week and time of day, the funds may not be available until the next day.

The Deed

The deed is the document that actually transfers legal ownership from the seller to you. Typically, it will say something like, "John Q. Seller transfers all title at 123 Main Street in YourTown, USA, to you for value received from you." It's dated and signed by the seller. In many cases, the signature will be *notarized* as well. Once it is recorded, the ownership transfer becomes a matter of public record.

After your loan documents have been signed and notarized, the lender funds the loan by transferring the loan amount to the escrow firm's bank for ultimate disbursement to the seller. The only thing left before you own the home is the recordation of the sale. The escrow company sends the documents that the local laws require be recorded to the local recorder's office for recordation. When recordation occurs, the escrow company is notified. They notify your agent and the seller's agent, and pass the information on to you and the seller. At this point, you are considered "on record." In other words, you own the home! Congratulations!

def•i•ni•tion

Notarized means that a notary public witnessed your signing of documents and placed her notary seal on each document certifying the papers. She will keep a record of each notarization according to the law in her state.

What to Bring

What to bring to the closing depends on whether it's an escrow closing or an attorney closing. In the states where you actually attend the closing, you will need some form of government-issued identification, so make sure you bring your driver's license or passport with you. Local law may vary from one state to another, so ask your agent if there are any other documents you need to have at the closing.

Remember, in an escrow closing, you are not present at the actual closing because your document signing takes place a few days prior to the actual close of escrow. In many cases, all of the funds are already in escrow by this time. Therefore, you don't need to bring any money. However, in some locales, you actually bring a check to escrow covering such items as down payment and taxes on the day of closing. You will also have to write a check to pay for the closing costs, which includes your escrow fee, title insurance premium, first year's homeowner's insurance premium (if not already paid directly to the insurance company), flood insurance premium (if it applies), and notary and recording fees. These fees will be deposited into an escrow account and later disbursed to the intended recipients by the escrow company at closing.

You, and any other parties named on the documents, must bring photo identification. If it's an escrow closing, in most states you bring it to the signing a few days prior to closing. If it's an attorney closing, bring it to the attorney's office where the closing will likely occur. You can bring a passport, driver's license, or other government-issued ID. A Social Security card is not a valid identification, and it even states so on the card. The need for identification may seem a bit much, given the fact that your agent has been dealing with you for some time now, but in order for your signature to be notarized, the escrow firm's notary must see some valid ID to prove to their legal satisfaction that you really are you.

What you bring to an attorney closing varies from state to state. You might need photo identification, and you may have to bring any funds that are part of the purchase price that you have not yet produced, as well as funds for your closing costs. These closings usually occur in your attorney's office, and the attorney will oversee such things as funds disbursement and document signing.

Sometimes the seller won't be in attendance at the closing due to family issues or because they are not physically able. In such cases, the one signing for the seller(s) will have a limited power of attorney that permits them to sign for the seller(s).

You should have your Realtor at the closing. She can answer any last-minute questions you may have. Also possibly attending a closing will be the notary, the seller, the seller's attorney, and possibly the seller's agent.

Commissions

Paying the Realtor commissions happens at closing. That is because a Realtor gets no payment for his hard work at all unless and until the purchase closes and title transfers. He may have worked like the proverbial slave, but if the deal falls apart, even at the last minute, he gets nothing for his efforts.

Traditionally, as the buyer, you pay nothing to your agent. His commission comes from the seller. The seller pays a total commission to his listing agent. The amount is open to negotiation between the seller and her agent, but the most common figure in the business seems to be 6 percent of the purchase price. That commission is then split between the seller's listing agent and your agent.

While there is no strict requirement that it be split equally, that is the most common circumstance. Sometimes, however, the commission is split differently, with a larger sum going to the listing agent. Remember, it's the seller's decision how the commission is split. In some cases, the seller and her agent might feel that an extra incentive is needed to sell the home. Therefore, the seller may decide to split the commission in your agent's favor.

Bonuses and Incentives

Sometimes, on the seller's instructions, there will be a bonus or some other form of incentive payment to the buyer's agent when the sale closes. Usually this is an extra chunk of cash over and above the commission that your agent is entitled to receive. However, this bonus doesn't have to be money. It can be a new luxury car—a Porsche, Lexus, or Mercedes—jewelry, a trip to some exotic vacation spot, or a week at a resort. Usually such incentives are offered when the market is severely slow or when the property has issues or faces an inordinate amount of competition in a slower than normal market. These bonuses are merely to encourage a little more aggressive work on the part of your agent as a buyer's agent.

> **Tips and Traps**
>
> In addition to agent commission bonuses and incentives, a seller sometimes pays a stipulated amount toward your closing costs as an incentive to get you to consider buying his property. This payment is made only if you complete the sale. It also may be an allowance for some work in the home, such as new carpet or interior paint.

When *You* Pay Your Agent's Commission

Sometimes the seller doesn't pay the buyer's agent's commission. The most common situation is when the property you are buying is for sale by owner (FSBO). The seller has no agent handling his end of the transaction and thus has no one to pay. When you and your agent first consider a FSBO, one of the first questions your agent will ask the seller is whether the seller will pay the buyer's agent a commission if that agent's buyer buys the home.

If the seller says yes, your agent will still get paid by the seller at closing. But what if the seller says no? Your agent will tell you that you're not obligated, but he wants to help you get a home and he needs to be paid for his efforts. He shouldn't just walk away without any explanation.

The solution is what's called a buyer-broker agreement. This is a contract between you and your agent that covers the situation when her commission is not being paid by the seller. It specifies that you will pay your agent's commission and the amount of the commission, either in dollars or as a percentage of the purchase price. It will also have an expiration date, but it can be extended. Should you end up buying a home where the commission *is* paid by the seller, then you do not also have to pay your agent. She gets paid only once.

Some agents propose a buyer-broker agreement at the start of the relationship so there are no surprises later. Other agents wait until they face this situation before discussing it. Either way is fine, although it is better to get it out of the way early on.

Escrow Fees and Other Expenses

The escrow company charges escrow fees for the work it performs in opening and managing your account. This is either a flat fee or a percentage of the purchase price, up to a maximum amount. The fees will be listed on your HUD-1, or closing, statement. The escrow fee is included in your closing costs.

You likely will find additional fees or expenses that you are responsible for. Many of these cover the premiums associated with specialized types of insurance, such as flood or earthquake insurance.

Insurance Premiums

Insurance premiums are the fees an insurance company charges to insure your new home against various types of damage or disaster. The most common is homeowner's insurance, which covers damage by fire, storms, wind, and, in some cases, landslides (although this depends on what caused the slide). The fees are paid annually, although some companies allow quarterly or monthly payments. The first year's premium is usually paid at the closing.

If you took out a mortgage to buy your home, you will share the beneficiary's position on the policy with the bank. The beneficiary here is the payee of the insurance policy in case an insured disaster actually takes place. This is to make the bank feel comfortable about the protection of its collateral for the mortgage it made to you.

Two other types of insurance may be placed on your home: flood or earthquake insurance. If they are, the premiums for each will also be paid for the first year at your closing.

Prorated Property Taxes

You will be paying some property taxes at closing. A portion of the tax bill will also be paid from the seller's sale receipts. You'll be paying property tax in advance for the portion of the tax year you are currently in the middle of that coincides with your ownership of the property.

Other Closing Charges and Fees

Other expenses must be paid at closing. They include, but are not limited to, the following:

◆ Loan or application fees that you are required to pay as a condition of your mortgage.

◆ Any points on your mortgage loan.

◆ Prorated interest. This covers interest on your mortgage for the initial period before your first payment is due. The first mortgage payment usually isn't due until the month after you take occupancy in the house, while your loan has been funded at the start of your occupancy. As a result, the lender wants to be paid interest for that initial period before the first payment is due.

◆ Attorney fees.

Documentation: The Transaction

So much paperwork is involved in buying a home, so when you finally are all settled into your new home, it's time to get that paperwork organized and filed.

Protect yourself by filing your documents so you can reference them if you need them at any time after you close. Organize the documents into two parts: transaction documents and closing documents. Transaction documents are all of your documents—inspection reports, proof of repairs or remediation, seller disclosures, purchase contract, counteroffers, contingency releases, and so on. Also include structural reports, permits, applications, final inspections, installations, and related items.

Closing documents are all the documents you received and signed at closing. You can keep a file at home or store your documents electronically. Many Realtors now provide documentation files for their clients on a CD or a thumb drive. This gives you access to your documents on a small, easy-to-store device that provides some security. Most states require the title companies and real estate brokerages to maintain copies of all document files. So feel confident that your documents are accessible if you lose them or if they're destroyed.

> **Quotes and Facts**
>
> My personal preference is to store closing documents on a thumb drive, since it has immense storage capacity. If you use a CD, however, something on the order of 700 MB of capacity is usually more than sufficient.

Once all the documents are signed, it's almost time to get the keys and move in. Congratulations!

The Least You Need to Know

◆ Depending on where you live, you will have either an escrow or an attorney closing.

◆ Be prepared to pay your closing costs, which depend on your type of financing and the agreement that you have made with the seller.

◆ Once you've reviewed and signed all the documents, get your keys to your new home and celebrate!

Chapter 17

Moving and Moving In

In This Chapter

- ◆ Arranging your move
- ◆ Closing up your old home
- ◆ Preparing your new home
- ◆ What to do if your new home isn't ready

It's finally moving day! It's time to leave your old home and move to the new one. But if you haven't carefully planned this day as thoroughly as you did your purchase, it could become a complete nightmare. As a matter of fact, moving is considered one of the most stressful events we go through in our lives, so it's vital for you to have a checklist to follow so you don't forget anything.

This chapter focuses on just that—making your move go smoothly, whether you hire a moving company to handle the job or you do it all yourself. We follow this from the time you get the keys at closing to the time you get your boxes moved in.

No matter how prepared you are, though, occasionally you'll run into glitches—perhaps the previous owner or tenant hasn't moved out yet and you need to get in. This chapter gets you through these glitches and also tells you how to get your basic remodeling—such as painting and carpet upgrades—done and how to set up the new home, including your utilities, before you even walk through the front door.

Finding a Moving Company

Moving is time-consuming and, at times, exhausting and stressful, so you might find it easier to hire a company to handle some of the details, including the packing and unpacking. Unless you've hired a moving company before that you were happy with, follow the same advice we gave you for choosing a real estate professional and mortgage lender. Start by asking friends and co-workers for recommendations, and ask them what they liked about the company and problems they had, if any. Then interview and get estimates from each company. Be sure to ask each company the following questions:

◆ Are both packing and unpacking included in the moving fee, or are they additional expenses?

◆ Do you hire subcontractors? If so, what are the names and phone numbers of each the contractors? (Check them out individually as well.)

◆ How is cost determined? Is it by pound or per hour? Are any additional travel expenses—such as gas, tolls, or other long-distances charges—added?

◆ How is payment made? Will you need a deposit up front, or does the company require payment in full at the beginning or the end of the trip?

◆ Do you have your required registration number with the Federal Motor Carrier Safety Association and the U.S. Department of Transportation?

◆ What kind of insurance do you carry, and what is your company's policy on anything the movers might break?

◆ Do you have your cancellation or rescheduling fees? (This is in case the closing gets pushed out for some reason or falls through.)

Tips and Traps

Need to move your car to your new location, but have nobody to drive it there for you? You have several options. Ask the moving company you've hired, and see if they have this option. Second, hire your own driver by putting an ad online or in your local newspaper (be sure to check out his references before giving him your car!). Third, you can hire a vehicle transportation firm that arranges (and handles the background checks) for a driver for your car. Check out Auto Driveaway at www. autodriveaway.com.

Protect Yourself from Fraud

The moving industry has its share of fraudulent companies and individuals, so be aware when you're checking out the credentials of the company you want to hire. The Federal Motor Carrier Safety Administration (FMCSA; www.fmcsa.dot.gov) is a federal agency dedicated to increasing safety and legitimacy of large trucks and buses. On the FMCSA site, you can examine the safety records of individual trucking firms for free with a Company Snapshot, a brief record of the particular firm. For a much more detailed Company Safety Profile, you can pay $20 via a safe online payment section or mail the fee to the company.

The FMCSA also warns of "rogue movers" who scam customers by providing a low-ball estimate—either by phone or through e-mail—without even visiting the home or seeing what the customer is moving. Once all of the stuff is on their truck, the drivers demand more money before they'll deliver or unload the items. The FMCSA says that your best defense against a rogue mover is to recognize the red flags. According to the FMCSA consumer website, www. protectyourmove.gov, avoid companies that have the following red flags:

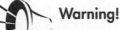 **Warning!**

If you are taking care of your own move, make sure you don't leave anything visible in the truck or car when you stop at rest stops or hotels for the night. Lock valuables in the trunk.

- ◆ The mover doesn't offer or agree to an on-site inspection of your household goods and gives an estimate over the phone or Internet—sight unseen. These estimates often sound too good to be true. They usually are.

- ◆ The moving company demands cash or a large deposit before the move.

- ◆ The mover doesn't provide you with a copy of "Your Rights and Responsibilities When You Move," a booklet federal regulations require movers to supply to their customers in the planning stages of interstate moves.

- ◆ The company's website has no local address and no information about licensing or insurance.

- ◆ The mover claims all goods are covered by their insurance.

- ◆ When you call the mover, the telephone is answered with a generic "Movers" or "Moving Company," rather than the company's name.

Warning!

Get a cell phone number or other emergency number to maintain contact with your mover's representative at all times. Emergencies don't always happen between 9 and 5 on weekdays.

♦ Offices and warehouse are in poor condition or nonexistent.

♦ On moving day, a rental truck arrives instead of a company-owned and -marked fleet truck.

Additionally, you can protect yourself against such "firms" by checking with the Better Business Bureau and asking the company for references from past clients. Get more than one or two, and check these references carefully.

Moving Out of State

If you are moving out of state and want to choose a local moving company instead of a well-known national moving company, your move may be handled by more than one company. Let's explain …. Say you're moving from New York to Ohio. Your local company may take your items only a certain distance out of state, and then contract with another local firm to finish the job. Smaller qualified moving companies are quite qualified to handle a moving job, even one from state to state, but just make sure you know who is handling the job from start to finish.

Insurance

In addition to any insurance the moving company may have, check with your own insurance company to make sure you're covered if something happens to your belongings. Policies differ, and you may find that your insurance policy doesn't cover your goods while in transit. Don't cancel your policy effective the last day in your old home until you find out. Similarly, if your new insurance policy isn't in effect until you are actually in the home, you may find your possessions uninsured in the event something happens.

Warning!

If you had a renter's insurance policy and not a homeowner's policy, ask your agent if your items are covered while in transit. If not, see if you can start your homeowner's insurance policy before your move, and ask your agent if it will cover the items before you actually move in.

This is especially important to keep in mind for your valuables—artwork, statues, jewelry, and so on. Are they covered, or are you required to purchase a rider to guarantee their coverage at full value? It's probably worth the extra cost of a rider if you truly have something of value or something difficult to replace.

Relocation

If you're moving because of job reassignment, chances are your employer will arrange your move and, typically, foot the bill. To make things easier, they might ask you to contact the moving company and make the arrangements on your own, including payment. Then they may reimburse you either the entire amount or up to a certain stipend. You can spend as much as you want, but over the limit, it comes out of your own pocket.

Doing It Yourself

An alternative to hiring a moving firm, of course, is to do the move yourself. You can rent a truck, pack up your belongings, and drive the truck to your new residence, whether across town or across the country. If it's a closer move, you can rent a van or truck and make multiple trips between homes. If the move is across the country, you'll need a truck that can hold all of your belongings in one trip. Rental trucks can become pricey when moving from state to state or across country, so consider your budget. Also consider whether this is a good idea if you have little or no experience driving a large truck.

There are two other areas of cost to consider as well. Check out fuel costs and mileage for the truck, and find out if the truck is gas or diesel powered. While costs of both fuels are similar, diesel still gets better mileage than gas in most cases.

The other cost item to be aware of is the boxes and packing material you buy. Buy a little more than you think is necessary to save yourself a trip back for more. Just be sure that the materials are returnable if unused.

If you're renting a van or truck from a company such as U-Haul (www.uhaul.com), make your reservations early. Confirm the vehicle's size and load capacity—you want to make sure it fits your furniture, household goods, clothing, kids' toys, artwork, and so on. General sizes run as follows:

- ◆ **Cargo van:** Holds up to two average-sized rooms of furniture/contents
- ◆ **15-foot truck:** Holds two to three rooms of furniture/contents
- ◆ **18-foot truck:** Holds four to six rooms of furniture/contents
- ◆ **24- and 26-foot truck:** Holds seven to eight rooms of furniture/contents

Make certain that the company provides moving supplies such as loading ramps, *dollies*, padding to protect the breakables, and boxes of all types and sizes. Some moving companies charge extra if they have to include boxes and packing materials. Get the boxes and packing materials before you get the truck. Ask the rental company what the rates are and what kind of roadside assistance they provide, in case the truck breaks down on the way to your new home.

def•i•ni•tion

A **dollie** is a small platform with wheels to assist in moving heavy objects. There are also special ones designed for handling the extra weight and bulk of appliances.

Also confirm what, if any, extra expenses there are, including expenses for dropping off the truck at a different location than where you picked it up, or expenses for special insurance, such as coverage beyond what your own auto liability policy may cover. Also be sure to find out their rules about the gas in the vehicle when you return it. (Do you have to return it with a full tank?) Finally, make sure you have a bunch of friends and family lined up to help you with the move!

Packing

Now that you've gotten the move arranged, it's time to pack up the old place and let everyone know where they can find you. Packing your belongings in an organized fashion is very important to making a smooth transition to your new home. If you need to be out of the home right at the closing, begin to pack as soon as you can. Some buyers wait until the closing is done, just to be sure, and then complete the task quickly.

 Warning!

Most moving companies will not transport gas, propane, or other volatile materials. Some will even dump out gasoline from mowers and other lawn equipment on the driveway.

Keep, Sell, or Donate

Decide what you want to keep and what you want to donate or sell before you pack it all up. No sense taking things you really don't need to the new home. You can have a garage sale, sell items on eBay (www.ebay.com) or on Craigslist, or donate items to your local church, Salvation Army, Goodwill, AmVets, or shelter. You can also check out various donation sites, such as Freecycle (www.freecycle.com), to find ways to donate or recycle your unwanted belongings.

Supplies

If you've hired a moving company, get your boxes and start packing as soon as possible. If you are doing the move yourself, either you'll need to get supplies from the rental truck company or you'll have to track down moving supplies on your own. You can purchase boxes from a moving company, an office supply company, a hardware store (such as Lowes), or even stores such as Walmart (or their accompanying websites), to name a few. You can ask stores such as grocery stores for extra boxes, or see if anyone has some through Craigslist or Freecycle. The latter few selections are generally cheaper than the truck rental firms.

Valuables

Don't send small valuable items, such as jewelry, by mover. Instead, safely pack them and carry them with you, if possible. Consider sending them by registered mail or Federal Express to the new house, but with adequate insurance to cover any eventuality of loss. This may sound a bit ridiculous, trusting your valuables to the Post Office—even by registered or Priority Mail—but, in case you didn't know, the Hope Diamond was sent Parcel Post in a plain brown wrapper to the museum that now houses it.

Tips and Traps

Save all of your moving-related expenses in a folder, since some moving expenses are tax-deductible. Visit www.irs.gov to obtain any moving-related tax forms. Check with your accountant about the rules for deducting moving expenses.

Packing Perfectly

Yes, there is a right way to pack your belongings, to help you get into your home quickly and more efficiently. Keep these tips in mind while you get ready to move:

◆ Have a centralized area for packing. Keep boxes, labels, markers, bubble wrap, plastic packing tape, and other supplies in this area.

◆ Number all boxes and color-code them, indicating what room the movers should place each box in. List rooms by color or have a floor plan that shows the colors that coordinate with the boxes.

◆ Use a record-keeping system. Write down the box number, color, and contents of that box. Keep your notebook in your packing section.

◆ Also color-code the furniture for each room. The movers can then place furniture in the correct rooms along with the color-coordinated boxes. If possible, put the color of the room on the door so that it is visible for the movers.

◆ Reinforce the bottoms of boxes with plastic packing tape, to make them more secure.

◆ Limit the weight of the boxes to less than 50 lbs., for easier lifting. Larger boxes should be used for lighter items, like pillows and light household items. Smaller boxes should be used for heavier items. Use original packaging for electronics and small appliances, when available, or secure them snugly in boxes.

◆ Utilize wardrobe boxes. They are perfect for lightweight items as well as hanging clothes. You can put bulky items like shoes, handbags, and sweaters on the bottom and hang clothes on the rod. This will eliminate some boxes while keeping closet items centralized.

◆ Pack off-season items early. If you are moving in the winter, pack summer items.

◆ Reduce the number of smaller kitchen appliances you are using and pack those you are not using regularly, such as the blender. Pack nonessential cooking utensils and cookware.

◆ When packing, keep things together. For example, pack the extension cord with the appliance, put screws and bolts in small baggies and tape them to the item, or mark the baggie and put it in with tools you need to put the items back together. Keep a special box for parts, cords, and cables, and code it as such.

◆ Cushion the bottoms, sides, and tops of the boxes for fragile items. Put an X in masking tape on all mirrors—this will keep the glass from shattering. Wrap all artwork. Be sure to pad the corners so items don't slide.

◆ Place heavier items on the bottom of the box and lighter items on top.

♦ Wrap the doors and drawers on the furniture with plastic wrap, to keep them secure and free from scratches.

♦ Keep a few boxes for last-minute items, such as bedding, toiletries, toilet paper, medications, cleaning supplies, coffeemaker, and so on. This will be the last box to leave the old house and the first box into the new house.

♦ Do not overstack boxes while waiting for moving day or when you place them on the truck. Stacking heavy boxes of books (or other heavy items) on top of one another will crush the boxes underneath.

♦ Unless you know it's being handled by the former owner, plan to cut the lawn soon after arrival. Keep your old mower easily accessible or plan to buy one shortly after arrival so you can get the mowing done.

On the actual moving day, remember to carry enough cash or traveler's checks, as well as your credit cards and ATM card, to cover any costs that may crop up during the move. This is at least until you've had an opportunity to establish banking at your new destination.

Shutting Down

Before you move, you'll have to contact several companies to turn off services, including phone, cable, utilities, and garbage. These include, but aren't limited to, the following:

♦ Electricity

♦ Gas

♦ Water

♦ Telephone

♦ Sewer service

♦ Trash collection

♦ Cable TV

♦ Internet service

♦ Home security service

Plan ahead to return equipment before your moving date.

Change of Address

To forward your mail, go to the post office and ask for a change of address form, or fill it out online at www.usps.com. Although the form notifies the U.S. Post Office to forward your mail, you still need to notify others about your address change. Here are a few reminders of where to send a change of address notification:

♦ Subscriptions. Update your address for magazine subscriptions as early as possible, since magazines often require six to eight weeks' notice. Call your local newspaper and cancel or change delivery to your new address.

♦ Charge accounts. You can update your mailing address for credit card accounts online, by calling, or through the mail. This will prevent lost bills or billing disputes.

♦ Friends and relatives.

♦ Department of Motor Vehicles.

♦ Bank and brokerage firms.

♦ Social Security and other government offices.

♦ Employment profit sharing or pension companies.

♦ Insurance policies. Just so you know, depending on where you are moving to, your auto, health, anti-theft, and life policies may generate changes in premiums.

♦ Banks. If you are moving out of your bank's service area, you may want to close your account and wire your funds to a bank at your new location or obtain a cashier's check.

♦ Schools.

♦ Doctors/dentists. You might need to find new doctors and dentists for you and your family members. If so, don't forget to obtain copies of your medical and dental records to give to your new ones.

♦ Organizations in which you're involved.

Tips and Traps _____

If you have any unopened canned food in the house that you don't want to move, take it to a local food bank. It benefits those not as fortunate as you and earns you a tax deduction. Try to plan your grocery shopping so that you use up whatever perishables you have before moving day.

Warranties and Manuals

If you have a collection of owner's manuals and warranties for home appliances and accessories—dishwashers, microwaves, refrigerators, and so on—leave them on the kitchen counter for the next renter or owner of your home or apartment. You can also include a list of the service people you used and their contact information.

The New Home

It's a great feeling to move into a new place knowing that everything is all ready for you and your family. Much of this involves preparation. Of course, planning isn't always possible, but it will make the move much smoother for you. For example, if you have time and the financial means, try to have any important repairs, remodeling, or decorating done before you move in. Throw a painting party, if you can. Repainting or recarpeting can be completed in just a few days. Minor repairs can be done in a short period of time, too. Even a new roof can be installed in one day. Hiring a cleaning person to clean your new home before you get there is a nice treat for yourself.

This is possible if you have a temporary place to stay, the money to book a room at a local hotel, or an overlap of days when you're in both your old and new homes.

Get Things Started

Next, call your new utility companies and local service providers—trash, cable, Internet service, and so on—and arrange service. If you need a new bank, visit one and arrange your accounts. Get the kids registered for school and check into local houses of worship.

For safety reasons, have your locks changed at your new home! You really have no idea who has a copy of the keys to your new home. While you're at it, don't forget to have the code on your new garage remote changed as well. Also, where applicable, check with the post office for a new mailbox key.

Tips and Traps _____

To save the cost of disconnect and connect fees, have the seller transfer the water, gas, and electricity from his name to yours. Don't forget to request refunds of service deposits from the utilities at your old home if you were required to make them to start services there.

Meet the Neighbors

You may have met your new neighbors when you were in the process of buying your home, but it's nice to go around and introduce yourself. You can meet your neighbors by going door to door or joining a neighborhood association. Once you're moved in, invite them over for a housewarming party or cookout. They'll probably quickly return the favor.

What If Your New Home Isn't Ready?

Let's say that, so far, everything about your purchase has gone perfectly. The offer was accepted, your mortgage was approved, the inspections went well, you closed on time, and now you're ready to move in. But what if the former owner hasn't finished moving out by the agreed-upon possession date? Worse, he tells you he thinks it will take at least another two weeks to finish. Or what if you're ready to move in and the repairs you've ordered aren't going to be ready for another week or two? What do you do now—particularly if you've moved a long distance and the movers are scheduled to arrive the next morning?

First, and most important, figure out where you and your family are going to stay while you resolve this—a hotel or motel may be okay for a night or two, but staying there and eating out for a couple of weeks won't be cheap.

Second, determine exactly when you'll be able to move in. If the contractor is holding up your move, find out exactly when he'll be done and get that in writing as well. If the problem is a tenant or former owner, get it in writing from the occupant and decide whether you want to charge him rent for the time he's occupying your home. You are entitled to it, but pushing the issue can make him determined to stay as long as possible just to make a point. You can also request a security deposit from him, but if it's only a relatively short period of time, it may not be necessary, and he may not agree to pay it. This is your decision. Ask your Realtor for advice.

If the newly agreed-upon date arrives and he still hasn't moved, check with your Realtor about the possibility of this situation coming under any mediation or arbitration clause in your purchase contract. Again, this may depend on local law. If not, contact your lawyer and begin proceedings to have him removed. How much time this will take varies from jurisdiction to jurisdiction. Make sure that you also have your lawyer seek reimbursement of your legal expenses from your holdover.

The Least You Need to Know

◆ Moving is extremely stressful, and planning and organizing can help reduce the stress and make your move more enjoyable.

◆ Check out your movers' backgrounds and licenses before hiring them.

◆ Before you move, clean out your home and donate, sell, or throw away what you don't need or want.

◆ Unpack as much as you can before you move so your home is ready when you arrive.

◆ If the tenant or previous owner doesn't move out by the agreed-upon possession date, find out when he will or contact an attorney for assistance.

Chapter 18

After the Fact

In This Chapter

- ◆ Dealing with problems you discover after moving in
- ◆ Determining who should take care of the problem
- ◆ When you should take the seller to court
- ◆ Statutes of limitations on taking the seller to court

Now that you own your home, you probably think you're done. You might be, but what if something suddenly "pops up" that you feel warrants action by the seller? For example, let's say that after you move in, you find a crack in the foundation that extends from one corner of the foundation to halfway up one side of the structure. You never saw it during the walkthrough and the inspector missed it. It isn't a recent crack, yet the seller never said a thing about it to you. Your warranty doesn't cover it, so what do you do? Do you take action against the seller for not disclosing this to you, or do you take action against your inspector for negligence in not finding or discussing the crack? Or do you just have to deal with it on your own?

This chapter focuses on what happens after you move in. You might think you're done dealing with the seller, but instead you might encounter something that forces you to talk to him and see if he knew about the problem. If he did, you then need to decide what's going to be done about it. This chapter takes you step-by-step through what to do if this happens to you.

Contact Your Realtor

If you've found something wrong with the house and it's something you believe you should have known about, the first thing you should do is contact your Realtor. Tell your Realtor why you thought the seller knew about it and didn't disclose it. She can then carefully review the disclosures you received from the seller to determine whether any mention of the problem was made in the documents. If the crack was mentioned in the disclosure documents, you are, unfortunately, stuck with repairing and paying for it on your own, and you likely have no recourse against the seller.

However, if your agent sees that there was no disclosure, you have a strong basis to pursue the seller for financial compensation so you can have the problem fixed. If the seller is willing to pay the repair costs, the issue is settled. If the seller refuses to talk about the situation, you must decide if you want to pursue mediation, arbitration, or litigation. See Chapter 13 for a discussion about mediation, arbitration, and litigation.

Knowledge of the Problem

When the seller is approached to find out if he knew about the problem ahead of time, a few things might happen. First, he might have lied about it during the sale process. A seller might do this because he didn't want to torpedo the sale, so he chose to remain silent in hopes you wouldn't uncover the problem until it was too late.

Second, the seller might have known about the crack, but he didn't intentionally hide it from you. For example, the crack might have been hidden from everyone's view because it was under the carpet of a finished basement. The seller had owned the home for a dozen years and intended to get it repaired, but as the saying goes, "Out of sight, out of mind." He might have forgotten about the crack and failed to disclose it to you, but this memory lapse doesn't excuse him from liability.

Third, he might have known about the crack, but considered it in the overall scope of things to be too insignificant to warrant mentioning. That's his error and will not protect him from liability.

Realtor Involvement

It's also possible that the seller's agent may have been involved in the efforts to conceal the defect from you. The agent may have been fully aware of it and chose not to disclose it as a way of pushing the price upward, an act that benefits both him and his client. In such a situation, both the seller and the agent can be found liable not only for the costs of remedying the problem, but also for fraud, which can produce much larger damages at trial.

Constructive Knowledge

Constructive knowledge of a problem means that the agent knew, or should have known, about the problem because of something else that was going on. For example, maybe you found mold that you didn't know about before. The seller's agent claims he didn't know about it, but he did know that the washing machine overflowed and not only soaked the floor and walls, but also leaked under the door to the downstairs room and soaked the wall-to-wall carpet in that room, too. As it turned out, this leak resulted in the mold. The seller's agent said the home never had mold but never told you about the leak that caused the mold. It costs you thousands of dollars to remove and replace all of the laundry room walls and the carpet in the family room. Even if the agent can prove that she had no direct knowledge of the mold, it is possible that she had constructive knowledge of the defect.

In another example, a seller told her Realtor she had remodeled the home two years ago, adding on 2,000 square feet of space to the home. The total square footage was listed as 4,500 square feet. Six months after closing, the buyer told her contractor that the home was 4,500 square feet of living area. The contractor immediately recognized that the number was not right, and that the square footage was much smaller than that, by more than a third. The seller's agent never questioned the size that the seller claimed, and he was held liable for fraud and nondisclosure. As a professional, he should have recognized that the square footage had been greatly exaggerated. Had the actual difference been minimal, such as 50 to 100 square feet of the claimed 4,500, the Realtor likely wouldn't have been held liable.

Both examples illustrate constructive knowledge of a problem that was not disclosed to a buyer. In such a case, you have a good chance of recovering your repair costs or the extra costs for paying for what you thought was a larger home. In most cases, the damages you'll recoup likely will be paid by both the seller and the Realtor, with the total not to exceed your damages unless you can prove deliberate fraud. In such situations, suddenly you may reap punitive damages in addition to your actual damages.

Inspector Negligence

What happens if the problem is something the inspector missed and the seller didn't lie about? You should ask your agent to talk to the inspector and find out if he saw the problem and, if so, why he didn't mention it. If he explains that he did see it but didn't mention it for whatever reason, it's up to you to decide whether you want the inspector to provide some compensation for this. If he admits he missed it, definitely consider seeking compensation from him.

What Repairs to Expect

It's inevitable—you'll move in and *something* will need to be fixed. When an issue with the home or any of its systems or appliances occurs after you close, it is very unlikely that the seller will agree to repair this type of defect. In most cases, the seller believes the sale is history and there's nothing further to discuss. You'll have to fix the appliance or system yourself. This is why these systems are turned on during the walkthrough—to check that they work. If you do want to talk to the seller, you can ask him to fix something. He may say no, and if you want to pursue it, you may have to go through mediation, arbitration, or a lawsuit. Or maybe he'll say yes and the problem is solved.

Tips and Traps

If you are having a dispute with your seller after you've already closed, check the purchase contract to see how to proceed—mediation, arbitration, or litigation.

Other Warranties and Their Coverages

Keep in mind that some appliances may still be covered under an existing manufacturer's warranty. Also, if you have a home warranty and included riders for appliances, you may be able to get an appliance fixed or replaced for a nominal service fee. Again, if the warranty expired and it's something you want to pursue with the seller, you may still have to go through mediation, arbitration, or litigation.

Other warranties are worth checking out if you have an issue with your new home. If it's a newly constructed house, a warranty may cover construction defects. It holds the builder responsible for any physical defects in the construction of the home and usually is good from one to three years. Notable exceptions exist, however. For example, Mississippi has a structural defects warranty covering six years from the date of construction. Although it didn't pass, Arizona voters in 2008 considered a 10-year warranty. Even though it was defeated, its mere existence on the ballot shows that the idea of extending warranty protection for home buyers is under consideration.

California has a 1-year specific warranty from the builder, but a 10-year implied warranty against construction defects exists under California law. However, in what can be called a balancing attempt between plaintiff buyers and builder defendants, the 10-year period may be tempered somewhat by the date you first discovered the problem and when you brought it to the builder's attention. Various statutes of limitations apply to the different types of defects you might discover. So the 10 years is the absolute maximum time you have under this implied warranty. But statutes of limitations aside, even if you're within the statute period, the fact that you delayed an appreciable amount of time may have caused further deterioration and you likely will not be permitted to collect for that portion of the damage. A final decision will be made by the arbitrator or court.

If you find yourself in this situation, you can go two places for guidance: your Realtor, or the local board of Realtors and your attorney. But whatever you do, don't wait. Any delay may void your warranty rights.

Uniform Commercial Code

The Uniform Commercial Code law, found in some form in all states except Louisiana, is not designed to cover a home purchase, but is designed to regulate commercial dealings of many different types. How does it relate to your home purchase? Well, some of its individual sections may have some connection. For example, implied warranties on appliances, fixtures, and building materials may protect you on those items, or application of liens on removable parts of the land parcel the home is situated on. This refers to mechanic's liens placed on fixtures removed from the land. Fixtures are items added to the property that are so attached they are legally considered as if they were an original part of the property. The implied warranties are unwritten warranties for a particular use or purpose related to a specific object. For example, if you bought a washer, there would be an implied warranty that it would wash your clothing. This is because it would be reasonable to expect that you bought it with that use in mind. Similarly, implied warranties could exist on materials used in the construction of the home you just bought because it would be reasonable to expect that they would be used in its construction and should be fit for the purpose.

In the former instance, *implied warranty of merchantability* or for specific use, any recourse would be back to the manufacturer or the dealer from which the item was purchased. Also check with an attorney to see if you have any other rights under the code.

def•i•ni•tion

An **implied warranty of merchantability** is one that assumes you bought an item for a specific purpose and therefore it is warranted to be good for that particular expected use.

Statute of Limitations

A statute of limitations is a legal time limit you have to start a lawsuit. In most cases, the clock starts running on your time limit either at the time the cause of your dispute initially occurs or, in some cases, when you first become aware of an issue.

Tips and Traps

Statutes of limitation vary from state to state. For information on a specific state's law, visit www.answers.com/topic/statute-of-limitations. This site details various statutes and refers you to additional detailed sources of statute information.

Rules and limitations vary from situation to situation and state to state. Therefore, the best advice is, do not delay when you feel you have an issue and your attempts at resolving it have been unsuccessful. Check with an attorney about how much time you have under the applicable statute of limitations law. This is not to suggest that you shouldn't attempt to resolve your dispute amicably before resorting to litigation, but don't waste your time doing so. When the statute has run out, it's over—and so are your chances of any further recourse.

The Least You Need to Know

◆ Although you'll want everything to run smoothly, there is a chance you'll uncover problems after you move in.

◆ The key to fixing a problem—or getting your money back for repair—is first finding out whether the previous owner knew that the problem existed.

◆ If the seller lied about a problem that you find after closing, contact your attorney and see if litigation is an issue.

◆ When you discover a problem, don't delay in taking action, since it can cost you compensation.

Red Flags—Beware

In This Chapter

- ◆ Know that your agent is working for you
- ◆ When to sever the relationship with your agent
- ◆ Red flags with the seller
- ◆ Warning signs to walk away from the purchase

So far, we've spent the entire book telling you how to buy a home—one that you desire, like, and can afford. Now we take a look at a few instances that scream, "Run away as fast as you can!" We truly hope you will face none of these possible scenarios, but it's best that we tell you about them so that if you do, you'll take heed. They frequently portend serious issues in your future regarding a particular house or Realtor if you don't pay attention to them.

Of course, you want your purchase to go perfectly, from finding the right real estate agent to finding the right home and getting to closing. Unfortunately, though, not every transaction goes smoothly, and not every agent/buyer relationship flows easily. There may be problems with the way the agent is handling the purchase, or you may be questioning his ethics.

Many real estate agents have been confronted with difficult scenarios, and their advice is almost always the same: forget about the house in question. This chapter focuses on potential red flags and what you need to do when something just doesn't feel right.

Real Estate Agent Problems

When you chose your Realtor, hopefully you followed the advice we gave you earlier in the book. Maybe you got a strong recommendation from a co-worker or family member who said that Joe Johnson, real estate agent from ABC Realty, was the best agent you could ever hope to find, or perhaps you completed your interviews with several Realtors, Joe included, and Sue Andersen outshone all the others by a mile.

Sue might have had more listings in the area you're considering or far more ads in the Sunday newspaper's real estate section. You thought, "How could she not be a good agent if she has all of this business?"

Conflict of Interest or Time Issues

Unfortunately, after hiring Sue, you've found that everything wasn't quite as good as it first seemed. You've been looking at properties in a number of locations and she shows you a home that she says is "perfect." Best of all, she says, it's at a great price in an up-and-coming area.

So you look at the property, visiting it several times to get a solid impression of its pluses and minuses. You think that the home is a possibility, but you have some reservations. The price seems too good to be true if the house is "perfect." You're uncomfortable with the proximity to the highway—something you stressed to your agent that you didn't want. You tell the agent you're not sure, and she listens, smiles, and says she understands. However, she is aggressive and tells you that it's a rare opportunity and "you're going to be sorry if you don't move on it." At this point, ask yourself, and definitely ask her, "Why the fixation on this particular home?" and "Why are you pushing for this one?" You need to figure out what her motivation is. True, sometimes your agent believes the home is a real bargain. She might just be trying to encourage you to make a decision so you don't lose the home by hesitating too long. However, she could also be pushing it because she has a personal or business relationship with the seller or developer.

This could be a conflict of interest. A relationship between your Realtor and the seller is not illegal, per se, and any ethics issue depends on exactly how she represents your interests in the house. If the agent has disclosed this relationship to you and thoroughly protects your interests in all circumstances, it's not unethical. However, if she fails to tell you up front of her relationship with the owner or developer and "overlooks" her fiduciary ethical obligations to you, there is an ethical issue here and you may wish to discuss the matter with her broker. Also, this is a good reason to consider ending the relationship. Have a serious conversation with her about her actions. Listen to her explanation before making any final decision. If you aren't convinced by her explanation, look for a new agent.

Most times you won't have signed any agreement with the agent, except if it's a buyer-broker agreement. If you've signed one of those, as a buyer, your only obligation is to pay the agent's commission if and when she succeeds in getting you a home that you buy and close on. No house, no obligation—definitely no lawsuit.

Tips and Traps

Keep in mind that your Realtor is ethically bound to act in your best interests and to place those interests ahead of hers in making a decision on your behalf.

Poor Inspection Advice

Another way your agent can fail you is with inspection advice. Let's say you finally find a home that looks practically perfect in every way—it has the number of bedrooms and baths you want, it seems structurally sound, it has the amenities that you are looking for, and it's in a good neighborhood with access to excellent schools and great shopping. This seems to be "the" home for you.

When writing the offer, your agent tells you he doesn't think it is necessary for you to get inspections completed on the property beyond the basic pest and contractors' inspections. In a more extreme case, he might tell you that this home is in such great shape that you can feel comfortable making your offer without worrying about inspections of any kind.

You question his advice. Instead of agreeing to condition your offer on the results of the inspections, your agent reiterates that you're "needlessly worrying about nothing" and that if you "don't hurry" with your offer, you'll lose the property. There's that aggression again, but this time, you trust his experience and decide to move forward.

Unfortunately, proceeding with the offer without any inspections, or with fewer inspections than might otherwise be advisable, could set you up for serious problems down the road. Imagine moving in and finding out that your septic system is broken or the entire roof needs to be replaced. You could be facing tremendous expenses on any problems that crop up after you close on the house. These expenses could run several thousands of dollars. Inspections are vital to your home-buying process, and nobody should try to convince you otherwise.

If your Realtor keeps insisting that you shouldn't waste any time (or money) on inspections, whether he is referring to *any* inspections or to supplementary ones that the original inspector may recommend based on his findings, and can't be dissuaded, you should sever the relationship and find an agent who is more willing to protect your interests.

In another version of this issue, the Realtor keeps insisting against all logic and information to the contrary that you *only* use one specific inspector. Ask your agent directly why he's pushing so hard for this one guy. If he can't come up with reasonable answers—and a few references for him or her—it's time to move on.

Quotes and Facts

In one situation, it can be reasonable for your agent to recommend avoiding inspections: if inspections have been performed on the home within the past one or two months and you have full access to the results and the inspectors who wrote them. Some agents are willing to forego contractors' inspections for up to six months since the last one, but they still recommend a pest inspection if more than two months have elapsed since the last one.

Suspect Mortgage Lenders Referrals

If you don't already have a mortgage lender and you receive a referral from your real estate agent to a lender or mortgage broker, that's okay. There's *nothing* wrong with her providing you with such a referral. However, there's something wrong with a Realtor who insists that, as a condition of working with her, you *must* obtain your financing from a particular mortgage lender.

Ask her why she's insisting that you use that lender. Then ask if she receives referral fees. If the answer is yes, the agent is required to disclose this information. Your agent may be placing her own best interests before yours. This is a breach of ethics on her part and is illegal. In addition to breaching her duty to provide you the best service without favoring her own interests, it violates a federal law, the Real Estate Settlement Procedure Act (RESPA), which specifically prohibits such kickbacks in exchange for business referrals. RESPA is a federal law passed to stop anyone in the real estate industry from benefiting by, among other things, referring their clients to mortgage lenders in the industry in exchange for a kickback of part of that vendor's fee. It is also intended to stop actions by Realtors and lenders that only increase those individuals' receipts while increasing the buyer's closing costs for no additional benefit. Violations of the act can result in civil and criminal penalties.

More properly, she should give you that individual or firm's name, along with at least one alternative so that you make the choice in the final determination. While strict interpretation of RESPA requires only that she not force you to use that one individual as a condition of her representing you, common practice is that she give you two or three references, which can include the one she favors.

If your agent keeps insisting that you must use her lender as a condition of working with her, the solution is simple. Find another Realtor—*fast*. Be aware that she may feel this way about a particular mortgage broker because he always is able to get the job done, no matter how daunting the buyer's credit is, or because she has had too many deal killers from other local loan brokers. But get some specifics from her about her insistence. If they don't ring true, my original advice stands—run!

Seller Problems

Let's say you put in an offer on a house for a price that is at or close to the seller's asking price, to secure a relatively quick close. However, as we've stressed, you also want to protect yourself and include contingencies for inspections and loan approval in your offer.

After reviewing your offer, let's say the seller has no objection to a loan contingency, but she is opposed to an inspection contingency. She says that her house has "always been maintained at the highest level," and she makes it clear that if you want the house, you'll buy it without inspections. This is a very clear warning that there are likely to be serious issues with the physical condition of this home.

If this happens to you and you really want the home, then reiterate your offer, including the inspection contingency request. If the seller still refuses, forget the home. There's obviously something the seller isn't telling you, and that would soon become your biggest headache.

Price Issues

The next red flag you see could be the price of the home. Let's say you find a home that has a price so far below comparable homes in the same area, you wonder if there's a catch. There probably is. It's one thing if the house is only a few thousand dollars cheaper than other homes in the same market. However, it's another thing if the home is more than 25 percent cheaper. Ask your agent to find out why.

It might be simply that the home has been on the market for a while or the owner needs to get it sold as soon as possible for personal reasons. Or the seller might be almost out of time on a short-sale deal or he wants to avoid foreclosure by cutting the price to the bone as an incentive. But it's also possible that the home has major structural issues and the seller is hoping that the low price will generate a sale anyway. Or something in the local environment might affect his ability to get it sold, so a low price could lure in a buyer. In this latter situation, a good example is that the home you are looking at is on an area bordering a former chemical manufacturing facility. However, the specific home you're considering not only is part of the bordering neighborhood, but it is the home closest to the now-closed chemical plant, and thus subject to the worst of the effects of the old facility.

While the seller isn't obligated to say why his price is so low, he is obligated to disclose to you any and all known defects in the property, as well as any environmental issues that may affect the value. Remember, the basic rule on any disclosure is that if something might affect the decision of a willing buyer, it must be disclosed. Clearly, something negative in the local environment fits this category. My own practice is that if I can think of it as a possible issue, I disclose it.

If nothing turns up in any disclosures, you may choose to proceed with the purchase, but be very careful. A major price reduction usually has a serious reason behind it.

Too Many Homes for Sale

If your agent tells you that typically there are three or four homes on the market at any one time in a particular location, and when you are visiting the area you see that about 90 percent of the homes have "for sale" signs in their front yards, this is a red flag.

In some cases, a larger than normal number of homes for sale in an area could be due to the foreclosure crisis as it affects an area, but this won't be the only reason for an unusually high number of sale signs in a neighborhood. Also, the foreclosure crisis hasn't hit all areas uniformly.

If there is a general economic turndown affecting the whole region, proceed with caution and due diligence. However, if you are not aware of such a situation and your agent is unable to enlighten you, this may be a good reason to look elsewhere. A good agent familiar with a particular area will be aware of anything serious enough to cause such a mass sale situation, but if she can't tell you, consider another area as well as another agent.

Odor Issues

We discussed earlier in this book how such things as a nearby major highway or airport can depress prices and negatively affect the quality of life in a particular locale. In addition to the expected issues that you would expect with either of these, such as noise, gas fumes, flashing lights at night, and physical shaking from large planes taking off, there are also other issues often not spoken of but every bit as annoying. These are odors.

Near a highway, the odor issue can be as broad as the different types of cargo hauled along the road. If a semi hauling hogs goes past, you'll know immediately—and probably for a while afterward. If one or more vehicles is burning oil or rubber, the smell can permeate your home for days on end—and as more vehicles in this shape go by, it becomes cumulative.

Airports in their own way are no different. Every time a plane takes to the air or makes its final landing approach, you can smell the JP4 burning. The effect is, like the highway gas fumes, cumulative. The more planes, the more fumes and the more smell.

Let's say that when you go on one of your neighborhood visits, you notice a particularly unpleasant odor. You hadn't noticed it before, but no matter where in the neighborhood you go, you can't seem to escape it. You ask your agent if she knows the source of the odor or if it's just a one-time thing. She tells you that it is a fact of life in that neighborhood. It is coming from a local manufacturing plant and there's really nothing you can do about it. She also tells you that some residents claim that after a while you get used to it and don't really notice it any longer.

If you're not one of those people who can get used to it, forget about buying that home. The odor could become a health issue and will probably make it harder for you to sell the home in the future.

Landslides

If your home is located on a hill or is bordered by hills, consider potential problems with landslides. Even small hills can cause slides, given the right set of circumstances. If you discover there have been previous slides on the home's site or somewhere in the neighborhood, consider looking elsewhere. If this truly is your dream home, get an inspection and analysis by a licensed geological or soils engineer. You may also want to have an inspection by a drainage engineer. Both specialists can tell you how severe the threat of additional slides is, but they'll also give you the disclaimer that they can't give you a guarantee. They can, however, recommend remedial steps you can take to protect the home and reduce the risk of slides, such as retaining walls and special excavation. It's your call, but we recommend you forget the property.

Warning!

In addition to a current license from either the state or the city, make sure any engineer you hire has current errors and omissions (E&O) insurance in case he incorrectly analyzes the slide potential at a location. E&O insurance covers any claims made against the engineer that are faulty due to his negligence. It's similar, in a way, to a doctor's malpractice insurance.

This chapter includes just a few examples of red flags that you might encounter during your home-buying process. The best advice I can offer is to use your common sense and listen to your gut feeling. If something seems wrong and you can't shake the feeling, forget the property. You'll avoid having your dream turn into a nightmare.

The Least You Need to Know

 ◆ Your agent should be working for you, not getting referral fees from lenders.

 ◆ If you're not happy with what your agent is doing, let her know.

 ◆ If your agent is doing anything illegal or unethical, sever ties with her immediately.

 ◆ Sellers who won't allow you to get inspections on the property are often hiding something—run, don't walk, away.

 ◆ Trust your instincts—if something doesn't feel right, it probably isn't.

Glossary

acre   A measure of land; equals 43,590 square feet.

adjustable-rate mortgage (ARM)   A loan on which monthly payments will increase or decrease over time based on changes in the ARM's interest rate index. ARM payments typically are adjusted every six months or once a year. Common indexes to which ARMs are tied include one-year T-notes and six-month T-bills.

amortization   The schedule of repayment of a mortgage over its term, usually monthly.

annual percentage rate (APR)   The true rate of interest you pay after compounding.

appraisal   A professional valuation of a piece of real property.

arbitration   A form of nonjudicial dispute resolution. Its decisions are binding on the parties.

as-is   A term used to denote that a piece of property is to be sold in its present condition, regardless of what the buyer may discover in inspections. In some extreme cases, a seller may agree to reduce the agreed contract price if unusually extreme damages to the home are found during the inspection.

assessment   1.) A one-time expense required of condo owners by their homeowners' association, usually to cover a sudden large expense for the condo complex. 2.) The value the local taxing authority assigns to real estate, as a basis for establishing its tax bill.

balloon payment   The final payment on a loan that is only partly repaid by the time it reaches its final due date. The balloon equals the remaining outstanding balance at that point.

bankruptcy   Legal processes under federal law to resolve indebtedness.

blog   Short for *weblog*, a blog is like a personal diary for a business.

buydown   The process of paying points to a mortgage lender, to get a lower interest rate charged to the mortgage.

capital gain   The increase in value of your property made during the period you own it.

change order   A change from original plans made during construction by the contractor.

closing   The final point in a home purchase, when you legally take title to a property.

comparative market analysis (CMA)   A survey of attributes and selling prices of comparable houses either on the market or recently sold. A CMA helps determine the correct pricing strategy for a seller's property and a buyer's purchase.

condominium   A type of residential property. Also, a legal form of ownership in which you own everything within your residence but have shared ownership of all common areas, such as grounds, pools, and other amenities.

constructive knowledge   When it is deemed someone should have known about a situation or defect due to his professional expertise.

contingency   A condition to your offer that allows you to cancel a contract within a specific period of time if you cannot be satisfied under the conditions of the contingency (for example, an inspection contingency or a loan contingency).

conventional loan   A mortgage with an initial principal amount not exceeding $417,000.

conveyance   Either 1.) the transfer of title, or 2.) the document, such as a deed, by which title is officially transferred.

creditback   An amount of money that the seller pays back to the buyer at the time of the purchase closing.

curb appeal   The attraction—or lack thereof—that a home shows visitors as they first arrive at the home.

deed   A legal document that formally conveys ownership of property from seller to buyer.

depreciation   An accounting process by which the paper value of real property is reduced. This benefits an owner from an income tax point of view, even though the property may actually be appreciating.

days on market (DOM)   Represents the time, in days, that a piece of real property has been on the market.

dry rot   A fungal form of damage to wood. Contrary to its name, it is caused by the exposure of wood to moisture.

duplex   A residential building that has two separate residential units. A duplex is often used as an investment property.

earnest money   A good-faith deposit that the buyer pays at the start of the purchase transaction. It accompanies the initial offer and becomes part of the buyer's overall down payment.

easement   A legal transfer of a right to a nonowner of property that affects the use of the property. Easements are granted in perpetuity (for example, a right of passage across a piece of land given by the owner to another person).

equity   The part of a property's value that is not part of the loans outstanding on the property. Also referred to as owner's equity.

Errors and Omissions (E&O) insurance   Covers a Realtor's liability for errors of negligence in his practice while representing a client.

Federal Emergency Management Administration (FEMA)   The federal government agency that oversees disaster emergency assistance.

FICO score   Credit score. Often used to help determine eligibility for a mortgage.

fiduciary   One who acts on behalf of another in any matter that requires a high level of trust. If violated by the one receiving that trust, it is dealt with harshly by the courts.

fixture   Any part of a structure that is, by its form of attachment, effectively an inseparable part of the structure. This may include built-in cabinets and appliances.

flood zone   A geographical area determined by the U.S. Army Corps of Engineers to be likely to flood at least once in a hundred-year period. Homeowners who have a mortgage in these areas are required to obtain flood insurance.

foreclosure   The process by which a lender takes possession and title of real property from its owner, usually due to nonpayment of a mortgage on the property.

FSBO   For sale by owner. The home is for sale by the owner, without an agent representing the owner.

GI loan   A federally guaranteed mortgage for military veterans, also known as a VA loan.

gift letter   A letter from the donor of a gift of money that is used to buy a home. It certifies that the funds truly are a gift and that the buyer has no obligation to repay them at a later date. The buyer provides this to a bank as part of the mortgage application package when down payment funds include a gift.

hazard insurance   Compensates for property damage from specified hazards such as fire and wind.

homeowners' association (HOA)   The group of all owners in a residential complex that enforces owners' covenants. Although it is a possibility in any group of homes, it is most often found in condominiums and townhomes.

implied warranty   Part of the law in many states to protect buyers of new construction. It generally holds that, for a specific period of time after construction, the original owner has a right to expect no defects from poor construction work.

impound   An account established by the mortgage lender to hold funds to cover property taxes and homeowner's insurance premiums.

installment sale/purchase   Transfer of property over a period of time, during which the buyer makes installment payments to the seller until the full agreed price is paid. Interest is charged to the buyer, and the legal title passes only when the seller receives final payment.

institutional lender   A traditional lender, such as a bank.

jumbo loan   A mortgage loan of more than $417,000. In some high-price areas, this can be as much as any loan over $724,000.

lien   A legal claim against the title to a piece of real property. Also referred to as a "cloud" on the title, something that calls its legitimacy into doubt.

liquidated damages   A contractually agreed-upon amount that must be paid to the seller if the buyer breaches the contract. This agreed amount avoids litigation and related expenses.

loan assumption   The situation when a buyer, as part of the purchase, agrees to take over the existing financing on the property. Some loans are assumable; others are not.

market value   The current value of real estate that a buyer is willing to pay and a seller is willing to accept.

mediation   A form of nonjudicial dispute resolution. Its decisions are not binding on the parties.

Megan's Law   A series of laws enacted in most states that provides a sexual offender database for buyers to see if an offender lives near their home.

mold   A living organism that, in a very few circumstances, can have serious harmful effects to people's health. Mold is usually caused by moisture in a confined area.

mortgage   1.) The term for the lien placed upon a piece of property by a lender to secure its loan on the property. 2.) A loan used to finance the purchase of real property.

mortgage broker   An individual who arranges mortgages for buyers by obtaining information and then presenting it to as many banks as he feels appropriate to get the best loan possible.

Multiple Listing Service (MLS)   The place where Realtors usually list their properties for sale.

National Flood Insurance Program (NFIP)   Special federally backed flood insurance program. This program is required of homes located in Army Corps of Engineers–designated flood zones as long as they have mortgages from FDIC-insured lenders.

notice of default (NOD)   The first legal recorded document when a homeowner breaches the terms of his mortgage. The breach is usually failure to make timely payments of the mortgage.

open house   When a property is open to the public for on-site viewing, with or without a Realtor.

per annum   Literally, "per year." The most common method of calculating interest on a loan.

PITI   Principal, interest, taxes, and insurance, forming the basis for monthly mortgage payments.

point   A loan fee equal to 1 percent of the principal amount of the loan.

preapproval   The process by which a lender fully analyzes a buyer's financial information and approves a mortgage. It may be conditioned on satisfactory title and appraisal reports.

prequalification   The process by which a lender briefly reviews a buyer's financial information to consider the likelihood of eligibility for a loan upon further in-depth analysis. This is not as good as a full approval.

principal   The amount borrowed when taking out a loan.

private mortgage insurance (PMI)   Insurance purchased by the buyer on the principal loan amount, guaranteeing repayment. Usually required on higher-risk mortgages.

proration   The process by which real estate taxes and interest on a loan, for a brief period at closing, are divided between the buyer and seller of a home.

real estate owned (REO)   Bank parlance for foreclosed property owned by the bank.

Real Estate Settlement Procedures Act (RESPA) statement   A precise breakdown of closing costs for both sellers and buyers.

real property   A possession that consists of real estate and any fixtures attached thereto (such as buildings), as distinct from personal property.

Realtor   A real estate sales professional licensed by her state to list and sell real property, who is also a member of the state or National Association of Realtors.

recordation   The process of legally recording documents related to a home, such as a mortgage, a deed, liens, and easements. Usually performed by a county official known as the county recorder.

relocation   The process by which an individual is moved from one location to another by her employer. The company often provides relocation assistance to ease the move. May sometimes refer to a voluntary move that is not job related.

reverse mortgage   A loan that is repaid on the sale of the property from the equity in the home. This loan is more common for elderly or retired homeowners living on a fixed income who have a lot of equity built up in their home.

secondary mortgage market   A market created by lenders selling their mortgage loans to other lenders to replenish lendable cash.

seller carryback   Occurs when the seller agrees to "carry back" a mortgage on the property he has just sold. The mortgage can be for the entire amount financed or just a portion of it. Principal amount, interest rate, and term of the loan are negotiated between the buyer and the seller.

setback   The distance from your lot's boundaries that local ordinances require you to place your walls when building or remodeling your home.

short sale   The sale of real property when the seller's price is less than the outstanding loan balances on the property. The bank holding the mortgage must agree to the sales price.

specific performance   A legal process by which one party to a contract can force the other party to perform under the contract. Most commonly used by the buyer in home buying when the seller breaches and refuses to complete the sale.

specific warranty of construction   Means that, by law, in the states that have it, a buyer of a new home has a statutorily defined period of time in which the builder/seller must remedy any construction defects.

tenants-in-common   A form of ownership in which all owners share a common ownership of the property but individually own a specific percentage of the whole. Each individual also gets his own financing.

term   The length of time a loan is made for. Also called tenor.

title insurance   Insurance to protect against claims made against legal title to a specific piece of real property referred to in the policy.

topography   The physical details of land—hilly, flat, sloping, and so on.

toxic mold   Certain types of mold that can cause serious health problems.

Uniform Commercial Code (UCC)   A legal code that deals mostly with non–real estate issues. The main real property exceptions to this are lenders' security interests in items of value that are removable from real estate, such as timber, crops, or extractive minerals.

VA loan   A federally guaranteed mortgage for military veterans; also known as a GI loan.

vesting   Conveying ownership.

virtual tour   A "tour" of a home by video or photos on a CD or website.

walkthrough   Buyer verification of a property's condition immediately before closing.

warranty   A form of guarantee of no defects in an individual item of merchandise or an object containing that merchandise. In certain formats, it may apply to a home or its components, systems, and appliances.

Appendix B

Resources

This is a collection of some very useful and informative books and websites that can provide plenty of help during your search. It is by no means all-inclusive; it's merely an assortment of useful books and websites that I have used and referred buyers to.

Books

Bach, David. *The Automatic Millionaire Homeowner: A Powerful Plan to Finish Rich in Real Estate.* New York: Random House, 2004.

Eldred, Gary W. *106 Common Mistakes Homebuyers Make and How to Avoid Them.* Hoboken, NJ: John Wiley & Sons, 2005.

Johnson, Randy. *How to Save Thousands of Dollars on Your Home Mortgage, 2nd Edition.* New York: Wiley, 2002.

National Association of Realtors, Blanche Evans. *The National Association of Realtors Guide to Home Buying.* New York: Wiley, 2006.

Robert, Irwin. *Tips and Traps When Buying a Home.* New York: McGraw-Hill, 2009.

Wasserman, Mollie, and Ken Deshaies. *How to Make Your Realtor Get You the Best Deal, Massachusetts Edition: A Guide Through the Real Estate Purchasing Process, from Choosing a Realtor to Negotiating the Best Deal for You!* New York: Partners Group, 2003.
If you're not from Massachusetts, try searching for a similar volume specific to your area.

Websites

www.bankrate.com
A good site for information on mortgages, changes in the laws, and regulations pertaining to them.

www.berkeleyhomes.com
A Cyberstar website. This site helps readers who are buying in the San Francisco Bay area, but it also gives all buyers a good idea of what a leading Realtor can offer.

www.car.org
The site of the California Association of Realtors. This site covers all you need to know about real estate in California. It also lists all Realtor members in the state.

www.cdva.ca.gov/CalVetloans/Default.aspx
Operated by the State of California. This site provides plenty of good, easy-to-follow information on Cal-Vet loans.

www.cleanoffer.com
Designed to assist home buyers in locating homes of interest. It has expanded from its original California-only base to now include Texas and Massachusetts. Your Realtor has to sign you up, after which you have free 24/7 access.

www.comehometomarin.com
My own website. It's the best you can find for Marin County, California. Drop in and let us help you.

www.cooperator.com
A publication for cooperative and condo owners, managers, and staff members. It offers great information on living in a co-op and condo. The information is targeted to New York and New Jersey but is informative overall.

www.crs.com
The site of the Council of Residential Specialists. It's another site for locating excellent agents around the country.

www.cyberstars.net

The home site of the Allen Hainge Cyberstars. If you're seeking a great Realtor, you can do no better. Click on "The Cyberstars" to see if there is a Cyberstar Realtor located near you.

www.epa.gov/mold

Operated by the United States Environmental Protection Agency. This site provides helpful information about mold in the home.

www.equifax.com

The website of one of the three major credit-reporting firms. It not only provides information about Equifax, but it also helps you get a credit report on yourself.

www.experian.com

The website of one of the major credit-reporting firms. It provides credit-related information and advice. You also can get your credit report here.

www.fanniemae.com

The website of Fannie Mae, the government-chartered, private shareholder-owned mortgage agency. It guarantees or purchases a major amount of the mortgages issued in the United States.

http://federalreserve.gov

The website of the U.S. Federal Reserve. It contains a seemingly endless amount of information on virtually anything financial in the country. Once on the site, click on "Consumer Information" and then "Mortgages." You'll find a wealth of excellent information about mortgages, including payment calculators, information about different types of mortgages, tips on avoiding foreclosure, guidance on shopping for the most suitable mortgage for your needs, and information about home equity lines of credit.

www.fema.gov

The Federal Emergency Management Administration website. On the home page, click on "Flood Insurance, Maps, and Information" for details about flood insurance and federally declared flood zones.

www.freddiemac.com

The website of the Federal Home Loan Mortgage Corporation, Freddie Mac. Freddie Mac is one of the two largest purchasers/guarantors of home mortgages (along with Fannie Mae) in the country.

www.freeforeclosurereport.com
A site for information about foreclosed homes you may be able to buy in all parts of the country. You must register, and to get to the site you have to initially get past a number of other offers that have little to do with foreclosure.

http://homebuying.about.com
A good website for all types of information on many aspects of buying and maintaining a home. It also refers you to other informational sites on any given home-related subject.

www.homeloans.va.gov
The U.S. Department of Veterans Affairs website. It gives details about the GI Bill or veterans' mortgages.

www.hud.gov
Operated by the federal Department of Housing and Urban Development. This site provides substantial information on many aspects of home purchasing. It also has information for the homeowner on buying and selling homes, foreclosures, home improvements, fair housing, and recently enacted HUD recovery programs.

www.inman.com
Inman News is the real estate industry's most authoritative source of market conditions, business trends, technology, and real estate.

www.mortgage-x.com
An excellent website for all types of information on mortgage loans and lenders. Included are directories of mortgage lenders and brokers, as well as a mortgage payment calculator.

www.multihousingnews.com/multihousing/index.shtml
MHN provides the leaders of the multi-housing industry with the most current and complete news, information, and analysis in print and online forms to help them run their businesses more efficiently and profitably. Consumers can find business information if buying in an apartment or co-op/condo is for them.

www.realtor.com
The largest real estate website, run by the National Association of Realtors. This site is the largest site in the world listing homes and Realtors. It provides good information, whether you're looking locally or in another part of the country.

www.realtytimes.com
This website includes informative real estate news broadcasts.

www.reoconnection.com
A way to connect with Realtors around the country who specialize in marketing foreclosed homes.

www.tdhca.state.tx.us/homeownership
This site provides quality information on loan assistance from the state of Texas.

www.transunion.com
The website of one of the three major credit-reporting firms. It provides information
about a variety of credit service and assistance. You can also obtain your credit report
here.

www.zillow.com
This website provides free real estate information. Search homes for sale, home prices,
home values, recently sold homes, mortgage rates, and more.

Checklist and Contacts List

This checklist, as well as the contacts list that follows, is designed to help you take notes or record contact information as you move through the various stages of your purchase. The timeline checklist helps you schedule each step of the home-buying process in the proper order, and have the information at your immediate grasp at any time. Consider both as ways to remind you of things to do and people to contact, as well as a brief summary of the information in the book. One thing to remember: don't be shy. Mark them up! That's what they're here for!

Timeline

Preliminary Preparation

❏ Surf the web for Realtor sites.

Sites I found:

_____

_____

_____

_____

❑ Interview Realtors.

Candidates:

_____

_____

_____

_____

❑ Find a mortgage broker.

Candidates:

_____

_____

_____

_____

Before Purchase Agreement

❑ Tour homes.

Check newspapers and websites for open house information and schedules:

_____

_____

_____

Appointments that the Realtor made for me to see homes:

_____

_____

_____

_____

Post-Purchase Agreement

❏ Inspections:

Times and dates (bring checkbook for paying inspector[s]; bring camera and notebook):

_____

_____

_____

_____

❏ Contractors:

Get references from Realtor and interview candidates.

_____

_____

_____

_____

❏ Closing staff:

Escrow firms: Get references from Realtor.

_____

_____

_____

_____

Closing attorneys: Call local bar association or Legal Aid for reference; get references from Realtor.

_____

_____

_____

Packing

❏ Companies/stores where I can buy packing materials:

_____

_____

_____

_____

❏ Packing materials needed:

_____

_____

_____

_____

Moving In

❏ Contact moving companies:

_____

_____

_____

_____

❏ Locksmith:

_____

_____

_____

_____

❏ Utilities—arrange service:

Gas: _____

_____

Electric: _____

_____

Water/sewer: _____

_____

❏ Other services to arrangement:

Telephone: _____

_____

DSL: _____

_____

Cable/satellite: _____

_____

Trash: _____

_____

Contacts List

List the contact information of everyone involved in the process of buying your home here:

Realtor

Name: _____

Address: _____

Telephone: _____ E-mail: _____

Notes:

_____

_____

_____

_____

Interesting Homes

Addresses/Details: _____

_____

_____

_____

_____

_____

Mortgage Broker/Lender

Name: _____

Address: _____

Telephone: _____ E-mail: _____

Notes:

_____

_____

_____

_____

Credit Reports

Date(s) requested:

_____

_____

_____

_____

_____

Insurance Agent

Name: _____

Address: _____

Telephone: _____ E-mail: _____

Notes:

_____

_____

_____

_____

Escrow Company

Company: _____ Name: _____

Address: _____

Telephone: _____ E-mail: _____

Notes:

_____

_____

_____

_____

Attorney

Name: _____

Address: _____

Telephone: _____ E-mail: _____

Notes:

_____

_____

_____

_____

Websites

_____

_____

_____

_____

Contractor(s)

Name: _____

Address: _____

Telephone: _____ E-mail: _____

Specialty: _____

Notes:

_____

_____

_____

_____

Inspector(s)

Name: _____

Address: _____

Telephone: _____ E-mail: _____

Notes:

_____

_____

_____

_____

Accountant

Name: _____

Address: _____

Telephone: _____ E-mail: _____

Notes:

_____

_____

_____

_____

Gardener

Name: _____

Address: _____

Telephone: _____ E-mail: _____

Notes:

_____

_____

_____

_____

Decorator

Name: _____

Address: _____

Telephone: _____ E-mail: _____

Notes:

_____

_____

_____

_____

Locksmith

Name: _____

Address: _____

Telephone: _____ E-mail: _____

Notes:

_____

_____

_____

_____

School(s)

Name(s): _____

Address(es): _____

Principal/administration: _____

_____

Telephone: _____ E-mail: _____

Notes:

_____

_____

_____

_____

Interviewing the Pros

The following are sets of questions to ask when you interview each professional that you are likely to utilize in your search for a home. I've developed these lists based on many years of experience.

You may not need to ask every question to every individual you talk to, or even use the same questions for each expert. Basically, this comes down to your personal comfort level and gut feelings about a particular person. Feel free to add to them according to your own interests when you talk with any particular professional at the time or based on your individual circumstances.

Realtor

1. How long have you been a Realtor?

   _____

   _____

2. Are you a full-time real estate agent?

   _____

   _____

3. Have you always been with this real estate company? If not, where else have you worked and with what types of properties?

_____

_____

4. Do you have any special designations? What are they?

_____

_____

5. Are you a broker?

_____

_____

6. Do you specialize in sellers or buyers?

_____

_____

7. Do you work only with a certain type of buyer? (If yes, what type?)

_____

_____

8. Do you specialize in certain areas of the town or county?

_____

_____

9. Do you specialize in certain types of properties/homes?

_____

_____

10. Do you have an assistant? If so, is she licensed?

_____

_____

11. Does your brokerage have a website, and if so, what is the web address/URL?

    _____

    _____

12. Is it possible for me to search for properties through the web/IDX on your website?

    _____

    _____

13. If you're not compensated by the seller's agent, how do you get paid?

    _____

    _____

14. If I have to pay you, what is the percentage of commission?

    _____

    _____

15. Do you regularly work with relocation clients and firms?

    _____

    _____

16. Are you familiar with foreclosed homes and/or short sales? Will you work on either type of transaction?

    _____

    _____

17. Can you give me at least three recent references?

    _____

    _____

18. Can you recommend a mortgage broker? What is your relationship with this mortgage broker?

    _____

    _____

19. If it becomes necessary, can you recommend contractors and other vendors to work on the property? What is your relationship with these contractors and vendors?

_____

_____

20. Is there any way for me to have 24/7 MLS access?

_____

_____

21. Are you able to assist me in getting information about local schools?

_____

_____

22. Who decides the amount of the offer—you or me?

_____

_____

23. Do you have E&O (Errors & Omissions) insurance? How much?

_____

_____

24. Will you be available on _____ to start conducting my search?

_____

_____

Mortgage Broker

1. How long have you been a mortgage broker?

_____

_____

2. Where are you licensed?

_____

_____

3. Do you charge anything for your services? How much?

_____

_____

4. Can you provide references?

_____

_____

5. Do you handle FHA/VA mortgages?

_____

_____

6. How do you decide where to present my application?

_____

_____

7. Will you present my application to only one lender or do you present to multiple lenders simultaneously?

_____

_____

8. How do you decide what lenders to use for a particular application?

_____

_____

9. What are interest rates doing now?

_____

_____

10. Where do you see rates going in the next few months? In a year? In five years? (This information will help you decide whether to get a fixed- or adjustable-rate mortgage.)

_____

_____

11. What would be better for me—a fixed-rate or an adjustable-rate loan?

_____

_____

12. What can I afford?

_____

_____

13. Are there any "special" loans or lending programs that I'm eligible for?

_____

_____

14. I'm self-employed. Does that present any particular hurdles for approval? Are there certain extra requirements I'll have to get past to qualify?

_____

_____

15. I have a bankruptcy in my past. What effect will that have on my application?

_____

_____

16. I had a foreclosure/short sale a few years ago. Can I still get a loan?

_____

_____

17. My credit is pretty bad and/or I have some bad debts. Will I still be able to get a loan?

_____

_____

18. How fast can I be approved?

_____

_____

19. What's my credit score and what effect does it have on my application?

   _____

   _____

20. I've never borrowed or had any credit cards before. Will that help or hurt my application?

   _____

   _____

21. How much effect do points have on the interest rate?

   _____

   _____

22. Besides interest and any points, are there any other costs for the loan?

   _____

   _____

23. What percentage of the purchase price can I get for a loan?

   _____

   _____

24. Would I qualify more easily if I'm buying a duplex instead of a single-family home?

   _____

   _____

25. What effect will a gift from my parents for the down payment have on my application?

   _____

   _____

26. Are there prepayment penalties?

   _____

   _____

27. Do you use only large banks, or do you also work with smaller ones?

_____

_____

Seller

Often, a buyer does not have the opportunity to talk to the seller directly. You can ask these questions through your agent.

1. Why are you selling?

_____

_____

2. What things did you like best about the home?

_____

_____

3. What things did you dislike the most about the home?

_____

_____

4. What problems exist, or existed, in the home?

_____

_____

5. What changes did you make to the home?

_____

_____

6. What repairs did you make?

_____

_____

7. Was all work on/in the home done with permits and by licensed contractors?

_____

_____

8. What are the neighbors like—good *and* bad?

   _____

   _____

9. How is traffic in the neighborhood?

   _____

   _____

10. Are there any major noise issues?

    _____

    _____

11. Have you had/noticed any industrial smell/pollution issues?

    _____

    _____

12. Do any safety issues exist?

    _____

    _____

13. Are there any weather-related issues? For example, during storms do you get particularly heavy precipitation or wind from any particular direction? Is this locale known for excessive heat or cold?

    _____

    _____

14. How close are schools?

    _____

    _____

15. How close are playgrounds and other public facilities?

    _____

    _____

16. How close is shopping?

    _____

    _____

17. If I want to make changes to the home, how are the neighbors likely to react?

_____

_____

18. Are there any good babysitters in the neighborhood?

_____

_____

19. Is there a Neighborhood Watch group?

_____

_____

20. Do you know of any planned development in the immediate neighborhood? What is it?

_____

_____

Inspector

1. How long have you been inspecting homes?

_____

_____

2. Are you a member of any professional associations? Which ones?

_____

_____

3. What experience qualifies you for being an inspector?

_____

_____

4. Exactly what does your inspection include?

_____

_____

5. Are you bonded/insured?

   _____

   _____

6. Have you ever been sued or forced into mediation/arbitration? What was the outcome?

   _____

   _____

7. Can you provide references?

   _____

   _____

8. What do you charge?

   _____

   _____

9. Are you paid at the time of the inspection or at closing?

   _____

   _____

10. How soon can I expect your written report?

    _____

    _____

11. Can I be present during the inspection?

    _____

    _____

12. Do you perform any of the repairs you find necessary in your inspection?

    _____

    _____

13. Can you estimate what the repairs you think are necessary will cost?

    _____

    _____

14. Can you recommend the appropriate expert to do whatever repairs you feel are necessary?

   _____

   _____

15. How do you decide when "further" inspection is necessary?

   _____

   _____

16. May I see an example of an inspection report that you provide after the inspection?

   _____

   _____

City Officials

1. What's the zoning at the property location?

   _____

   _____

2. Does the property sit in a particular "special" safety or historic preservation area?

   _____

   _____

3. What setbacks (the distances back from the parcel's boundaries that you have to observe to put up a structure) or size limitations exist for the property?

   _____

   _____

4. I'm thinking of doing an addition. Will that be possible at this location?

   _____

   _____

5. What will I be permitted to do at that location? What will I not be permitted
    to do?

    _____

    _____

6. What will permitting and other fees for a project or remodel cost?

    _____

    _____

7. What does the process of obtaining permits entail?

    _____

    _____

8. How long does the approval process take to receive necessary permits?

    _____

    _____

9. Is there any history of code violations on the property?

    _____

    _____

10. What is the permit history of the property?

    _____

    _____

11. What are the property taxes?

    _____

    _____

12. Are/will there be any new assessments?

    _____

    _____

Contractor/Architect

1. How do you bill—hourly or by the project?

   _____

   _____

2. What is your availability?

   _____

   _____

3. Are you bonded/insured?

   _____

   _____

4. Are you licensed?

   _____

   _____

5. What professional associations do you belong to?

   _____

   _____

6. Have you been the subject of any arbitrations or lawsuits? For what?

   _____

   _____

7. How long have you been doing this type of work?

   _____

   _____

8. Can you provide references?

   _____

   _____

9. Can you suggest design ideas?

_____

_____

10. How often are changes in the plans (known as change orders) necessary?

_____

_____

11. What will this project cost? (If you have a specific project in mind.)

_____

_____

12. How much time will the project take to complete? (If you have a specific project in mind.)

_____

_____

13. (For contractors) Do you handle all of the work yourself or subcontract out certain parts of a project?

_____

_____

14. How much of the time will you be on the site?

_____

_____

15. Who's in charge in your absence? What's their experience?

_____

_____

16. Can I purchase materials myself, or do you supply everything?

_____

_____

17. How many employees do you have?

   _____

   _____

18. How many jobs do you work on at a time?

   _____

   _____

Escrow Officer

1. What are the fees and costs involved?

   _____

   _____

2. What exactly happens in an escrow?

   _____

   _____

3. Do you employ a notary?

   _____

   _____

4. Do you provide a title report and do the research to ensure clear title?

   _____

   _____

5. Do you provide for title insurance?

   _____

   _____

6. What will closing costs be?

   _____

   _____

7. Is my money safe here in case the deal falls apart?

   _____

   _____

8. Can anyone get access to my funds before closing?

   _____

   _____

9. If the deal falls apart, how easy is it for me to get my deposited funds back?

   _____

   _____

10. Do you prepare copies of the documents for my use when I file my tax returns?

    _____

    _____

11. (Only in an attorney closing state) How closely do you work with my attorney to determine when to disburse funds?

    _____

    _____

Attorney

1. Are you a member of the bar? If so, in which state(s) do you practice?

   _____

   _____

2. What's your legal specialty?

   _____

   _____

3. What is your role in a real estate transaction?

   _____

   _____

4. How many home purchases have you worked on?

_____

_____

5. What do you charge to handle a real estate transaction?

_____

_____

6. Do you do the research to ensure a clear title?

_____

_____

7. Do you carry malpractice insurance?

_____

_____

8. Have you ever had any disciplinary rulings/penalties against you?

_____

_____

9. Can you provide references?

_____

_____

10. If there are any legal claims resulting from this purchase, will you also represent me in such a situation? If not, would you refer me to an appropriate attorney? If such claims go to appeal, do you handle the appeal? If not, will you refer me to an appellate attorney?

_____

_____

Appraiser

1. What do you charge?

   _____

   _____

2. Are you paid by me or the lender?

   _____

   _____

3. How do you establish the value of the home?

   _____

   _____

4. The house is in a flood zone (wildfire, landslide, etc.). Will this affect the value you set, and if so by how much?

   _____

   _____

5. How long have you been appraising? How many homes have you appraised?

   _____

   _____

6. Are you independent, or do you just work for specific banks/mortgage brokers?

   _____

   _____

7. (If the appraiser's not from the local area) How are you able to accurately establish value if you don't normally work this area?

   _____

   _____

8. For how long can I reasonably rely upon the value you set for the home?

   _____

   _____

Insurance Agent

1. What will a policy cost me?

   _____

   _____

2. What is covered in that policy?

   _____

   _____

3. Do I need any special coverage or riders for valuables such as antiques, art, or jewelry?

   _____

   _____

4. Does such coverage need specific current professional appraisals?

   _____

   _____

5. What is the deductible?

   _____

   _____

6. Are floods covered under a basic homeowner's policy?

   _____

   _____

7. Are landslides covered under a basic homeowner's policy?

   _____

   _____

8. What is flood insurance?

   _____

   _____

9. When is flood insurance required?

   _____

   _____

10. Does flood insurance carry a deductible?

    _____

    _____

11. The home is in a flood zone. Is there are way I can avoid having flood insurance?

    _____

    _____

12. Must I have earthquake insurance if my home is in a quake area?

    _____

    _____

13. How much extra must I pay for earthquake insurance?

    _____

    _____

14. What is the deductible for earthquake insurance?

    _____

    _____

15. Are my personal possessions covered by my homeowner's policy? What about when I'm moving from my previous residence to my new home?

    _____

    _____

16. I've had some minor claims in the past. How much will these affect my insurability and my premium cost?

    _____

    _____

17. Will I get any discount on premiums if I have my other policies, such as automobile and any professional coverage, with the same firm?

_____

_____

18. Do the home insurance policies you sell provide full replacement value, even in an increasing value economy? If so, will such replacement result in a higher premium?

_____

_____

Appendix E

Sample Purchase Contract

In this appendix, you'll find a sample real estate contract from New Jersey. You and the seller sign this contract once you have agreed to all the terms of your offer. Although most of the clauses in this contract are standard in any state, your state may have additional or different clauses. This is just to show you what a real estate contract may look like. If you have any questions regarding your own purchase contract, ask your real estate salesperson.

Remember that the actual home-buying process may be a bit more involved than just signing the contract. For example, if your offer is not completely rejected by the seller, she may return a counteroffer noting what she agrees to and what she wants to change. You can accept these changes and proceed to a signed contract, or you can counter her counteroffer. This can go back and forth as many times as you and the seller feel necessary until you reach agreement or give up and move on. Each time you counter, you (or the seller) will sign the offer, noting that the seller's signature is subject to agreement on the newest counteroffer. When you finally reach complete agreement, you and the seller will sign the contract, which will include the counteroffers. We covered this process in more detail in Chapter 13.

Provided by Scott A. Breyer, marketing and sales associate at Walter R. Breyer Real Estate Co. in Bergen County, New Jersey (www.breyerrealty.com).

N.J. CONTRACT FOR SALE OF REAL ESTATE   PLAIN LANGUAGE

"THIS IS A LEGALLY BINDING CONTRACT THAT WILL BECOME FINAL WITHIN THREE BUSINESS DAYS. DURING THIS PERIOD YOU MAY CHOOSE TO CONSULT AN ATTORNEY WHO CAN REVIEW AND CANCEL THE CONTRACT. SEE SECTION ON ATTORNEY REVIEW FOR DETAILS."

CONTRACT FOR SALE OF REAL ESTATE

This Contract for Sale made on _____, 200__, BETWEEN

(Purchaser)_____

Address_____ Phone _____

_____

AND (Seller) _____

Address _____Phone _____

_____

1. Property. The property to be sold consists of the land and all the buildings, other improvements and fixtures on the land, the property being more commonly known and referred to as:

in the County of _____, and State of New Jersey. It is shown on the municipal tax map as lot(s) _____ in block _____. Approximate lot size is _____

2. Purchase Price. The total purchase price is $_____

3. Payment of Purchase Price. The Purchaser will pay the purchase price as follows:

Cash deposit on signing of this agreement, for which this a receipt. $_____

Additional cash deposit within _____ days of the dates of this agreement.

                                                                                          $_____

Balance to be paid at closing of title, in cash or by certified or bank cashier's check (subject to adjustment at closing). $_____

By proceeds from a first mortgage, _____ type, for a term of _____ at an interest rate of _____ for which the Purchaser will apply immediately through the offices of the named Real Estate Broker or a Lender of his or her choice. $_____

                                        TOTAL PURCHASE PRICE........ $_____

4. Mortgage Condition. This contract is conditional upon the Purchaser obtaining a mortgage commitment on the above terms, within _____ days. The Purchaser further agrees, in addition to applying promptly for his needed mortgage financing, that he will supply to the mortgagee all documentation required by the Lender. If the Purchaser fails to obtain such mortgage commitment or fails to waive this contingency during the _____ day period and any agreed-upon extensions, either party may cancel this contract. In that event, all deposit monies paid by the Purchasers shall be returned.

5. Deposit Monies. All deposit monies will be held in the non-interest bearing trust account of SELLER'S ATTORNEY until closing of title, or returned to the Purchaser in the event this contract is voided as provided for herein.

6. Time and Place of Closing. The closing date cannot be made final at this time. The Purchaser and Seller agree to make on or before _____,20 _____, the estimated date for closing. The closing will be held at the offices of the Purchaser's attorney or such other place as may be mutually agreed upon.

7. Adjustments at Closing. Rents, water rents, real estate taxes, interest on any mortgage to be assumed by Purchaser, fuel, and insurance premiums, if any, are to be apportioned as of the date of actual closing of title.

8. Type of Deed. At the closing the Seller agrees to provide a deed known as _____, including full legal description. The Seller will also provide proper affidavit of title.

9. QUALITY OF TITLE. This title will be subject to easements, restrictions of record and existing tenants, if any.
(a) Such state of facts as an accurate survey might disclose, provided none of these render the title unmarketable.

(b) The title shall be free and clear of all encumbrances. (c) The title shall be insurable by a reputable title insurance company licensed to do business in the State of New Jersey.

10. Personal Property and Fixtures. Included in this sale are gas range, gas and electric fixtures, chandeliers, window shades, screens, storm sash, and venetian blinds, if any, not belonging to any tenant of said property and now on said property. The following items are also specifically included:

11. Assessments. All assessments which may be imposed by the municipality for public improvements which have been completed as of the date of this agreement are to be paid in full by the Seller or credited to the Purchaser at the closing.

12. Possession. At the closing the Purchaser will be given possession of the property, unless an extended date is agreed upon in this contract.

13. No Assignment. This contract shall not be assigned without the written consent of the Seller.

14. Inspection of the Property. The Seller agrees to permit the Purchaser to inspect the property at any reasonable time before the closing. The Seller will permit access for any inspections provided for in this contract.

15. Physical Condition of the Property. This property is being sold "as is". The Seller does not make any claims or promises about the condition or value of any of the property. The Purchaser has inspected the property and relies on this inspection, and any rights provided for in this contract. Seller agrees to maintain the grounds, buildings, and improvements in good condition subject to ordinary wear and tear. The premises shall be in "broom-clean" condition and free of debris on day of closing. Seller represents that all electrical, plumbing, heating, and air-conditioning systems (if applicable), together with all fixtures included in the sale, are now working and shall be in proper working order at time of closing. This provision shall not survive closing of title.

16. Building and Zoning Laws. The Purchaser intends to use the property as a   family home. The Seller states that this use does not violate any zoning ordinance, building code or other law.

17. Property Lines. The Seller states that all buildings, driveways and other improvements on the property are inside its boundary lines. Also, no improvements of adjoining properties extend across the boundary lines of this property.

18. Risk of Loss or Damage. The Seller is responsible for any loss or damage to the property, by fire or otherwise, except for normal wear and tear, until the closing.

19. ATTORNEY REVIEW.

A. Study By Attorney

The Purchaser or the Seller may choose to have an attorney study this contract. If an attorney is consulted, the attorney must complete his or her review of the contract within a three-day period. This contract will be legally binding at the end of this three day period unless an attorney for the Purchaser or the Seller reviews and disapproves of the contract.

B. Counting the Time

You count the three days from the date of delivery of the signed contract to the Purchaser and the Seller. You do not count Saturdays, Sundays or legal holidays. The Purchaser and the Seller may agree in writing to extend the three-day period for attorney review.

C. Notice of Disapproval

If an attorney for the Purchaser or the Seller reviews and disapproves of this contract, the attorney must notify the REAL ESTATE BROKERS and the other party named in the contract within the three-day period. Otherwise, this contract will be legally binding as written. The attorney must send the notice of disapproval to the REAL ESTATE BROKERS by certified mail, by telegram or by delivering it personally. The telegram or certified letter will be effective upon sending. The personal delivery will be effective upon delivery to the REAL ESTATE BROKERS' office. The attorney may inform the REAL ESTATE BROKERS of any suggested revision(s) in the contract that would make it satisfactory.

20. Broker's Commission. The Seller(s) agrees to pay a commission of   of the purchase price on closing of title.

21. Entire Agreement. This contract contains the entire agreement of the parties. No representations have been made by any of the parties, or their agents, except as set forth in this contract.

22. Termite and Home Engineering Inspections. This agreement is subject to a termite and home engineering inspection being made of these premises, at the Purchasers' expense, within ten (10) days of the date herein. In the event the termite inspection reveals termite infestation, and/or termite damage, and in the event the home engineering inspection reveals any structural, mechanical, and/or material defects, then both parties hereto will have the option of allowing the Seller to make all necessary treatments and repairs at Seller's expense or either Seller or Purchaser may void this agreement. In the event this agreement is voided as hereinbefore provided, then all deposit monies tendered shall be returned to the Purchaser and all further rights, liabilities, and obligations of all parties shall immediately cease and terminate. Written notice must be given by Purchaser to Seller within said ten (10) days as to the discovery of termite infestation, structural, mechanical, and/or material defects as a result of said inspections or this contingency shall be of no further force and effect.

23. Inspection for Radon Gas. Purchasers, at their own expense, may have the premises inspected to determine whether or not there are elevated levels of naturally occurring radon gas as defined by the New Jersey Department of Environmental Protection (DEP). This inspection shall be made within 15 days of the date herein. In the event the radon inspection reveals elevated levels of radon gas as defined, then the Seller will be required to remedy this condition at his expense, prior to closing. Seller shall supply to the Purchaser proof that the work was performed by a certified radon contractor. In the event the Seller is either unwilling or unable to correct the elevated levels of radon gas, then the Purchasers, at their option, may waive this contingency or void this contract. In the event the contract is voided, there shall be no further liability from one party to the other and all deposit monies will be immediately returned to the Purchaser.

24. Purchaser Financially Able to Close. Purchaser represents that he has sufficient cash available (together with the mortgage or mortgages referred to in Section 3) to complete this purchase.

25. Consumer Information Statement. Purchasers and Sellers acknowledge receipt and full disclosure of the Consumer Information Statement. In this transaction Walter R. Breyer Real Estate Co., Inc., is acting as the   and is representing the

26. Megan's Law Statement. Under New Jersey Law, the county Prosecutor determines whether and how to provide notice of the presence of convicted sex offenders in an area. In their professional capacity, Real Estate Licensees are not entitled to notification by the County Prosecutor under Megan's Law and are unable to obtain such information for you. Upon closing, the County Prosecutor may be contacted for such further information as may be disclosable to you.

Witness	Date	Purchaser
Witness	Date	Purchaser
Witness	Date	Seller
Witness	Date	Seller

Index

I

Q-R

S

6^2

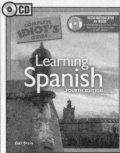

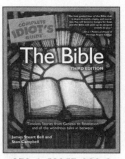
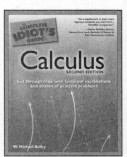